Why It Is Good to Be Good

Why It Is Good to Be Good

Ethics, Kohut's Self Psychology, and Modern Society

John H. Riker

JASON ARONSON

Lanham • Boulder • New York • Toronto • Plymouth, UK

Published by Jason Aronson
An imprint of Rowman & Littlefield Publishers, Inc.
A wholly owned subsidiary of The Rowman & Littlefield Publishing Group, Inc.
4501 Forbes Boulevard, Suite 200, Lanham, Maryland 20706
http://www.rowmanlittlefield.com

Estover Road, Plymouth PL6 7PY, United Kingdom

British Library Cataloguing in Publication Information Available

Library of Congress Cataloging-in-Publication Data

The hardback edition of this book was previously cataloged by the Library of Congress as follows:

Riker, John H., 1943–
  Why it is good to be good : ethics, Kohut's self psychology, and modern society / John H. Riker.
      p. cm.
  Includes bibliographical references (p.   ) and index.
  1. Ethics. 2. Self psychology. 3. Psychology and philosophy. 4. Kohut, Heinz.
I. Title.
  BJ45.R55 2010
  170—dc22   2010021380

  ISBN: 978-0-7657-0790-1 (cloth : alk. paper)
  ISBN: 978-0-7657-0791-8 (pbk. : alk. paper)
  ISBN: 978-0-7657-0792-5 (electronic)

Printed in the United States of America

To David Terman
and
the Chicago Self Psychologists

CONTENTS

have a core psychological structure to be intact in order for our lives to feel vitalized and meaningful and the fact that this structure is highly vulnerable to injury, and, therefore, in need of others to sustain it is exactly the kind of psychology that can ground an understanding of why we need to become ethical human beings. It stands in strong contrast to the self as conceived by economic modernity as an independent individual who is fundamentally concerned with satisfying personal desires and establishing a legitimated status in the socioeconomic realm.

Not only does Kohut's theory give us a ground for moral life, it also allows us to see how modernity's misunderstanding of the self has led to patterns of living that undermine the development and sustenance of the psychological self, resulting in both a loss of motivation for being ethical and an immense increase in the number of persons suffering from such narcissistic symptoms as intolerable feelings of inner depletion, extremely fragile self-esteem, and the tendency to treat others as objects.

In brief, I argue that the best life for individuals involves feeling dynamically and intensely alive and that this experience of elevated vitality is essentially dependent upon one's having a coherent self that grounds psychological activity. Because self structure is so highly vulnerable to injuries, persons must have others who can play self functions for them in times of stress or trauma. For others to be to willing to provide selfobject functions in adult life, one must be able to reciprocally provide selfobject functions for them. However, persons can be selfobjects for others only if they have developed an ability to empathize with others, the moral virtues as described by Aristotle, and an abiding sense of fairness (the essential feature of the moral point of view according to Rawls). I then contend that the virtues and ethical concern must be extended beyond reciprocal relationships to all human beings in order for the self to retain a core integrity. I conclude that if the best personal life is one that is grounded in a coherent self, then we need to become integrated, virtuous, empathic persons who can extend ethical concern to all human beings.

Since the self for Kohut is largely unconscious, I also develop a way of understanding ethical life that incorporates unconscious intentions and strivings. This way of conceiving ethical life as based in a mature narcissism and including unconscious processes is, I believe, original and important, for it includes all of human functioning in the ethical sphere rather than just conscious motivations and does not demand that moral actions be generated by "unselfish" intentions. The key ethical development that needs to take place is not from egoism to altruism but from an infantile narcissism to a mature self-love. With this focus, the book presents a vision of ethical life that differs radically from the leading contemporary views that see ethics as derived from a pure rationality (the Kantians), an attempt to maximize, organize, and distribute pleasure (the utilitarians and economists), or the exercise of altruistic sentiments (religious morality). In short, the book is an attempt to interweave psychoanalytic theory and moral philosophy into a significant new moral psychology.

The theoretical orientation that seems most in conflict with this project is that of postmodernism. Postmodernism's critique of theory, foundationalism, and ethics emerges from its beliefs that there is no higher purpose to life than life itself and that life is best conceived of as spontaneous responsiveness, adventure, and encounter with otherness. It emphasizes multiplicity over unity, fluidity over stability, process over structure, and openness over closed systems of meaning. Life is not best lived by fitting everything into an organized system and repeating its codes, for life is irreducibly diverse, singular, and creative. Postmodernism asks us to live without foundations—to face the reality that there are no justifiable grounds for a "best" way to be human. Rather, life needs to be lived in openness, spontaneous responsiveness, and creative activity.

Insofar as what I am doing in this volume is positing a theory of moral psychology that is meant to be foundational, it appears that I am violating every major tenet of this life-affirming philosophy that has been such an important corrective in Western thought. As opposed as my project and the postmodernist framework seem to be, there are profound agreements. First, I thoroughly concur that life is for the sake of life, that what the psyche most seeks is an intensity of experience, and that the affirmation of each person's particular being is crucial to living most lively. I also agree that creative responsiveness, adventure, and chaos are essential for experiencing a depth of liveliness.

However, to say that chaos, dissonance, and disorganization are essential to life is not to say that order, harmony, and organization are not also essential, for they are. "Deadliness" comes in two forms: the overly organized and the deficiently organized. The chaos in the mind of the psychotic is not the zenith of life but one of its saddest deformations. Some forms of organization, such as those of the psychological defenses, stultify life; while others, such as the organization of personal energy around achieving a cherished value, greatly enhance it. Some disorganizing events lead to new ways of perceiving, creative shifts, or moments of heightened intensity, but other disorganizing events are traumatic and leave a person less able to live with full vitality.

The crucial question is not whether to favor structure or chaos but to determine what kind of psychological organization most enhances the life of the soul.[1] The argument of this book is that the optimal organization for the psyche is one centered on a vital coherent self. This self is not a "foundation" in the traditional sense that is so inimical to the postmodernists, for the self which Kohut describes has multiple parts, is engaged in a lifelong adventure of development, and can tragically fail. It is not a "substance," but the fragile experiential process that constitutes the core of who a person is and which is in constant negotiation with the other parts of the psyche and the world. The self is also not foundational in the psyche in that it does not take on a ruling function, as reason does for Plato, Aristotle, Kant, and most of the other ethical thinkers. Rather than being a dominant part of a hierarchically organized psyche, the self is related to other psychological functions as a member of a complex ecosystem.

Insofar as I claim that the best way to sustain the vitality of the self and with it the aliveness of the whole psyche is to become an ethical person, my argument seems to stand in opposition to Nietzsche's critique of morality as normalizing and constricting.[2] However, the central ethical virtues of self psychology—empathy and concern for the well-being of other singular individuals—do not require conformity to a generalized concept of a good life nor do they demand that all moral persons be alike in any way other than having the abilities to be empathic, engage in reciprocity, and sustain integrity. These virtues are not imposed as limitations on the self but are the traits any person needs to sustain a self that can have the kind of creativity and vitality that Nietzsche champions. The acts of moral shaming and the instilling of guilt that Nietzsche rightly condemns are known by self psychologists to be deeply injurious to the self. But there are fundamental differences between Nietzsche and a self psychological approach to ethics: self psychology understands that personal vitality depends on a depth of human relatedness, while Nietzsche glorifies the lonely Zarathustra sitting on a mountain top.

In short, the self psychological vision of the soul will constitute a genuine alternative to the rational soul of the Greeks, the irrationally passionate soul of the Romantics, the willful soul of Nietzsche, the spiritually longing soul of the religious philosophers, and the desiring/laboring soul of economic society. It is a soul organized around a fragile self in need of empathic human relatedness in order to engage in the adventure of fully becoming itself. This self psychological concept of the soul opens up a new way of being human and of constructing human lives.

There is one final issue that must be raised before proceeding. From Plato's *Dialogues* to the present day, philosophy has identified the self with the subject of conscious experience—the ego—and has located all important intentions, structures of meaning, and acts of agency as conscious productions. My claim that the self is predominantly an unconscious structured process calls into question this fundamental orientation of the West. I will not attempt to offer a defense for the notion of unconscious mentality except to say that if I can show that it is only with this concept that we can both achieve an adequate notion of the self and establish a ground for ethical life, then we will have the best reasons possible for taking this concept seriously. There is no value of greater worth to society than having a compelling way to explain why it is good to be good. If the concept of unconscious mentality proves necessary for this explanation, then it will be integrated into the web of concepts through which we understand human life.

Locating the fulcrum of ethical life in unconscious mentality constitutes a Copernican revolution in ethics. Previously, ethicists have proclaimed that the rational ego with its conscious intentions and ability to understand and predict consequences to be the psychological agency responsible for generating moral life. It is true that there can be no ethical life without the critical powers of the rational ego; however, this is not the same as saying these powers are sufficient for the production of moral life. I will attempt to show that the neglect of unconscious motivation in general and the needs of the unconscious self in particular have severely distorted the West's concept of ethical life, making it both impotent to deal with substantial forms of evil and tending to create a kind of judgmental, self-negating person rather than a self-affirming, life-affirming one. Admitting that the unconscious plays an essential role in moral life has the great advantage of inviting all of our psychological activity into this realm rather than limiting it to that which is organized by the rational ego. Ethical life can now be based on the reality of who we are rather than revolving around the fantasy of a conscious subject who fully knows and controls all of his intentional actions.

NOTES

1. I will use the term "soul" as equivalent to "psyche" and mean by it primarily a set of psychological functions that concern meaning, intention, and action. I follow Jonathan Lear in his *Open Minded: Working Out the Logic of the Soul* (Cambridge: Harvard University Press, 1998) in wanting to reclaim this powerful and evocative word from its capture by a religious model of life and return it to its Aristotelian naturalist home.

2. See especially his *Genealogy of Morals* in *The Birth of Tragedy and the Genealogy of Morals,* tr. F. Golffing (Garden City, NY: Doubleday, 1956).

Acknowledgments

The thinking that has come to fruition in this volume began in the fall of 2003 when I was invited by Jonathan Lear and the Committee on Social Thought to be the Kohut Professor at the University of Chicago. Jonathan's books, lectures, and friendship have been immensely vitalizing during the period of writing the book. While I was the Kohut Professor, Arnold Goldberg and other self psychologists in Chicago invited me to address their group, and their response to my ideas was so encouraging that I set out on the journey to write this book. I especially want to thank Arnold Goldberg, Allen Siegel, Ernest Wolf, and the late Marian Tolpin for their encouragement and friendship. The most important member of this group has been David Terman, director of the Chicago Institute for Psychoanalysis for the past eight years. More than anyone else, David encouraged me to write the book, read an earlier draft, gave me excellent advice for revision, and significantly enhanced my understanding of Kohut's theory. Without his friendship and dedication to this project, I am not sure it ever would have come to fulfillment.

Others need to be thanked. My colleague Jonathan Lee read an earlier version and gave me, as always, astute comments. His friendship and his unparalleled philosophical acumen have sustained and inspired me through the years we have shared at Colorado College. Eric Santner of the University of Chicago has also been highly stimulating for my thinking. Colorado College has been extraordinarily generous with its funds for a sabbatical, a research grant, and travel to conferences, all of which helped with the production of this volume. The students of the college have been very receptive to the ideas of the book when I have tried them out in various courses, and I am always grateful for their vivacity, responsiveness, and intelligence. Last, I must thank the person who always means the most to any and every thing I do, Marcia. Our shared life is a joy beyond reckoning.

ONE

THE MORAL PROBLEM OF MODERNITY

IS IT GOOD TO BE GOOD?

When Socrates first developed the concept of what it means to live an ethical life, the Sophists confronted him with a critical question, one that threatened to turn the offspring of this philosophical midwife into a still-born child: "Socrates, we get what you are saying about what it means to live an ethical life—doing what is right or good rather than simply doing what you want to do, but why would anyone who had the power to choose how to live their lives ever choose to live this form of life? Why live an ethical life if you can get more personal satisfaction simply by being out for yourself?" In short, before they would accept that being an ethical person was the best way to live, they demanded that Socrates show why it is (personally) good to be a (morally) good person.

Socrates' answer to this question of why it is good to be good was extraordinarily powerful.[1] He claimed that to have a life[2] one had to have an organized enough soul to be able to choose one's life and enough self-control to abide by one's choice. Conventional persons living out the codes of their social orders do not choose their lives in any significant way. Nor can a person bent on achieving personal satisfactions choose a life, for desires are too impulsive and disorganized to provide a genuine ground for choice. The only kind of person who can choose a life is one whose soul has enough organization to control the passions, weigh different options, think into the future and the likely possibilities it holds, and understand what is good for one over time and enough self-discipline to abide by one's decision. The only kind of soul that can perform these functions is one in which reason is the dominant faculty and which has developed the moral virtues of *sophrosyne* (temperance, moderation, self-control), justice (allowing for high functionality of each part of the soul), courage (to do what one knows is right), and wisdom. Without wisdom—especially about what is right—reason does not have the authority to

1

guide the soul. Hence, it is only the person who knows what is good and has developed the moral virtues who can freely choose to have a life. More than any other experience the act of freely choosing how to live one's life is the most humanizing and enlivening of all possible acts, and a life that is well-chosen is the best of all human lives. Thus, only the ethical person truly lives a life fit for a human being.

Quite an argument!

However, from the very beginning, the validity of this argument has been questioned. The Sophists claimed that one could have an organized enough soul governed by pragmatic reasoning rather than an abstract ontological grasp of objective moral principles—principles which they doubted had any valid grounding in reality. They proclaimed that the pragmatically organized, self-seeking person lives the best life because such a person will be freer to seek personal satisfactions than someone who restrains himself by moral concerns. We don't need wisdom to optimally direct our lives, we just need to know what will most satisfy our desires over time.

In response to this powerful counterargument, Socrates supplemented his philosophical account of the ethical life with myths of how each soul would be judged according to its moral goodness in the afterlife. These myths were absorbed into Christian theology in which the firmest answer as to why it is good to be good was given: if you are morally good, you get rewarded with eternal bliss in a heavenly afterlife; if you fail to be good, you will suffer in the afterlife in proportion to your moral failings, a suffering which includes the possibility of an eternal damnation. These are compelling reasons for being a good person, but they depend upon a very questionable metaphysics and an oppressive religious authority.

With the coming of modernity and its renunciation of religious authority, dismissal of metaphysics, adoption of a Darwinian naturalistic account of human beings, and emphasis on the freedom of individuals to pursue their own satisfactions, the religious and metaphysical reasons for being good were cast aside and the question about why it is good to be good once again became a compelling issue. It became even more compelling as modernity transformed into an economic world with astronomically increased opportunities for reaping pleasures through cheating, stealing, lying, and physical mayhem. With so many personal satisfactions available in the modern world and the means to them so subject to intense competition, contemporary persons seem to be asking whether it is better to appear to be morally good while really being out solely for their own perceived interests. The question asked so powerfully by the Sophists when ethics was first invented is again being put forward, but now with even greater force: why is it personally good to be a morally good human being? Why is it good to be good?

When modern persons look to contemporary society for reasons as to why they should want to be good persons, they can locate none that are compelling. Modern society is principally an economic world in which persons are supposed to pursue their own individual satisfactions by doing as well for themselves as they can in market interactions by selling their goods and/or services for as much as they can and buying goods and services for as low as they can. In this world of individuals pursuing personal pleasures in a highly competitive setting, morality is seen as a set of limits to what one can do to achieve those satisfactions. The question then arises as to why persons should constrain their quests by adopting these ethical limits.[3]

Modern society cannot offer as a good reason for being good the rewards one will receive from a divine being either in this life or an afterlife, since by definition modern persons have an empirical orientation and need to have all explanations for values relate to this world. Since modern society is fundamentally an economic one, can an economic reason be given for why persons should be moral? While it is true that economic society could not function unless people in general were honest, private property safe, and the pursuit of satisfactions not personally dangerous, this constitutes a compelling reason only for why a market society needs to generate moral persons. It does not constitute a compelling reason as to why I, as an individual, should be good if I can get more satisfactions by not being good and not getting caught. Indeed, since economic society's highest value is the pursuit of personal happiness, it predisposes its members toward this orientation.

If modern economic society can offer no compelling reasons for why it is good for individuals to be good, can modern philosophy? Modern philosophy has spawned two great ethical systems that are necessary in order for the essential structures of democracy and a capitalist market economy to flourish: utilitarianism and the deontological ethics of Kant. Kant held that persons could pursue their own happiness in any way they want so long as they do not violate basic moral laws—they can seek their own advantage in any way except by lying, cheating, murdering, making false promises, and so on. The utilitarians realized that a society based on a market economics by necessity had to produce a group of people who lose in the competitive struggle. Hence, they proposed that moral persons must concern themselves with the general welfare. For the most part this obligation can be satisfied by rationally engaging in market interactions (as such activity has the consequence of lowering the cost of goods to the lowest level—thereby benefiting everyone), paying taxes to a government that has programs to aid those who have lost out in the competition, and generally having a compassionate attitude toward those who suffer.

In short, modernity has generated the two kinds of ethics it most needs: one that justifies a set of restrictions on how far individual pursuits can be taken and another that strongly validates the satisfaction of desires as the ultimate goal of individual lives and commends a compassionate attitude toward the less fortunate. Ethicists over the past century and a half have fought over which of these is the superior ethic, but, clearly, both are needed in order for a society of economic and social individualism to flourish. That is, modernity has produced a fairly adequate concept of what it means to be a good person for this kind of world: play fair, don't violate basic moral laws that everyone needs to follow in order to have a trustworthy enough economic society, work on increasing general utility, and develop compassion for those less fortunate. This concept of what it means to be a good person might have difficulty with situations in which conflicts between these values arise, but these situations seem fairly rare. They occur most often in the counterfactual examples raised by philosophers. For the most part modernity seems to have a "good enough" sense of what it means to be moral, and we are, in general, held accountable to this concept.

However, the question remains as to whether these philosophical systems of ethics can offer modern persons compelling reasons for following their principles. The utilitarians, especially John Stuart Mill, claimed that we should want to be good because we are fundamentally social by nature. Morality is grounded in our natural inclination to help our fellow human beings. However, they also admitted that we have selfish, self-serving sentiments. There is no apparent reason why one kind of sentiment should be privileged over the other when they conflict.

The primary tendency of philosophy since Kant has been to answer the question of why it is good to be good by showing that rationality itself demands that we follow moral laws or the principles of justice—that they are built into the very concept of a rational life.[4] Like the Greek philosophers, Kant found the faculty of reason—pure practical reason—to be the only kind of human motivation that could be free, lift us above our animality, and counter the numbing forces of social conditioning. If there is any one crucial tenet to what constitutes rationality, it is consistency. To be fully consistent means that we cannot expect others to act on principles which we do not hold for ourselves. Ergo, all rational agents must find themselves constrained by moral laws that hold for all persons.

However, Kant recognized that there were two forms of rational self-direction, one that seeks personal happiness and acts on hypothetical imperatives—maxims which state what we should do in order to optimize our happiness—and another which states what is categorically required of us to be moral. Our question is why should a person favor one form of rationality over the other when the two conflict. If someone can get ahead by cheating while proclaiming the glories of honesty, then why should he prefer to be rationally consistent? In some situations consistency might not be a virtue but, as Emerson said, "the hobgoblin of little minds." There is no way of showing why a universal kind of reasoning is superior to individualistic scheming without presupposing that one kind of rationality is more rational than another.[5]

Some astute philosophers, seeing the failure of utilitarianism and Kantianism to provide an adequate answer as to why persons should be moral, have returned to Aristotle's virtue ethics. Aristotle, like Socrates and Plato, held that we need to develop the moral virtues in order to be able to self-direct our lives, for the virtues moderate the power of the passions enough to give us time to think about how best to respond to situations. In order to have a life that is self-determined rather than thrown this way and that by situations, emotions, and desires, we need to develop such character traits as courage, temperance, and justice. However, the character traits that allow us to have self-chosen lives are just the traits of the kind of person who sustains communities—the traits of a moral person.

Aristotle's argument is impressive, but it has three major problems addressing the moral problems of modernity. First, for Aristotle all good persons are alike—they are all virtuous men living the life of reason in both its practical and theoretical forms. The best of all lives is that of the philosopher. As such, Aristotle's ethics cannot respond to the radical individualism of modernity in which the singularity of each person is affirmed rather than a general type of person—the virtuous rational man. A variation of this problem is that Aristotle's ethics cannot respond to issues of diversity—cannot respond to different groups of people valuing genuinely different forms of life. Second, character traits, including the virtues, seem to operate contextually—we can use them in some situations and turn them off in others. We can be gentle and kind with our friends and ferociously cruel to our enemies. This contextualization of the virtues means that we can ask whether we want to be virtuous in any particular situation, especially situations in which it seems counter to our interests to act virtuously. We still need an answer as to why it is good to be good. Third, the virtues do not seem to be able to regulate unconscious motivations. The most virtuous of persons can suffer from obsessions, unconscious rage that works in stealthy ways, sexual compulsions, and so forth. In short, Aristotle has an inadequate moral psychology for explaining not only what the best life is but why we should live it.

Since deontology, virtue ethics, and utilitarianism more or less exhaust the possibilities for non-religious ethical thinking in the modern world, it appears that neither modern society nor philosophy can say why it is good to be good.[6] The only reason for being moral in the modern world is the Hobbesian one of fear of what will happen if one gets caught, and this is not a convincing reason for those who think themselves sly enough to avoid detection. This failure is not just one among many of the failures of modernity; rather I consider it to be *the failure,* for it stands behind three of the most problematic aspects of modern culture: the relentless presence and power of religious fundamentalism, the moral enervation of liberal modern persons who are good but who cannot explain to themselves or their children why they are, and the catastrophic increase in cheating with a concomitant rise in oppressive instruments of public surveillance and punishment.

While the causes of religious fundamentalism are complex, I believe that a major factor in the emergence of this powerful political and social force is modernity's inability to provide a justifiable ground for ethical life. Fundamentalism's response to modernity's problem is to regressively reinstate an absolute moral authority in the form of God, whose will and law is known with certainty by a sanctioned religious institution. The tightness, vindictiveness, self-certainty, willingness to impose values on others, and lack of epistemological humility that characterizes this movement make it a counterforce to modernity, one that threatens the great gains modernity has made in the realms of individual and political freedom.

Modern persons who eschew the mind-set of religious fundamentalism have the difficulty of explaining to themselves and others why they are being good persons. Insofar as good persons cannot give a coherent account for why they are good, their lives have a core senselessness in them. They can only say "I am good because that is what I choose to be" or "It's just the way I was brought up" with the first answer admitting the groundlessness of the choice and the second succumbing to a morbid developmental determinism. It is difficult to be energized by one's own goodness if one has no explanation for why one chooses to be good. One of the consequences of this moral groundlessness is a tendency to engage in tepid childrearing, one that overemphasizes freedom and personal choice and fails to provide a strong sense of what constitutes living as a good person. This lack of moral energy in liberal modern people explains in large part why the fundamentalists have become such a significant political force in modernity.

The third consequence of modern society's not being able to give an adequate account of why it is good to be good is the phenomenal rise in cheating. I want to focus on this phenomenon because I think it is the defining characteristic for how modern persons are most likely to morally fail. If definitive moral vulnerabilities for previous societies were tendencies to abuse power and privilege, become devastatingly overwhelmed by passions, or overidentify with a group ideal that required undeserved aggression against other groups, cheating seems to be the way contemporary persons are most likely to morally fail.

A PLAGUE ON OUR TIMES

According to David Callahan's *The Cheating Culture*, America is suffering an epidemic of cheating. It seems that in every area of life—government, sports, marriages, business, the stock market, law, the provisioning of health care, schoolwork, entertainment, and even academia—cheating is both rampant and growing. Like a plague—it is catching, spreads fast, and is deadly, for it has the power to undermine the basic social and economic institutions of modern life. Indeed, one can say that the catastrophic economic downturn of 2008 was due in large part to bankers and financiers following at best morally questionable policies in terms of their honesty and at worst, like Bernie Madoff, participating in downright fraud.

The extent of cheating in the United States is simply staggering. The IRS estimates that Americans, both rich and poor, cheat the government out of $250 to $500 billion a year on their income taxes. Americans file about $20 billion of fraudulent insurance claims each year. Half (half!) of all resumes contain lies. Half of all college students cheat at least once. (With this amount of cheating, are transcripts still meaningful accounts of accomplishments?) A number of surveys estimate that close to 50 percent of married persons cheat on their spouses. There have been endless recent business scandals—Enron, World Com, Merrill-Lynch and a number of other Wall Street firms, Martha Stewart, Adelphia, and so on, seemingly forever—in which a number of the most highly paid and esteemed executives cooked their books. Callahan reports that it is a common practice for lawyers, even in highly respected major firms, to cheat their clients by padding their hours; for doctors to prescribe unproven drugs and supplements in order to get subsidies from drug companies; and for professional athletes to use banned substances to enhance their performance. It is so common for young people to pirate music and videos off the Internet that it is almost accepted as ordinary practice rather than seen as stealing. One can see the practice of sub-prime lending that shattered America's economy in the early twenty-first century as a kind of cheating, for it was perpetrated by individuals and institutions trying to get as much as they could for themselves while playing fast and loose with the rules of sound banking practice.

A cheater is someone who does something he knows to be wrong and tries to get away with it by disguising what he is doing. That is, in cheating we do not wonder if what we are doing is morally right or wrong; we know that what we are doing is wrong but do it, nonetheless. These actions are not meant to heroically challenge the reigning moral order but to get away with something. That is, cheating always involves pretense. The student cheating on an exam pretends that she has studied and knows the material. The husband cheating on his spouse pretends that he is, indeed, a faithful partner. The business executive committing fraud pretends that he is a paragon of business integrity.

Cheaters want rewards both from the appearance of being good and from cheating. They want positive approbation for being the good people they appear to be but don't want to do the moral work that is required for this esteem. The student who gets an A because he cheated did not study; the businesswoman who gets rich through fraud did not play on an even field with others who were doing honest work to get ahead; the spouse who cheats expects to get all the rewards of marriage without paying the price of limiting his sexual adventures to those with his marriage partner.

Strangely, many cheaters wish to hide their cheating not only from others but from themselves. Since they know what they are doing is wrong but do not want to think of themselves as bad or weak persons, they try to conceal their cheating from themselves. How can they both cheat and think of themselves as good human beings? Simple—they either deny that what they are doing really is wrong and/or proclaim that there is some unusual condition which excuses them from having to be moral. The denial/excuse often takes the form of a rationalization, such as a student saying to himself, "I promise to learn this material later; I just don't have time now. I shouldn't be penalized by an exam occurring at a bad time, for I really am a good student. It is just that life has been impossible lately." The business executive might cook this quarter's books and tell herself that it is really ok because the company will recover in the near future and there is no need to jeopardize its standing on Wall Street with a disastrous quarterly report. That is, cheaters not only want the world to think well of them; they also want to think well of themselves. They both know that what they are doing is wrong and refuse to acknowledge their wrongdoing.

This ability to deceive ourselves when we are cheating means that we can also cheat on ourselves. In this surprising but immensely common event the person doing the cheating and the person being cheated are one and the same. When we do what we know is harmful to ourselves but simultaneously disavow its harm, we are cheating on ourselves. A dieter might rationalize the eating of a piece of chocolate cake by promising himself that he will exercise later, although he has not kept such promises to himself in years. He eats the cake knowing that it will fatten him, while simultaneously denying that an increase in weight will occur.

If we assume that most persons who voluntarily injure their health and possibilities for personal happiness are in some way cheating on themselves—doing something they know is injurious while simultaneously denying they are doing it or that it is really wrong—then the enormity of the problem of cheating expands astronomically. Two thirds of Americans are overweight with a third being obese; 16 percent are alcoholic or problem drinkers; about 10 percent have significant gambling problems; 22

percent smoke, and upwards of 80 percent of unmarried sexually active persons do not practice safe sex. Credit card debt is astronomical in this country as people buy far more than they can afford. In all of these cases the factors working to produce the lack of self control are complex, usually involving social pressures and biological predispositions, but they often also involve persons violating their own values—they involve people cheating on themselves.

The number of lives that have been lessened or ruined by overeating, compulsive gambling, alcohol and drug misuse, compulsive spending, smoking, and other forms of self-cheating is staggering. When we add the devastations of persons cheating on themselves to those in which others or "the system" are cheated on, then we see more fully how widespread and ruinous the effects of this moral problem are. Personal lives, social and political institutions, and economic well-being are all being significantly undermined by the tendency of modern persons to cheat.

Cheating is not a horrifying moral crime like the genocides of Hitler or Stalin. It typically involves no violence and often does not target specific victims. And, yet, when we look at the effects of cheating in the socioeconomic sphere, politics, academics, marriage, and personal life, we can see that the coherence of social life is being fully undermined. Cheating is a small, almost invisible, moral failure, but like a hidden cancer it is destroying the integrity of both persons and modern society.

Why are contemporary Americans cheating so much? Callahan thinks that the fundamental cause of the epidemic of cheating is the cut-throat economy that commenced during the Reagan years and continues unabated into the present. It is an economy in which winners get huge rewards and losers fall far behind. There is so much to gain by being on top that Americans will do almost anything to be a winner—including cheating. Even people not playing for high stakes will cheat if they perceive that their economic security is threatened. Callahan reports that when Sears went to a compensation system for its auto mechanics that was short on base pay and long on remuneration for doing major repairs, the mechanics filed a massive number of fraudulent reports. Sears was sued for millions of dollars and lost much of the prestige it had carefully built up for over a century. Callahan writes: "Want to know what happens when bottom-line pressure puts ordinary people under intense financial pressure? The answer is not very surprising: They will sacrifice their integrity before their economic security."[7]

While I agree with Callahan that the recent bottom-line market is responsible for tempting Americans to cheat, market pressures do not explain why spouses so readily cheat on one another, why dieters cheat on their diets, why students who are bright enough to get A's with a little work prefer to get A's by taking papers off the Internet, or why young persons think it is quite all right to get music and movies without paying for them. Economic conditions do not exert equal pressure on all kinds of human beings; some will respond to economic stresses more readily than others. It is my contention that what underlies modern persons' strong tendency toward cheating is a concept of self which causes us to see what is moral and what is in our self-interest as often being opposed and which also helps generate social conditions that undermine the possibility of establishing personal integrity. When a society undermines the social conditions necessary to sustain essential psychological structures due to misguided conceptual commitments, it has the tendency to foster the kind of person who not only will cheat but who will have a tendency to develop a host of other social ills that haunt modernity—excessive greed, entitlement behavior, a gnawing sense of emptiness that demands to be filled by everything from food to oversized houses, rage that can break out at any moment, and addictions to alcohol, drugs, food, shopping, and gambling.

MODERNITY'S BELIEFS ABOUT THE SELF AND SELF-INTEREST

If we try to unpack how the cheater is thinking of himself and his interests, I think we will find a set of basic assumptions that govern the way modern people in general think of themselves, namely, that (1) humans are independent organisms, each basically wired to be concerned for their own interests; (2) their interests are conceived of as a maximizing of satisfactions and a minimizing of pain; (3) there can be no universal concept of good, as what gives pleasure and pain differs for individuals; (4) individuals occupy a world of scarce resources and must compete for its goods—compete for everything from winning the most desirable mate to acquiring the basic necessities of life; and (5) there is no authority over an individual's life that is higher than the individual himself. These tenets were developed during the course of modernity, especially in the eighteenth and nineteenth centuries. They constitute the naturalist view of human nature that undergirds market economics, much of the social sciences, Freudian psychology, Darwinian biology, and utilitarian ethics. In relation to this modern view of human nature, morality is understood as a set of constraints that set limits on the pursuit of satisfactions.

    In short, modern persons understand themselves as pleasure-optimizing organisms engaged in an intense competition with one another for satisfactions. They also recognize that if this competition were entirely unregulated, it would probably doom us, in Hobbes' famous words, to a life that is "solitary, poor, nasty, brutish, and short." Without a general respect for moral norms and the law, few of us would fare very well. Since society is in such dire need of moral, lawful persons, it has created ever more effective means of surveillance and a massive arsenal of disciplinary punishments for wrongdoers—everything from doses of shame, humiliation, shunning, and guilt to confinement and death. However, modern society's need for moral citizens and its penalties for violating the moral and legal restraints on the pursuit of self-interest are not compelling to someone who believes his self-interest will be enhanced by cheating and who is confident he will not get caught. There is no intrinsically compelling reason for a person who believes in the naturalistic conception of human nature to be moral. Why constrain oneself with moral rules when one can get more personal satisfactions by appearing to be moral but cheating when there is little chance of getting caught?

THE PSYCHOLOGY OF THE CHEATER

It is not simply the belief systems of modern persons that predispose them to cheating; their psychological make-up also does. Modernity's misunderstanding of the self tends to foster social conditions (especially in childrearing practices, the competitive workplace, and extraordinary pressures to be mobile—see chapter 7) that destabilize and fragment the self, resulting in narcissistic vulnerabilities and symptoms.[8] I want here to examine five symptoms that characterize both cheaters and persons suffering from injuries to the self: (1) psychosocial splitting and/or dissociation; (2) a high degree of grandiosity; (3) a desire to get something for nothing; (4) an intolerable feeling of inner emptiness; and (5) an exceptional fragility concerning self-esteem.

1. Splitting

In order both to do something wrong and to retain their positive approbation of themselves, cheaters need to hide themselves from themselves. They perform this feat by splitting their psyches into two parts such that one part does not acknowledge or own what the other part is doing. This kind of splitting involves a type of vertical psychological repression that is different from the horizontal repression analyzed by Freud. Horizontal repression involves psychological material being dynamically held out of consciousness by a defensive barrier. We cease being conscious of it and cannot recall it to consciousness without working through defenses. The cheater has a different kind of split—a vertical split. In Arnold Goldberg's terms, the cheater suffers from "being of two minds," and, as such, is like the pervert who is conscious that he is engaging in a perversion as he is doing it but denies that he is doing it at the same time.[9] Persons with vertical splits refuse to fully acknowledge what they are doing and, hence, keep their questionable actions apart from their self-concepts.

Vertical splitting is hardly noticed in contemporary society because we are called upon to adopt many roles, each requiring us to adopt different attitudes, values, and personas. This parcelization, so well documented in sociological literature, makes us not even notice the lack of an integral self so long as we are capable of successfully functioning in the different contextual roles in modern life: business person, spouse, parent, friend, sports fan, etc. Each of these roles has its own pressures for how to act in the right way and its own criteria for success.

Zygmunt Baumann, one of the most significant interpreters of modernity, uses the term "liquidity" to describe modern personalities.[10] We need to have different character traits, values, and orientations in order to successfully engage the multifarious situations that face us daily, so we become "liquid" and flow from one personality style to another. Robert Jay Lifton mirrors Bauman's notion of liquidity with his concept of the "protean self"—one that shifts and changes itself to meet different demands in different parts and times of life.[11] Irving Goffman does not even think there is some singular authentic self beneath the roles; rather, he thinks we are nothing but the roles we play.[12]

In short, there is a strong tendency in modern life to compartmentalize ourselves and to try to achieve success in the most important contexts of our lives. As innocuous as this might seem, this kind of conventional role playing has been found by Hannah Arendt to be the primary cause of the most unspeakable evil ever witnessed in the West: the Holocaust. She found that many Nazis who committed horrendously inhuman crimes against Jews were loving spouses and fathers at home and kind, warm, empathic friends. They did not consider themselves mass-murderers of innocent people but simply persons performing their jobs with a great deal of efficiency and success. Arendt stunningly found that lurking behind the evil of the Holocaust was not some monstrous force of darkness but the banality of small men thoughtlessly following social codes.[13]

The problem with ethics in relation to parceling one's life into contexts is that moral values are supposed to be context-independent—they are supposed to hold for all contexts. As such, there is a profound tension between being a moral person and being someone who is successful in the key contexts of life. Moral values, especially the value of integrity, often get in the way of success.

There is also a profound tension between parceling oneself up and the development of a core self. A core self, like ethical values, wants to be present in all of a person's life, not just now and then. This is not to say that people with core selves can't contextualize themselves, for they can and, indeed, must. But if a person pays too much attention to the demands of the situations, he can become neglectful of the self and deaf to its voice. Modernity as a highly compartmentalized society can make it difficult—even disadvantageous—to have a self.

The primary context in a socioeconomic world is, of course, the workplace. Both people with core selves and those who compartmentalize their personalities find themselves having to commit to the values and procedures of their professions. But there is a difference. When pressures in professional life push one toward a violation of moral values, persons with integral selves will have some ballast to fight these pressures, while those without access to such a self will probably succumb to them. Scott Sullivan, the chief financial officer of WorldCom and a kind, generous, caring person to those who knew him, was the primary architect of one of the worst frauds in American history. When his fraud was exposed, WorldCom's stock plummeted and $175 billion in equity value disappeared and with it the retirement hopes of many were dealt severe setbacks (including mine and other professors as their retirement fund TIAA-CREF was heavily invested in WorldCom).[14] Scott Sullivan does not appear to be a malignant man out to hurt others, and, yet, the harm he caused far outdoes what a mean-spirited, vicious local bully could ever do. Why did he do it? I am not privy to his personal psychology, but my guess is that one of the crucial factors is that the only way he could save face as a top business financial executive was to cheat. He identified with his successful persona and when cheating was the only way he could make himself and WorldCom appear to be stunningly successful, he cheated.

2. A High Degree of Immature Grandiosity

The modern tendency to consider oneself the final authority in making decisions about one's life has profound reverberations with the megalomaniacal traits of pathological narcissism. All human beings are to some degree narcissistic and self-centered, but there is a difference between mature and immature forms of narcissism (chapter 2 will fully explore this difference). In mature states of narcissism a person can respect others, understand personal limitations, and, while still feeling special, have an accurate grasp of the reality of his life. Immature narcissists have an overly inflated fantasy of themselves, tend to use others for their own aggrandizement, and think that they deserve more than their fair share.

This last trait leads to the entitlement behavior so ubiquitous in contemporary times that it is not uncommon to be assaulted by it on a daily basis. It can be witnessed in persons thinking they *deserve* to drive as fast as they want and feeling rage when they can't, in persons cutting into lines ahead of others without waiting, in persons demanding perfect service at restaurants as though they were the only guests, and in persons expecting such grandiose gifts at Christmas time that families go into massive debt to meet the expectations. It is an excess of grandiosity and entitlement that allows the cheater to not be terribly concerned about whom he is cheating and fuels his belief that he is entitled to cheat in order to get what he wants.

Narcissistic grandiosity (in distinction from a healthy feeling of specialness and self-importance) is a pathology of the self. It typically involves an over-inflated, overly self-centered way of being that arises as a defensive compensation for an injured, deflated, or under-nourished self. While this psychopathology is not caused by faulty concepts and values but by a lack of psychological nourishment and/or trauma, it has such strong connections to the way the market society envisons the best of lives that modern society must be implicated in the pervasiveness of this psychopathology. Like modern market individuals, narcissists tend to dislike limits and restrictions on their freedom. Both narcissists and market individuals want to feel as though they are the kings of the universe and that the world is theirs for the taking. They resent limits being set on them, just as a two-year-old does. Both narcissists and market-driven people tend to see others as objects that can be used and discarded when they are no longer useful. In short, if the primary value system of modernity is an economic one that emphasizes the individual pursuit of pleasure and power, then the society fosters not only a tendency toward cheating but one also toward pathological narcissism.

Further, insofar as the value system of the culture tends to over-emphasize a self-gratifying perspective, it will result in persons who will be less able to provide the psychological supplies the young need to develop healthy selves. Parents and other caretakers are often conflicted between spending endless hours giving the attention, empathy, and care that children need and pursuing what the society says is best for them: the maximization of personal pleasure. This conflict often results in sub-optimal care for their children. Deprived children then tend to grow up to be persons who have narcissistic vulnerabilities, one of which is to feel it is all right to cheat—to put themselves above the rules—if this is the easiest way to get what they want.

3. Getting Something for Nothing

The cheater wants to get something for nothing. He wants a good grade, social advantage, wealth, status, and such. without having to work or pay for it. In this, the cheater is like the gambler who wants wealth without working for it or the drinker who wants to feel on top of the world without doing anything to produce that feeling except imbibing some alcohol. This motivation also seems to lie behind the hordes of people purchasing lottery tickets and much of the gratuitous stealing that occurs—stealing whose major motivation is the desire to get something for nothing.

Wanting to get something for nothing seems a natural enough motivation and, therefore, not symptomatic of a psychological problem. Yet, many mature human beings prefer the satisfactions that derive from accomplishment to those that are unearned. They have little interest in lottery windfalls, sexual pleasures gained without commitment, or highs gained by imbibing substances. They do not idle away time dreaming of a pot of gold at the end of a rainbow or fantasizing about the immense fame they will have when they are discovered as the next great star. They are active in producing their lives, not passive in hoping some miraculous change of fortune will make everything work. It is not that they are adverse to getting something for nothing every once and awhile, for this is akin to grace. However, they not only take responsibility for producing their lives but deeply enjoy this production. They prefer getting something for something.

Wanting something for nothing might not be a compelling motivation for mature adults, but it is a natural motivation at an earlier time in life—the time of infancy and early childhood. Infants deserve love, nourishment, care, and full attention for no other reason than that they exist. They do not have to earn the goods they enjoy—they are entitled to them just for being born. If a child has empathically attuned parents, these most important gifts of life will be lovingly and freely given. In time the child will be asked to slowly relinquish her position of narcissistic entitlement, but this transformation to a person who understands that he must accomplish to receive rewards will be non-traumatic. If this early stage of life is not done well—if the child has been deprived of freely given love and care, spoiled, or overly pressured to prematurely give up childhood, then an unconscious propensity will develop for wanting to get the kind of good he did not get enough of (or too much of): something for nothing.

Hence, what a cheater reveals in wanting something for nothing is that part of his psyche exists in a regressed place, a place caused by an injury to the self's early (therefore, appropriate) narcissistic grandiosity. If one does not get enough something for nothing in infancy and childhood, or was overindulged (often these two go together, as parental failures to give consistent nurturance are often compensated for by the over-giving of extravagant gifts), then one will seek this kind of nourishment for a lifetime (unless there is some form of psychological intervention).

In sum, I believe that behind many, if not most, of the cases of cheating, addictive gambling, compulsive drinking and drug use, and gratuitous theft lies a child who did not receive the empathic mirroring or calm consistent nurturance that she deserved in infancy and early childhood. Here is further evidence that what lies behind the immoral tendencies in modern culture is not a lack of moral education or a perverse turning away from the good but an early injury to the self that generates compulsive needs and a narcissistic orientation.

4. Inner Emptiness

Often cheaters cheat when they find themselves in a situation in which if they did not cheat, they would lose a sustaining status, be exposed as deficient, or not be able to satisfy a pressing desire. They cannot tolerate feeling empty, deprived, or worthless and proceed to cheat to avoid these dreaded states of feeling. While all persons encounter experiences of frustration, deprivation, and defeat and must learn to tolerate the emptiness connected to these states, persons harboring injuries to the self are at much greater risk for being traumatized by such experiences, for they threaten to reveal an inner deadness at the core of themselves. Rather than experiencing a nuclear self that can persist through difficult situations, they find the not-being of a self, and this is the most dreaded of all psychological experiences. We will do almost anything to avoid this horrifying experience of the abyss at the core of who we are, including cheating, lying, and stealing to sustain an illusion of wholeness.

One of the most common ways to flee an intolerable psychological emptiness is to convert it into a tolerable stomach emptiness. In these conversions, persons feel an incessant craving to eat, drink, and fill themselves up. If cheating is the moral plague of our times, overeating is the health plague. While overeating and obesity have many causes, I think that a primary one for many persons is the lack of an integral self, for without a self one both feels starved and has insufficient self strength to stand up to the craving to eat. While many causes have been proffered to explain the catastrophic rise in obesity—the seductive fast food industry, larger portions of food at restaurants, the overavailability of food for a species programmed to deal with scarcity, and so forth—I think that we must include a sense of inner emptiness that comes from modernity's failure to nourish the self as one of the primary factors in this epidemic. I believe that those who cheat on their diets, abuse alcohol and other drugs, or who compulsively gamble are all attempting, desperately, to ward off falling into the dark emptiness that lies at the core of their souls.

Another way of dealing with inner deadness is to project it into the world. A fear then ensues that the world might turn out to be empty of life—that is, boring. I have been a college professor for four decades and have found that one of the most consistent patterns over these years has been the fear of my students, who are just on the verge of adulthood, that life might turn out to be boring. The worst thing that can be said about a professor or a class is that they are boring. If a student wants to condemn an event, movie, video game, or another student, he does not proclaim them to be evil or malignant or even stupid. He declares them to be boring.

Flaubert, Kierkegaard, Adam Smith, Marx, and Heidegger are only a few of the profound interpreters of modernity who have located boredom as a central problem of modern life. That modern life might be exposed as boring is highly paradoxical, for it is the richest, most variegated, freest form of existence that humanity has ever invented. If modernity is boring, it is not because it lacks adventures but because the persons on those adventures project their own inner emptiness onto the world and, hence, find it always on the verge of being boring. No matter how many affairs Emma Bovary might have, if she does not have a self, they will be experienced merely as a set of pleasures that soon need to be replaced by other pleasures—endlessly. Such a life is boring and all partners will be found to be wanting. Nothing exterior can fill a person who has an emptiness where the self is supposed to be; only repair of the self can make one feel full.

Modern persons tend to ward off feelings of boredom, inner emptiness, and the horror of empty time by making sure that they are always busy. As soon as modern people get up in the morning, their day is already fully accounted for with things they must do. Efficiency becomes a virtue not just in professional situations, but in all of life, for the more efficiently we can accomplish our tasks, the more we get to do. And everything we do is for the good. However, the sum total often does not calculate to a full, abundantly enjoyed life but one that feels so rushed that we do not have time to enjoy it—do not have time to be present in our own lives. Rather than being aware of life's cornucopia, we concentrate on scarcity and what we do not yet have or have not yet done. If modern life has any defining characteristic, it is an incessant busyness. While this busyness can be partially explained by the pressures of modern life, I agree with Heidegger that it is a form of tranquilization, an attempt to avoid the emptiness we harbor within.

Finally, if I am right that persons with injured selves have difficulty tolerating situations that signify emptiness, then we should find modern persons having trouble dealing with loss, especially with the greatest of all losses, death. As Becker, Kübler-Ross, and many others have found, this is the case. We avoid thinking about death and go to insane lengths to ward off death for as long as possible—using up immense resources to prolong life for a few extra months. Kohut thinks that much of what passes as the fear of death is actually a fear about the disintegration of the self. Since the self is a developmental achievement whose coherence is always mutable, it can disintegrate. If modern life is constantly putting stresses on the self—making us forgetful of it, presenting us daily with narcissistic injuries, and failing to provide adequate conditions to support the self, then the anxiety about self-disintegration will be highly intensified and express itself as an inordinate fear of death.

In sum, cheating, addictive consumption of food and intoxicants, and incessant busyness are not accidental features of modern life but symptoms of a society that is systematically undermining, injuring, and starving the selves of its inhabitants.

5. Self-esteem Fragility

A fifth characteristic of the cheater is a tendency to experience extreme fluctuations in self-esteem, going suddenly from a feeling of "I am the greatest" to "I am worthless." Self-esteem fragility explains why so many cheaters need to hide their cheating from themselves—they cannot tolerate thinking of themselves as flawed. Both high and low states of self-esteem seem to be present in acts of cheating in which one feels superior to the moral law but is acting to ward off emptiness or worthlessness. Persons with fragile self-esteem tend also to need to bolster their sense of worth with constant supplies of what feels nourishing—food, sex, praise, success—and will cheat if those supplies are endangered and cannot be gotten through legitimate channels.

Signs that self-esteem fragility deeply affects an extraordinary number of contemporary persons are ubiquitous—extreme difficulty dealing with criticism, being haunted by a constant low-level edginess and tenseness, as though one's worth were under constant attack, a persistent need for reassurance that one is worthy, along with being hyper-vigilant to signs of disapproval.

The flight from self-doubt about one's worth often takes the form of identifying with some form of greatness—a prestigious automobile, a large home in the right suburb, or a winning sports team. These forms of external greatness are attempts at compensation for an inner (unconscious) feeling of insignificance that stems from a failure to develop a self in childhood. Large homes often have interiors that feel like vast empty spaces, thereby metaphorizing the state of the self: grandiose and inflated on the outside, empty on the inside. These homes are often thought of as the solution to all of one's problems ("If I live there, surely I will feel great about myself"), and when the home fails, as it must, to give this feeling of self-worth, then a quiet despair (and, often, increased drinking or drug use) sets in.

The modern world is addicted to sports partly because of the sense of narcissistic triumph we feel when our team wins or our hero has a spectacular performance. We feel elated, as though we ourselves had triumphed (this is also a variation of getting something for nothing). It is, of course, an illusion that we have triumphed and the elation can't be sustained. I have talked with a Colorado psychoanalyst who said that he always keeps a number of open sessions on the days following Denver Bronco games, for if the team loses, the amount of fragmentation in some of his clients rises to almost intolerable heights and they need emergency sessions.

MODERN INDIVIDUALS, MORALITY, AND THE CONCEPT OF SELF

The modern individual represents a new way of being human. This kind of person not only has become the predominant kind of person in the West but is rapidly becoming a global paradigm for how to be human. The modern individual, above all, declares that freedom to pursue his own life to be his highest value. If premodern persons found their identities embedded in traditions and place, modern individuals rebel from any embeddedness in traditional structures of social life, such as religion, gender roles, caste roles, or family imperatives. If premodern individuals sought to reproduce the form of life they were born into, modern individuals despise any form of reproduction of the same as boring, arbitrarily authoritative, and limiting. If premodern persons lived in a social world with severely limited opportunities for change or adventure, modern individuals live in a world of ever expanding opportunities and choices for love, work, recreation, where to live, with whom to live, how long to stay at any place, what to eat, who to politically champion, and so on.

This new kind of human being is stunningly adventurous, inventive, dynamic, flexible, and creative. She is far more embodied than her forerunners and validates her desires and impulses as having worth in a way that would be unrecognizable in the previous age. She does not distrust the spontaneous or the novel the way her predecessors did and she lives for the enjoyment of this life, not some fantasy life that might come after this one is over.

Yet, as with all goods, modern freedom comes with a price. A number of the great commentators on modern life, such as Weber, Durkheim, Marx, Nietzsche, and Heidegger, have found modern individuals to be shallow, prone to boredom, alienated, abstract, restless, driven by power, anxious, and wavering on the verge of nihilism. We have also seen how they suffer from a high degree of personal vulnerability and tendencies toward feeling inner depletion balanced by an excessive grandiosity. And, as I and others have claimed,[15] they have trouble with morality. Modernity has given rise to just the forms of morality it needs in order to function as a complex economic society in which market exchange, self-interested search for material well-being, and socioeconomic status are fundamental—namely, a set of restraints on the pursuit of self-interest (Kant), the affirmation of individual pleasure as the end of life (utilitarianism and economic theory), and the production of the general well-being of all as the fundamental social goal (utilitarianism). However, it has been unable to produce compelling reasons for why it is personally good to constrain or altruistically modify one's pursuit of self-interest to become a morally good person. This failure is most apparent in the epidemic of cheating that has swept over the United States, devastating its economy, undermining family life, and destroying individuals' abilities to be honest with themselves.

I claim that the primary reason why modernity cannot offer a compelling reason for becoming a moral person is located in its concept of the self as an independent agent fundamentally separate from other individuals and often in competition or conflict with them and in its concept of self-interest as attaining both personal satisfactions and the power to continue satisfying desires into the future. With such a definition of the self and self-interest, morality must be seen as a set of limits on personal freedom and self pursuit—limits that must be justified to modern persons. But since the only compelling kind of justification that can be given to self-interested persons is to show that morality is really in their interest, all attempts at justification must fail, for morality is clearly a constraint on self-interest, not a component of it.

I have further maintained that modernity's misunderstanding of the nature of the self has led to its undermining of the social conditions necessary to develop the self in childhood and sustain it in adulthood (see especially chapters 7 and 8 for a full accounting of the social institutions and values that undermine the vitality of the self). In creating conditions that undermine the self and not giving persons adequate concepts by which to grasp their genuine self-interests, modernity tends to injure the self-structure of individuals, predisposing them to develop narcissistic symptoms, symptoms which in turn profoundly predispose persons to want to cheat.

There are further profound connections between narcissism and the inability to be a moral person. Persons suffering from injuries to the self tend to treat others as objects rather than subjects having intrinsic worth, and they harbor unconscious narcissistic rage that seeks to destroy or punish innocent others who happen to be associated to the injuries through transference or projection. The narcissist is so needy that he can't fully recognize the legitimate claims of others for care and is so enraged that he often unawares seeks to harm those he loves. (These claims will be amplified in chapter 2 when we will explore the psychological dynamics that occur when the self is injured.)

In short, I am claiming that both the moral problems and general psychological miasma of modern life are profoundly related to the concept of the self that developed in modernity. This concept of the self did not arise by chance; without it, it is doubtful that liberal democracies and a market economy could have fully come into existence. And yet this concept of self now threatens to destabilize the moral structures that the liberal institutions of modernity need to function and undermines the psychological self-structures which modern persons need to live robust, fulfilling lives. That is, the very concept of self that is foundational for modernity must be overcome if modernity is to sustain itself. The concept of self that needs to be developed cannot be a regresson to a spiritualistic soul but must be founded in the empirical inquiries of those working closest to self-structure—especially injured self-structure, namely, those engaged in psychoanalysis.

NOTES

1. Indeed, my whole argument will be a variation of the Socratic one, for I will claim that it is ethical persons who are best able to sustain the psychological structure humans need in order to feel coherent and zestfully alive. The Socratic variation of this argument fails because Plato was working with a faculty concept of the psyche rather than one grounded in a self that is largely unconscious and that comes into being through a developmental process.

2. Jonathan Lear in his *Happiness, Death, and the Remainder of Life* (Cambridge, MA: Harvard University Press, 2003) brilliantly claims that the most important conceptual innovation of Socrates was the notion that human beings could have lives rather than just live them.

3. Although I have distinguished them in previous books, I will use "morality" and "ethics" interchangeably in this book. "Morality" tends to have the sense of a set of social values that governs our relations to others and is justified independently of established custom. "Ethics" tends to be associated with the personal quest to find a set of values by which an individual can live a good human life. Since I will be

arguing for a theory in which the best way for an individual to live is in empathic social relations with others, the ethical and moral come together.

4. For instance, see the works of Rawls, Gewirth, and Hare, all of whom adopt variations of Kant's stance that we are required to be consistent with ourselves as the key reason for why we need to universalize our values. In chapter 5 I will try to show why rational consistency is not a compelling value but that psychological consistency—integrity—is.

5. Bernard Williams makes this point in one of the most important books in moral philosophy of the past half century, *Ethics and the Limits of Philosophy* (Cambridge: Cambridge University Press, 1982).

6. Note that the recent work in neuroscience that has found that altruistic thoughts and acts can activate pleasure centers in the brain does not give us a good reason for being moral, although it does point to a biological basis that allows us to be moral. Since there are a number of different kinds of experiences that activate our pleasure centers, the biological discovery that we are "wired" to get pleasure from generous or altruistic acts does not really help, for we can still ask why getting pleasure from moral deeds is to be valued over pleasure from selfish deeds, especially when it appears that the selfish deeds will produce more pleasure.

7. David Callahan, *The Cheating Culture* (New York: Harcourt, Inc., 2004), 31.

8. I am, of course, hardly the first commentator to see modern persons as exhibiting narcissistic traits. The best known work is Christopher Lasch's *The Culture of Narcissism: American Life in the Age of Diminishing Returns* (New York: Norton, 1991). Lasch (and most of the other commentators) is morally condemnatory of narcissism rather than seeing it as an affliction from which modern persons are involuntarily suffering. Inflation, grandiosity, entitlement demands, willingness to use others, etc. are not traits chosen by excessively self-centered persons but symptoms of persons who are suffering from a psychological disorder.

9. See Arnold Goldberg's *Being of Two Minds* (Hinsdale, NJ: Analytic Press, 1999) for the fullest account of psychology of vertical splitting. Goldberg was close to Kohut and one of the key persons responsible for the self psychology movement.

10. Zygmunt Bauman, *Liquid Modernity* (Cambridge: Polity Press, 2000).

11. Robert Jay Lifton, *The Protean Self* (New York: Basic Books, 1993).

12. See especially Irving Goffman, *The Presentation of Self in Everyday Life* (New York: Doubleday, 1959).

13. See especially her *Eichmann in Jerusalem: A Report on the Banality of Evil* (New York: Harper & Row, 1963).

14. Callahan, *Cheating*, 98–104.

15. See especially Ross Poole's *Morality and Modernity* (New York: Routledge Press, 1991). I take much from Poole's book in locating the failures of Kantianism and Utilitarianism and grasping that modernity's problem with morality is not one of inadequate ethical systems but of there being a profound tension between adopting the stance as a market individual and being moral. Interestingly, Poole thinks that some notion of an inter-subjective subject is needed to solve the problem but does not know where to find this concept. My book is an attempt to develop the concept that Poole calls for. Alastaire MacIntyre's *After Virtue* (South Bend, IN: University of Notre Dame Press, 1981) is also a stunning commentary on morality and modern life.

Two

Kohut's Theory of the Self

KOHUT'S CLINICAL DISCOVERY

Kohut began his clinical career as a Freudian analyst for whom the heart of the therapeutic process was the analysis of the transferences.[1] However, he found that he had a number of patients who were unable to form traditional transferences, for they were so self-absorbed and self-referential that they could not relate to Kohut as a separate person. That is, they were narcissists. Freud had held that narcissists were unanalyzable because in order for traditional transferences to develop, a person must be able to relate to others as independent of himself. Kohut, in contrast, found that these patients developed another kind of transference—what he termed a narcissistic transference—and also found that such persons could undergo successful analyses if he attended to these transferences. Some of these patients instituted a mirror transference in which Kohut needed to sustain their sense of the self's greatness and specialness, while others formed an idealizing transference in which Kohut became an idealized object with whom they could merge. Whenever he failed to empathically mirror the first kind of patient or interrupted the idealization of the second, these patients then exhibited symptoms of fragmentation, rage, and depression. However, if he attended to these mirroring and idealizing transferences and worked through the ordinary disruptions of them, his patients improved and their symptoms alleviated.

From working with these narcissistic transferences, Kohut drew a number of conclusions that departed from Freud's theory of narcissism and led not only to new clinical practices but also to a new concept of what the self is, how it is formed, and what the conditions are that lead to its fragmentation and enfeeblement. First, he found in distinction from Freud that the primary psychic function was not the discharge of the drives but the development of a self. Indeed, Kohut came to see that drive-behavior (drivenness) was not normal but symptomatic of a fragmented self.

Humans do have basic needs, emotions, and desires, but these have very different psychological dynamics depending on whether they occur in a psyche organized around a coherent self or a fragmented self. He also found that the self was a dynamic core of energy that could invest psychic life with vitality if it were intact and deplete its sense of liveliness if it were injured. In contrast, Freud's ego has none of its own power; all the psychic energy comes from the id.

Third, Freud thought that narcissistic libido, like childhood toys, needed to be given up and replaced with object love, while Kohut found that the retention of narcissistic energy is crucial if we are to feel fully vitalized. He would agree with Aristotle that the love of the self is necessary in order to love others. What we need to do is not to overcome our narcissism but rather to develop it into more mature forms. We might say that Kohut does for narcissism what Freud did for sex. For Freud, it is not only all right to affirm one's sexuality and seek to satisfy its imperatives, it is necessary if we are not to fall into a neurosis. For Kohut, it is not only all right to love oneself, it is imperative if we are to have vital, meaningful lives. The aim is not to relinquish self-love but to transform it from infantile forms to mature expressions. It is infantile narcissistic traits carried into adult life that are devastating, not self-love per se.

THE DEVELOPMENT OF THE SELF: TRANSFORMATIONS OF NARCISSISM

Both Freud and Kohut thought that humans start life in a stage of primary narcissism. This stage is characterized by Freud as one in which an infant experiences itself as perfect, acts in a grandiose manner—full of "megalomania"—and has "an overestimation of the power of its wishes and mental acts."[2] In this state of primary narcissism, the child is "His Majesty, the Baby."[3] Kohut added that in this stage we have exhibitionistic urges to show off our greatness and that narcissism contains a reservoir of psychological energy which he termed "grandiosity."

The child experiences itself as an all-powerful being. As soon as it has a wish, the world (in the form of a caretaker—typically, Mom) mobilizes to satisfy it. The baby feels hungry and a breast appears; it feels sleepy and finds itself tucked into a crib; it wants to be comforted and gentle arms appear to cradle it. With a world so responsive, the baby might well imagine that it is omnipotent and undifferentiated. There will, however, be empathic and responsive failures. The breast does not appear exactly when it is wanted; the mother misunderstands a cry of stomach distress as a call for food and un-empathically forces food on the distressed child. With these failures, the child soon comes to understand that it is not an omnipotent god but the most dependent and vulnerable of all the earth's creatures. These failures are the beginning of the transformation of narcissism, a development that takes two different paths.

1. The Formation of the Idealized Pole of the Self

The first path involves the transformation of the baby's sense of perfection. This path begins when the child binds the anxiety that erupts when her sense of omnipotence is shattered by projecting her perfection on to her primary caretakers, metamorphosing them into gods. By doing this the child once again becomes safe, for she is now under the care and protection of invincible deities. The glow and extraordinary specialness that children typically experience their parents as having derive from the projection of their own narcissistic perfection. However, the child also retains her specialness, for she is the deities' primary object of concern. The perfection, however, is located in the caretakers only for safe-keeping. They get it for early childhood, but then the child needs to re-introject that perfection back into herself and turn it into her own idealizing abilities between the ages of four and six. This can occur because the child can now recognize flaws in her parents and is no longer so utterly dependent on their being perfect. Hence, the arena of perfection moves from "I am perfect" to "You are perfect" to "I have ideals as to what, if I could realize them, would make me perfect." This teasing apart one's actual being from perfection and then re-relating to the perfection in terms of ideals is crucial for retaining the energizing vitality that comes from perfection without identifying with it—a condition that, to the extent it does occur, makes one megalomaniacal.

According to Kohut, it makes all the difference that the sense of perfection "has passed through a cherished object before its re-internalization" for this "accounts for the unique emotional importance of our standards, values, and ideals."[4] The very ability of a person to hold ideals that feel meaningful and can motivate one to action is profoundly affected by this process of the projection of one's perfection into another and then re-internalizing it in the form of one's own ideals. What is psychologically crucial in terms of self-structure is not so much the content of ideals, as this varies over time, but the sense of meaningfulness and worth with which one can endow ideals. People whose perfection has been held in early childhood by a beloved caretaker will have, all things being equal, a much greater sense of living a meaningful life toward special ideals than those who have suffered traumas or severe disappointments in this process. When we turn to questions of ethics, the content of ideals will, of course, take on a central importance; but ethical ideals will not be able to motivate persons unless they first have the ability to love ideals and the desire to guide their lives by them.

The importance of meaningful ideals to the life of the soul can be seen most clearly when an important ideal collapses, such as when one finds after studying organic chemistry that he is not going to be the physician he had imagined himself being or when an idealized partner reveals that he is untrustworthy. I attribute much of the loss of vitality and direction associated with "sophomore slump" (a very real phenomenon) with the loss of ideals. Many students will have had as a major goal getting into a good college and then, once there, proving that they are worthy. Good students accomplish these goals in the first year and so their chief motivating ideal is no longer operable. For many students sophomore year is the first time in their lives that they must generate their own ideals rather than adopting those of their parents and class, and they don't know who they are or where they want to direct their lives. The structure of ideals collapses and they go into a situational depression, sometimes drop out, and often engage in such disintegrative activities as the over-consumption of alcohol, meaningless sexual "hook-ups," and excessive "hanging out."

2. The Formation of the Pole of Ambitions

The second path of narcissistic transformation deals with the narcissistic energy that is connected to feeling special, wanting to exhibit oneself, and wanting to be admired. Kohut says that the primary transformation that needs to occur in this sector of the self is the change from feeling special just because one exists to feeling great because of what one has achieved. When this energy is fully transformed it acts as a strong motivation to achieve, which, when it becomes organized, forms what Kohut terms "a pole of ambitions." For Kohut, ambitions "push us," in distinction from ideals, which "pull us." Ideals are "gazed at in awe" and represent what we would like to be; but the narcissistic self (the pole of ambitions) "wants to be looked at and admired."[5] This side of the self carries the exhibition-istic side of narcissism; it wants itself to be recognized as great and special (rather than its ideals). Ideals might give meaning to life, but it is the "ambitious" kind of energy that gives us restless energy for achievement in the world.

Ambitiousness in Kohut is close to what the great nineteenth-century philosophers termed "will." To will something for Nietzsche or Kant is not simply to want or desire something but to act from a source of autonomous, spontaneous energy that operates more like a prime mover rather than as an event in a series of causes and effects. Wants, desires, and needs are typically instilled in us by non-self forces; the will is different. It is a self-moving kind of power and is, I believe, what Kohut means by the pole of ambitions. When the pole of ambitions is coherent and mobilized it allows us to feel a strong sense of personal agency, a sense that we can generate our worlds. I believe that Kohut is right in making ambitions only one pole of the self rather than stand for the whole of the self as Nietzsche and Kant seem to do. The concept of will, by itself, is too abstract and impersonal to stand for the core of what it means to be an individuated vitalized agent—ideals, traits, talents, and a playful *jouissance* need to be added.

The transformation of this grandiose sector of the self from "I am great because I exist" to "I am great because I accomplish" occurs through a process Kohut terms "optimal frustration." A situation is optimally frustrating if a child (or anyone) performs a task that extends their skills, energy, or intelligence. For instance, when a young child is invited for the first time to use a toilet, he is being asked to give up the grandiosity of eliminating his wastes whenever and wherever he pleases and to use instead a rather horrifying contraption. The loss of privilege constitutes a narcissistic blow, but one, which, if the child is ready, will be nontraumatic. If the toilet training goes well, the child will convert injured grandiose specialness into accomplishment pride. The feelings of specialness and greatness are retained, but the infantile behavior is forsaken. A situation will be non-optimally frustrating if it is either too easy for the child (resulting in boredom) or too difficult (generating either genuine frustration or trauma).

This path of optimal frustration includes Freud's concept of development through the introjection of lost objects. If a mother withdraws herself as breast-feeding nurse at the proper time, she is asking the child to be able to accept more mature (less demanding) forms of sociality and nourishment. The child will be able to accept these more mature interactions only if he is able to supply some of the earlier soothing functions by himself. Kohut says that through a process of "transmuting internalization" we take part of the psychic abilities of the selfobject and convert them into our own "psychic protein." Kohut differs from Freud in seeing the introjection of lost objects to be only one part of the structuralizaton of the self rather than its essence. One might say that the whole situation of challenge along with selfobject responsiveness and care is what generates self.[6]

Kohut found that the narcissistic energy associated with grandiosity is inherently tied to a self-concept—an idea/evaluation of who one is. "While the exhibitionistic-narcissistic urges may be considered as the predominant drive aspect of the narcissistic self, the grandiose fantasy is its ideational content."[7] One's self-concept needs to transform over time from a "fantasy" of greatness into a more realistic understanding of one's specialness. Always, of course, one's self-concept is tinged with fantasy, for in reality very few achieve the importance needed to realistically support the feeling of specialness they carry. More than any other factor it appears that having a positive and strong self-concept is crucial in health and vitality of the ambitious pole of the self.

Kohut also discovered that a person's self-concept is highly vulnerable to environmental responsiveness. If children are empathically mirrored during the first several years of life, they will continue to feel a sense of sustaining greatness and specialness, which in turn will sustain their vitality and allow them to ebulliently explore the world and assert themselves without shame or timidity. However, exhibitionistic grandiosity is easily ignored, shamed, put down, or ridiculed. If these devastations to one's self-concept occur chronically or in non-repaired traumas, they can severely deplete a person's sense of vitality and make her reluctant to assert herself in the world. If the defeated grandiose energy then diverts into the idealized pole, life can become frozen in fantasies of greatness rather than actual accomplishment.

3. The Playful Remainder of Narcissistic Energy

There is a third branch of grandiose/exhibitionistic narcissism that Kohut almost never writes about, for it is less likely to be subverted and in need of therapeutic repair. This kind of narcissism retains the initial feeling of being special just because one exists. With this side of narcissistic energy we feel a kind of joyful delight in ourselves and the world. I believe this sense of being delighted in oneself is crucial for the abilities to play, have aesthetic experiences, be intimate, and be creatively productive. Ideals guide us but also pressure us to realize them. Ambitions push us to be productive. The third form of narcissism neither pulls like ideals nor pushes like ambitions but resides in a profound sense of our own singular worth beyond accomplishment and ideals-to-be-realized. With this form of narcissistic energy we can be creative not because we have to but because we affirm ourselves so profoundly that we want to generate new worlds, new meanings. I believe it is this sector of narcissism that we express when we spontaneously pronounce our delights and dislikes.

This playful, self-affirming energy does develop but typically without pressure from the world, for this form of narcissistic energy seems spontaneously to seek higher forms of complexity. No one forced me to give up the grandiosity I felt as a young child for having mastered the game of checkers. It just became boring as my skill and intelligence level passed beyond it, and so I moved on to more complex games. I believe that it is this kind of playful, life-affirming narcissism that Nietzsche champions— sometimes to the neglect of the other forms of narcissistic energy.

Kohut did not pay much attention to this form of narcissistic energy as it is not where severe injuries to the self are most likely to occur. Traumatic injuries seem to be more deeply associated with failures in caretakers to

empathically mirror grandiose energy, hold idealizations, or optimally frus-
trate the growing child without shame or spoilage. If this sector of playful
narcissistic energy has a transference associated with it, it is the "twinship"
transference. Injuries here involve some kind of limitation on spontaneous
expression and the experiencing of oneself with joyful delight. They might
have happened when one was shamed—not for failure but for showing off
or exhibiting oneself. Since such injuries tend to push a child into a state of
isolation and feeling ashamed for his spontaneous likes and dislikes, ges-
tures and movements, repair for these injuries comes in twinship transferences. In a twinship transference I feel that it is all right to be just who I am
because, in her being like me, my "twin" confirms the worth of the kind of
person that I am. I think that mature love relationships involve a great deal
of twinning, for this sector of the self is extremely fragile as it is not supported by estimable ideals or a history of accomplishments. It expresses in
a quite vulnerable way one's singularity.

Although Kohut does not address how these three kinds of narcissistic
transformations need to be balanced, it is important to see that too much
or too little of one of them can result in a distorted life. Persons with too
much self associated with ideals will be prone to depression, for they will
always find themselves lacking in comparison to their ideals. So much of
their selves resides in the perfect ideal of who they should be that they
don't have enough energy to perform the actual feats necessary to realize
their ideals. They can become immobilized in guilt. If too much energy is
connected with ambitions, a person feels driven. He cannot rest but must
always be accomplishing in order to feel good about himself. If he finds
himself "wasting" time, he goes into paroxysms of self-loathing. There is
little or no time for play and often the work is deficient in meaningfulness.
It is work for the sake of doing, not for the sake of meaning. Finally, if too
much narcissistic energy is located in playful self-delighting grandiosity,
one might be overly tempted to simply enjoy life rather than produce it.
One will be deficiently pushed by ambitions and will not be motivated to
achieve ideals. As nice as this might seem, it can soon lead to boredom, a
sense of meaninglessness, and a decline in vitality.

THE NUCLEAR SELF

These three strands of narcissistic energy need to combine with a person's
idiosyncratic traits, gifts, and abilities to form what Kohut calls the nuclear self.

I obtained the impression that during early psychic development a process
takes place in which some archaic mental contents that had been experienced

as belonging to the self become obliterated or are assigned to the areas of the non-self while others are retained within the self or added to it. As a result of this process a core self—the "nuclear self"—is established. This structure is the basis for our sense of being an independent center of initiative and perception, integrated with our most central ambitions and ideals and with our experience that our body and mind form a unit in space and a continuum in time. This cohesive and enduring psychic configuration, in connection with a correlated set of talents and skills that it attracts to itself or that develops in response to the demands of the ambitions and ideals of the nuclear self, forms the central sector of the personality.[8]

Like the nucleus of an atom, the self is that set of psychological functions around which all the other psychological functions revolve. The self is the central fulcrum of the psyche that holds all of the diverse motivations and centrifugal forces together. When it is coherent, the psyche can function well. However, when it is injured the psyche can have massive to moderate amounts of non-functionality depending upon the age of the injured person and the severity of the trauma.

Although the core of the "bipolar nuclear self" consists of the poles of ideals and ambitions, Kohut emphasizes that it is not so much the content of the ideals and ambitions that give the self a sense of continuity—"the sense of our being the same person throughout life"—as it is "the abiding specific relationship in which the constituents of the self stand to each other."[9] Since ideals, ambitions, and traits all are subject to change, the relationship between them, while having some kind of abiding structure, must be understood as a dynamically structured identity. Later self psychologists, such as Joseph Lichtenberg, envision the self as a "non-linear dynamic system."[10] That is, the self is not an abiding entity but a structured process. The self has a stability—a nature—because it has a structure, but this structure responds to environmental inputs and internal adjustments. It shifts, develops, mutates, but all in a continuity with itself. Hence, this is not a foundationalist theory in the sense of locating one permanent unchanging ground upon which all rests. There is a foundation—the self— but the self has a fluidity, a dynamic flow, a set of relational tensions that call for constant re-adjustment and re-alignment. The self is a ground, but its being is its becoming. It is not so much a thing as an adventure—a structured adventure with continuity—but an adventure, nonetheless.[11]

It is precisely because the self has multiple sectors (ideals, ambitions, spontaneousness, traits) and each of these sectors has multiple parts (we typically have more than one ideal or ambition or trait that needs expression) that it is more correct to say that the self exists as a relational tension than that it is a thing or an organization of properties. "Just as there is a gradient of tension between two differently charged (+, -) electrical poles that are spatially separated, inviting the formation of an electrical arc in which the electricity may be said to flow from the higher to the lower level, so also with the self. The term 'tension gradient' thus refers to the relationship in which the constituents of the self stand to each other."[12] In locating the self not in a set structure but in a dynamic relation between ambitions, ideals, and traits, Kohut reflects the discovery of the great nineteenth-century German philosophers—Hegel and Kierkegaard—that the self must be conceived of as an activity interrelating oppositions rather than as a merely objective container of personal identity.

This model of the relational self will become even more dynamic and complicated when we add the intersubjective element to it in the next section. For now, what is important to understand is that the self consists of different parts each of which is capable of change and development and between which there is a dynamic tension that is also capable of development. When the sectors of the self harmoniously work together, we feel most vibrantly like ourselves. That is, self-experiences involve the realization of ambitions within a field made meaningful by our ideals and which utilize our most cherished skills.

The fundamental tension in the self that Kohut addresses is that between our ideals and our ambitions. Yet, he rarely goes further than saying that our ideals "lead us" and our ambitions "push us," or that we cherish our ideals but not our ambitions. I understand this tension to be akin to the tension Hegel found between identifying with a worthy ideal (which must be stated in some kind of universal or general terms) and asserting the greatness of one's particularity.[13] Universality gives meaning to life but generalizes it. The zest in life comes from the particular human being asserting and enjoying her unique singularity. However, such singularity is deficient in its ability to provide meaning for life. The self, to feel whole and alive, needs both ideals and ambitions, both a depth of meaning and a robust, spontaneous particularity. But they have an internal tension. When this tension is successfully negotiated such that in realizing our ambitions we also realize our ideals, experience takes on the glow of joy.

While we can often name or identify ideals and ambitions that we consciously hold, these might not be the same as the ideals and ambitions located in the unconscious nuclear self. We can be mistaken about ourselves. While we might not be able to name or systematically organize the nuclear self's values/concentrations of energy, we can come to know what experiences or relationships are most aligned with the self by paying attention to when we feel most zestfully alive. That is, we can distinguish self-experiences from both defensive experiencing—which tends to be tight, repetitive, driven, manic, and/or inflexible—and an everyday kind of experiencing, which has a kind of flatness to it. Both defensive experiencing and everydayish experiencing can involve pleasures, even intense pleasures.

But something else happens when our nuclear selves are present in experience—we feel intensely alive, engaged, and present, or what Kohut terms "joy." Pleasures, like those accompanying eating, sex, or going to a good movie come and go, but the joy of self-activities propels us into a realm where life feels buoyant, meaningful, and profoundly worth living.

Being mistaken about one's ideals, ambitions, or talents is one thing—its penalty is a certain lack of vitality and coherence in experience—having an injured or fragmented self is quite another. When the nuclear self is traumatized to such a degree that its cohesion is compromised, three psychological reactions occur: (1) the experience of intense disintegration anxiety, (2) an explosion of narcissistic rage, and (3) the construction of defenses that cocoon the injured part of the self so to prevent consciousness from experiencing the disintegration anxiety, narcissistic rage, and injuries to the self.

Disintegration anxiety is the fear that the self will be so injured as to permanently break apart, leaving the psyche without a center and in a state of insanity. For Kohut disintegration anxiety is the most debilitating of our anxieties and must be fended off at all costs. It often masquerades as the fear of death, for the loss of a coherent self is the equivalent of psychological death. In contrast to Freud's claim that castration anxiety stands at the heart of psychological dynamics, Kohut sees the need for psychological defenses to deal mainly with disintegration anxiety. For him disintegration anxiety includes anxieties about castration (anxiety about the loss of potency/agency), death, and the loss of love: "Not only the fear of loss of love, or the fear of death, but also the fear of a loss of contact with reality or the fear of psychosis can be compared with the feeling of horror that self psychology understands as disintegration anxiety."[14] When the self disintegrates, the psyche loses its ability to organize experiences, its sense of reality wavers, and selfobject relations shatter. While an intact self can sustain itself with difficulty through a loss of love, the reduction of potency, or the approach of death, a fragmented self in the midst of disintegration anxiety feels the possibility of losing all of its functionality.

The second product of trauma is the eruption of narcissistic rage. Narcissistic rage differs from anger at obstacles that stand in the way of the self in that once it exists, it remains in a diffuse state, ready to attack any surrogate object with the cruelty of revenge and punishment. Kohut distinguishes narcissistic rage from "the aggressions mobilized in the service of eliminating an obstacle to our goals: the first is characterized by unforgiving hatred and cruelty, the second by the absence of the need to hurt the opponent unnecessarily and the subsiding of aggression altogether when the goal in question is reached."[15] Narcissistic rage seeks to destroy any person who gets associated with the trauma suffered by the self, and no amount of inflicted pain will satisfy its demand for revenge.

This effect of trauma to the self is, as we will see, of extraordinary importance to ethical life. My supposition is that ordinary anger and aggression, while responsible for much misery and conflict, are not the primary causes of massive human evil. Ordinary life simply involves conflicts, anger, and aggression. Narcissistic rage, on the other hand, harbors cruelty, an inability to forgive, and diffuseness in terms of the objects it seeks to destroy. It wants to annihilate others, and no amount of annihilation satisfies the underlying rage. The only way the rage can be dissolved is through repair of the self; un-repaired selves remain enraged for a lifetime, a lifetime in which the rage seeks—overtly or highly covertly—its victims for destruction.

The third consequence of trauma to the self is the erection of defenses to protect the injured self by sequestering it from further blows and to keep narcissistic rage and disintegration anxiety from consciousness. In Freudian theory the defenses are attempts to avoid acknowledging psychological conflicts, and proper therapeutic technique involves attacking the resistances and defenses in order to expose the conflict. In self psychology, on the other hand, the defenses come into being largely to protect an injured self and contain the traumatic by-products. They are not so much avoidances of disagreeable emotional material as protections against further ruptures to self-structure. A person will not voluntarily give up these protections until there is some restoration of the self and they are no longer needed. Hence, the analyst needs to repair the self while simultaneously easing the rigidity of the defenses.

Persons with injured selves can exhibit a variety of symptoms, including feeling an inner deadness—often covered over by manic activity, a lack of motivating ideals, a chronic sense of inner depletion (often converted into fear about not having enough money), and a feeling of being always overburdened (because the self is so weak). They have tendencies to be non-empathic with others, isolate from others, or demand that others always allow them to be center stage. They suffer from shallow emotional connections and can be prone to the perversions, for different parts of the self operate independently from one another. In sum, having an intact nuclear self vitalizes a person's life as no other psychological factor can, while injuries to the self can cause a person to harbor profound disintegration anxiety, boil with narcissistic rage, and suffer from symptoms that severely compromise her ability to enjoy life, attain agency, connect with others, and treat others with respect and love.

Although an injured self might be sequestered by the defenses from fully engaging in experience, it is not absent from experience. Often a fragmented self will express itself as a kind of constant feeling that life is a bit disjointed. Usually there will be a few areas of experience that are felt as safe in which the self can be more present, and these feel joyous. However, when experience involves a reminder of the fragmenting trauma, then the defenses immediately re-appear and the self retreats to its protected sanctuary. This is tragic, for it means the self typically cannot avail itself of the help it needs, as help occurs in caring relationships—just the kind of relationships in which early trauma tends to occur.

THE SELF AS UNCONSCIOUS SUBJECTIVITY

The strangest and most difficult claim about the self that Kohut's theory entails is that the self is largely an unconscious structured subjectivity. I will explain the difference between the conscious ego (usually taken to be the self) and the self in chapter 4; for now I need to clarify what it means to call the self an unconscious form of subjectivity.

First, to call the self an unconscious structured subjectivity is to indicate that it cannot be accessed by conscious introspection. This agrees with what Hume and Kant found to be true about the self—it did not (and could not) appear as an object to consciousness. This is true both because the self resides at a level of unconscious psychological processes and because it is a form of subjectivity. Since the self cannot be known through conscious introspection, it can never be fully clear to anyone what the nature of her self is, whether or to what degree it is coherent, or how the self is experiencing a situation differently from how the conscious ego is experiencing it.

Second, although the self is not knowable through conscious introspection, it can be known in the way that other unconscious phenomena are known—through signs, symptoms, and dreams. When a person's self feels safe in a situation and something about the activity directly connects to the self's ideals and/or ambitions, the person will feel an increase in aliveness, buoyancy, and engagement. If the self finds little to connect to in a situation, the person feels her experience to be somewhat flat. If the situation is traumatizing or has reminders of previous traumas, then the person will typically feel increased levels of anxiety, dissociation, depression, and perhaps as a counter to the depression, an increase in manic energy. Kohut writes that if he has somehow failed to give a patient's self the empathic mirroring or holding an idealization that it needs, the patient will often come to the next appointment with socks that don't match, hair disheveled, or exhibiting other manifestations of fragmentation. In short, although the self is not available to be known through conscious introspection, it issues signs as to how it is experiencing the world.

The self also expresses itself in dreams. Kohut and other self psychologists present a number of case studies in which dreams play a crucial role in symbolizing the self states of patients. In contrast to Freud, who sees dreams fundamentally as wish fulfillments, Kohut theorizes that dreams can have a number of functions, including the symbolic expression of self-structure, self-strivings, self-injuries, and so forth. Careful attention to dreams and how they shift over time can be strong indicators of structural changes occurring in the self.

An injured self reveals its deficits, traumas, protections, and compensations in symptoms. For instance, one of the common symptoms of a narcissistic disorder is to have a persona that exhibits an extraordinary self-inflation that easily flows into arrogance, pomposity, or theatrical posturing. This symptom reveals both the lack of genuine self-love, an internal feeling of gnawing deflation, and a compensatory external grandiosity.

Third, to say that the self is unconscious means that it participates in unconscious dynamics. When the self is traumatized, the dynamics of dissociation, defense, resistance, and symptom-formation get mobilized. This kind of dynamics means that an injured or traumatized self is even harder to know than an intact self, for it is now not simply in the unconscious but cocooned behind imposing guards, sentinels that are wary of having it appear even when psychological growth has occurred and the defenses are no longer needed.

It is because the self is an unconscious structure and protected by unconscious dynamics when it is injured that it cannot be aided by the self-help procedures so in vogue today. Self-help procedures, such as saying mantras that proclaim one's goodness, being kind to oneself, doing nice things for oneself, or consciously accepting oneself, do not work. The acts of acceptance, affirmation, and restoring coherence to the self that need to occur are unconscious events that have little to do with what a conscious ego is thinking or saying. If the self were part of consciousness, such procedures would be curative and life would be much easier. When our conscious egos suffer injury from someone and the offender apologizes, we calm and feel restored. That injured selves seem almost impervious to this kind of correction is significant evidence that they reside at an unconscious level. Repair of a traumatized self can take years of painstaking empathic responsiveness by a seasoned therapist.

Fourth, to say that the self is unconscious entails that it participates in a form of experiencing governed by primary process thinking. This is the most difficult feature about the unconscious self to understand—that the unconscious self is a form of subjectivity that experiences the world; forms ideals; has wishes and ambitions, hopes, and a remembered past that is different from the way consciousnesses experiences the world; holds values; acts; and remembers the past. Thus, while Kohut says that the self has ideals and ambitions, these terms cannot be taken to work exactly like the ambitions and ideals of consciousness. In primary process thinking, ideas, beliefs, values, and ambitions do not have the critical clarity of their conscious cousins. They are not carefully articulated in relation to reality and tend to collapse differences into identities. The girlfriend who reminds the conscious person of Mom can, in the unconscious, be equated with Mom and stimulate all the unresolved problems that growing up with one's particular mother involved. In consciousness, time is clearly organized into events that have a historical sequence; in the unconscious, time is collapsed. Although decades might have passed since a trauma, the unconscious can expect to re-experience it at any moment, especially when certain reminders of it occur.

Ideals and ambitions in the unconscious are a type of proto-ideals and proto-ambitions (to use Jonathan Lear's term).[16] These two poles of the self are, initially, the abilities to have meaningful ideals and a sense that one can act in the world rather than highly specified ideals and ambitious goals. When these unconscious parts of the self suffer traumatic injury it is not only this ideal or that ambition that is injured but the very ability to be motivated by ideals or act assertively in the world. The self's unconscious poles are not, however, totally indefinite and capable of adopting any definite ideals and ambitions consciousness might have; rather, when a conscious ideal or ambition aligns with a propensity in the self, it leaps out as something we simply must do or try to achieve. We entertain countless ideals and ambitions over time, but only several "call" to us as being just the right ones for us. The calling that singles out ideals and ambitions as ones that we should adopt is the voice of the self.

Because the self experiences differently from consciousness a person can simultaneously be having two different experiences of the same event or object. One might consciously experience a professor's lecture as a compelling presentation of material while unconsciously be associating the professor with a domineering father. The unconscious connection might never come to consciousness, but a need to strongly criticize the lecture or instantly forget the material might overcome the person. Consciously, one's parents might be remembered as strong persons with well-organized worlds, but the self might have experienced their fragmented nuclear selves and harbor some anxiety about their repressed narcissistic rage.

Finally, now that I have given the ways in which the self is unconscious, let me say that it also seems omnipresent in consciousness. It is present not as an object to be experienced or even as the "I" which is the subject of experience, but as a qualification of that "I," a qualification that can be experienced but not fully articulated or grasped. When a healthy self is present, the "I" that is the subject of ordinary experience feels more robust, more present, more engaged than when the self is fragmented or depleted. When the self is fragmented or not fully present, the "I" can feel somewhat disconnected or distant from its own experience. Experience is happening, but it is not fully my experience. When the self is injured, there seems to be a general sense in the "I" that life is troubling or not quite right. So, para-doxically, even an injured or absent self is "present" in its fragmentations or lack of presence. Fine clinicians can experience this "absence" or "fragmentation" even when it is not being noticed by the patient.

THE FRAGILITY OF THE SELF AND ITS NEED FOR SELFOBJECTS

Once one understands the self as a precipitate of a developmental process that is inherently and essentially relational, it becomes clear how interwoven self-structure is with the presence of others. The child's sense of specialness and worth depends on its internalizing of the empathic mirroring of its caretakers. The child's ability to mobilize active energy is built on the empathic attunement of others to its ever-changing capabilities. The child's ability to be motivated by ideals is grounded in others' abilities to accept idealization and not betray it. The permeable child transmutes the gleam in the mother's eye into an internal self-glow, the sensitive encouragement of others into a sense of self-confidence, the calming presence of others at moments of failure or distress into its own ability to self-soothe, and the strength of others who hold its idealizations into the strength of ideals.

Kohut discovered that the role of others in establishing and sustaining a self did not end in childhood but continued throughout life. Experience always presents us with blows to our esteem and confidence, blockages to our ambitions, failures to realize ideals, and the loss of those we count on. The level of stress such events put on the self can disorganize, deplete, or traumatize the self. To repair these injuries, the self needs help from selfobjects—others who are willing to perform self functions for us. Selfobjects are not persons who just help us in an external kind of way, the way a chair helps us to sit at dinner, but actually perform self functions for us when we are not able to do so ourselves. The feeling of well-being and general sense of safety in the world is dependent on one's having others who can perform self functions when one is unable to. "Self psychology holds that self-selfobject relationships form the essence of psychological life from birth to death, that a move from dependence (symbiosis) to independence (autonomy) in the psychological sphere is no more possible, let alone desirable, than a corresponding move from a life dependent on oxygen to a life independent of it in the biological sphere."[17]

As Kohut says, the most important constituent in the creation of a healthy self is "the gleam in the mother's eye." It is this "gleam" that assures us that we are wonderful and special, that we are inherently good, and that we deserve to feel robustly alive. Later in life, we are sustained by seeing our friends' eyes light up when we come into their presence, and rarely can anything make us feel more alive or vital than seeing a lover's eyes gleam at us in the fullness of love.[18]

Since the self is always in relation to others, disruptions in one's selfobject relationships often result in fragmentations of the self. When an important friend moves away, we typically experience a loss in vitality and buoyancy with the possibility of experiencing acute depression. This seems to be especially true for those at fragile stages of self-development, such as during the teenage years. In the extraordinarily mobile world of contemporary life, it is rare for a child or young person to live through many years without having significant selfobject abandonments or disruptions.

Kohut's emphasis on the fragility of the self is—and I cannot emphasize this enough—a monumental shift in how Western society conceives of the self. It is much closer to a Confucian model of self-construction than it is to Plato, Aristotle, Spinoza, or Nietzsche. For Confucius, the self is always located in community and cannot conceive of itself outside of its relations to family members, clan members, and the rituals and practices that hold the community together. That is, for both Confucius and Kohut, the self develops and flourishes only in a web of selfobject relations.

In contrast, the West has been obsessed with individuals freeing themselves from social entanglements and becoming, in Aristotle's terms, "self-sufficient." The model for the self that riveted the ancient world and still persists as the defining model of individuality is Socrates at his trial and death. Nothing can move him or perturb him. Society can hate him and execute him, but it cannot change him or alter his relation to himself, for he is the master of himself. He needs nothing other than his mind in order to be fully complete. Aristotle, for all of his wisdom about how a good life involves virtuous interaction with friends and participation in the polis, claims that the best kind of life, in the end, is one of isolated contemplation, as this form of life is the most self-sufficient.

This model of achieving a self-sufficient, fully independent self is carried forth in Descartes' concept of the self as independent substance and Nietzsche's radical individualism that wants to surgically excise all social influences on the self. It is also found in the less rarefied tradition of the American frontiersman who needs nothing from society and can forge his own worlds through craft, ingenuity, and strength of spirit. It appears in Thomas Jefferson's ideal of a country of small independent farmers. Economically, the self-sufficient individual is identified with a person wealthy enough to buy all the services and goods he needs. When we look to the great hero literature of the West, we again find the ideal of the self-sufficient individual. From Odysseus to Indiana Jones, to be a hero is to be an independent maverick, secure in himself and needing nothing other than himself to conquer the most difficult of life's trials.

In sum, whether we look up to the austere heights of philosophy, probe our hero literature, engage in economic society, or simply go to the movies, we find ourselves confronted with an image of whom we should be: the self-sufficient, independent, invulnerable hero. In contrast, Kohut's concept of the self implies that no one is a self-made person and that our psychological well-being is dependent upon our relations with others. The self is built through the mirroring of others, the transmuting internalization of others, and others allowing us to merge with their idealized greatness. In short, others lie at the core of the self. We are social all the way down—there is no pure core of independent self.

Even if we live as hermits, it will be because we carry the mother's gleam in our souls and our father's merged-with strength in our bones. In our hermitage we would still carry the optimal frustrations and the transmuting internalizations upon which our selves were built. However, we must not carry this image too far, for from the viewpoint of self psychology, no isolated individual is ever really fully able to consistently sustain a vital self. Without selfobjects actively helping to support us we must rely on psychological structures other than the self—typically the ego or the persona (terms that will be explained in chapter 4).

If lifelong dependency on others is a hard enough pill to swallow for those who have been raised on a conceptual diet of frontier independence, it is even more difficult to acknowledge another conclusion that irrevocably follows from Kohut's concept of the self: much about our lives is fated. Our personal destinies depend in large part on what others do to us in early childhood when we have no choice in the matter. With empathic, sensitive, resonating parents whose care for us is not traumatically interrupted by illness or crisis, we have the nourishing environment needed to grow strong, vital selves. If our caretakers are non-empathic, inconsistent (such as with alcoholic parents), toxic, or traumatized, then, depending on the severity of their deficiencies, no self might develop (as in the psychoses), a severely injured one that cannot be fully repaired (as at the borderline level of pathology), or a self injured in one of its primary sectors and which might be restored later with good luck or therapy. Added to the fate of the early environment is the fate given to us by genetics—some people are simply more resilient than others in dealing with less than adequate environments. Often children in the same family confronted with the same poisonous environment will develop highly different responses with variable degrees of health.

To say that we always need others to support the self is not to say that all forms of dependency are equally appropriate at all times of life. The maturation of narcissism necessarily requires the development of selfobject relations. The infant depends on others for everything, is unable to be reciprocal, and tends to merge with or devour his selfobjects in order to get their psychological nourishment. Adults in satisfactory situations ought to be able to provide the material means for their subsistence, make independent judgments about what is best for them, enter into reciprocal forms of giving and receiving with others, and be able to take in psychological nourishment without primitively merging with others. The difference between archaic selfobject relations and mature ones is so important that Kohut made it the key factor in indicating whether an analysis had been successfully completed.[19] The abilities to depend on others without merging with them, to use them without destroying their independence and autonomous worth, and to be willing to provide for them when they are in need of selfobject repair define mature selfobject relations.

The Kohutian insight that the self is essentially interrelated with others has led a number of recent psychoanalytic thinkers—relationalists and intersubjectivists—to proclaim that the self is fully constructed out of its relations to others.[20] They find no remainder to the self outside of its selfobject relationships. Not only are we social all the way down but in every way. While I think that there is no aspect of the self unaffected by relationships to others, there is a residue that is uniquely individual. It is that which responds to others, finds their input soothing or traumatic, intrusive or distant, caring or mechanical. This primitive responsiveness to the social input into the self from others reveals that there is a core self already there able to convert selfobject supplies into its own psychological protein, resist pressures that are foreign to its nature, or be injured by traumatic intrusions, disruptions, or deficiencies in care. We might say that the Kohutian self mirrors the discovery in physics that every piece of matter is both a particle and a wave. The self is both a singular structure in an individual and an extended set of relationships.

The Western tradition has, in general, overemphasized the singular side of the self, while some feminist theory and intersubjective theory tend to overemphasize the relational dimension of self construction. While I think it is true that no aspect of the self is unaffected by our selfobject relations, it is also true that our selfobject relations do not constitute the totality of the self. There is a root, irreducible center of activity and responsiveness. Without some core self, it is hard to develop a concept of ethical responsibility that applies to a person rather than an inter-relational nexus. But without the inherent need for others to sustain the self, there will be no compelling need to be ethical, for there will be no compelling reason to engage in reciprocity. For humans to be ethical persons, they must have both a core self that grounds individual responsibility and an intrinsic social need for others that gives them a reason to be ethical. This is precisely Kohut's concept of the nuclear self.

In short, the self is a dynamic non-linear system that must constantly adjust its ideals, ambitions, and traits as these develop and shift, and it must do this in a context in which others are understood as a part of the self. If in a friendship, one person injures the other, both are likely to cut one another off from the nourishment each needs to have genuinely satisfying days. Oh, they will go on with their days and probably be quite productive, but they will not be good self-days. They are both likely to be edgy and tense. Ego needs will be met and social goals achieved, but they will not be deeply gratifying, for selves are not fully present in them. The fragmentation will not go away until the partners engage in repairing their relationship.

Ruptures and disruptions are, of course, an unavoidable part of any friendship or love relationship and when they occur they have a destructive effect on self-structure. Hence, one of the most important personal skills for Kohut is knowing how to repair and restore a selfobject relation when it has been rent. It is not by chance that Kohut's most important book was not called *Creating the Self* or *Actualizing the Self* but *Restoration of the Self.*

THE MATURE SELF

We have already noted that persons who have developed coherent nuclear selves can accomplish all the major self functions. They can regulate self-esteem, self-soothe when narcissistically injured, utilize others as selfobjects when needed, offer empathy and selfobject functioning to others, feel a core strength and vitality, harbor a robust energy available for work, love, and play, feel spontaneously alive, have meaningful ideals that give their lives a significance beyond their mere particularity, and feel as though all these major psychic sectors are harmoniously working together. Kohut adds to these structural traits of a healthy self five character traits that define the highest level of narcissistic development: humor, empathy, transience, wisdom, and creativity. All of these traits express mature ways of negotiating the conflict between the narcissistic impulse to think of ourselves as significant, special persons and the inescapable knowledge that we are mortal, flawed, limited, and in the end not very important.

Laughing at the misalignment of our narcissism with reality both acknowledges the absurdity of the human condition and triumphs over it. Kohut, quoting Freud, states that "'humour has something liberating about it;' that it 'has something of grandeur;' and that it is a 'triumph of narcissism' and 'the victorious assertion of . . . invulnerability.'"[21] Instead of being defeated by the knowledge that our narcissistic wishes to be immortal and the center of the universe will never be met, we laugh. Since the conflict between our narcissistic wishes and what we really are is the constant backdrop for human life, a fine sense of humor is called for in order to live maturely in the robustness of life. Nietzsche would agree: laughter is the defining characteristic of the overman; it is the overman's affirmation of life in the face of cosmic meaninglessness.

The ability to empathize is a second characteristic of mature narcissism. Kohut points out that an empathic way of being in the world is truer of childhood than adulthood, when we tend to be objective and detached. Being empathic recalls the earliest, most narcissistic form of life when the empathy of our parents was our primary environment and the protein out of which we built ourselves. The maturation of narcissism involves taking the empathy we have received as a gift and giving it to others, a gift which recalls both the joy of early narcissism and the acknowledgement of our indebtedness to others. While the adult world often calls upon us to be competitive, judgmental, and dismissive of others, a person with a mature self retains an empathic responsiveness to others, for empathy is the only environment in which selves can flourish.

A third trait of mature narcissism is the acceptance of our mortality. "Man's capacity to acknowledge the finiteness of his existence, and to act in accordance with this painful discovery, may well be his greatest psychological achievement."[22] While this acceptance of our transience appears to be the work of a rational ego defeating narcissism, Kohut says, "I believe that this rare feat rests not simply on a victory of autonomous reason and supreme objectivity over the claims of narcissism but on the creation of a higher form of narcissism."[23] The acceptance of our transience might be the most difficult of all optimal frustrations, but if we can accomplish it, we achieve a "quiet pride." When we openly face our inevitable plunge into non-being and still affirm the goodness of life, we overcome the greatest general obstacle to living with full vitality and meaning.

In his acknowledging the acceptance of death as the act which opens up the fullness of life, Kohut's ideas reverberate with those of Heidegger. According to Heidegger's *Being and Time*, almost everything we do in life is encoded by societal values. In general we live as generalized beings. However, we die as singular beings. It is only when we accept death that we can locate our authentic particularity and discover our ownmost possibilities rather than those we have fallen into by being members of a society. Acceptance of death is not a defeat of narcissism but the only way for the self to fully experience its individual greatness.

The fourth trait Kohut associates with mature narcissism is creativity. Creativity carries traces of early narcissism—closeness to one's surroundings, spontaneous responses, and the "narcissistic-idealizing libido" with which the creative artist invests her work. As the narcissistic child spontaneously creates without worry about conforming to standards, being acceptable, and so forth, so the creative adult asserts, over against the standardization of adults in modern culture, an original responsiveness that is grounded in the narcissistic conditions of feeling special and having worth. This trait does not mean that persons with mature selves need to be artists but that they originate their lives from an inner source that is singular and spontaneous rather than organizing them according to standardized codes and pressures from others.

The fifth trait that Kohut posits as characterizing mature narcissism is wisdom. "Wisdom may be defined as a stable attitude of the personality toward life and the world, an attitude which is formed through the integration of the cognitive function with humor, acceptance of transience, and a firmly cathected system of values."[24] In wisdom we gather who we have been through time: we retain the strongly cathected values of youth, the humor of middle age, and the acceptance of transience that usually comes with advanced age. The wise person acknowledges her finitude, laughs at how in the midst of death, suffering, radical shifts of fortune, and webs of power that hold us all in their irrational nets we still can assert the goodness of human life. Further, the wise person, while not giving up her singularity of being, merges her personal values with more universal ones, giving her life a significance beyond its finite particularity. The self-centered narcissism of childhood is transformed into a kind of "cosmic narcissism."[25]

When wisdom and humor go hand in hand, the result is often the adoption of an ironic way of being in the world. "And in contrast to an attitude of utter seriousness and unrelieved solemnity vis-à-vis the approaching end of life, the truly wise are able in the end to transform the humor of their years of maturity into a sense of proportion, a touch of irony toward the achievements of individual existence, including even their own wisdom. The ego's ultimate mastery over the narcissistic self, the final control of the rider over the horse, may after all have been decisively assisted by the fact that the horse, too, has grown old."[26]

Living ironically is a way of being in the world—a way of being in which we take life seriously while knowing that it has no ultimate ground, no final meaning. Socrates' irony was not an accidental trait but deeply tied to his way of being in the world. Jonathan Lear explains Socrates' essential irony as his knowing that he is human and yet not knowing what it means to be human—knowing that in order to be fully human, he must not know what it means to be human.[27]

Although Kohut does not include the adoption of an ethical way of being as part of the transformations of narcissism, the traits he mentions indicate that becoming an ethical person is part of this transformation into maturity, for ethics typically demands a creative, empathic response to the world that is guided by ideals that are higher than those of personal fulfillment. In addition, it is difficult to imagine people who have fully come to terms with their mortality and finitude and adopted an attitude of irony being cruel and insensitive to others. I will show in chapter 5 that what is implied here is in fact a necessary consequence of Kohut's vision: the mature narcissist must adopt ethical values as part of her wider vision of life.

CONCLUSION

I have tried to show how Kohut's conception of the self is remarkably different from any conception in which the self is seen as having a set identity and as being present in a stable unchanging way from birth to death. The self for Kohut is a dynamic system that develops from infancy through adulthood. A self does not just come into being and remain the same but, given favorable conditions, continues to change and grow for a lifetime. As such it can fail to come into being, come only partially into being, or come robustly into being. Further, the self needs others to develop and sustain itself. It is inherently intersubjective while at the same time remaining singular and itself.

The self's two major poles are ambitions and ideals. It is, therefore, an organization of energy for engagement with the world and a set of values that give meaning to life. When these poles cohere with favored traits and skills and allow for the emergence of a playful, spontaneous responsiveness, a nuclear self is formed. If this self fully develops, it will exhibit the traits of humor, empathy, creativity, acceptance of death, and wisdom. However, when the self is traumatized, the psyche experiences disintegration anxiety, emptiness, and narcissistic rage, all of which can remain unconscious and seriously distort life and one's ability to be an ethical person.

We have two more tasks to accomplish in exploring this notion of the self before we can attend to its social and ethical implications. First, we need to relate it to the rich history of philosophy concerning the nature of the self. I will try to show how Kohut's theory can integrate Aristotle with Nietzsche, Plato with Hegel. Further, I hope to show that when one amalgamates Heidegger's notion of authenticity with Kohut's concept of the unconscious self, an extraordinarily powerful vision of what it means to be an authentic self arises.

Second, we need to make a careful distinction between the ego and the self, between the "I" that is the subject of experience and the self. This is a difficult and extraordinarily important distinction both for theory and for common living. Without it, we can be easily confused about who we are and how to locate the self. I will discuss this distinction in chapter 4.

NOTES

1. For a biography and important discussion of Kohut's works, see Charles Strozier, *Heinz Kohut: The Making of a Psychoanalyst* (New York: Farrar, Straus, and

Giroux, 2001). For the best general account of Kohut's works, see Allen Siegel, *Heinz Kohut and the Psychology of the Self* (New York: Routledge, 1996). For the best clinical account of self psychology, see Ernest Wolf, *Treating the Self* (New York: Guilford Press, 1988).

2. Freud, "On Narcissism: An Introduction," in *The Standard Edition of the Complete Works of Sigmund Freud*, vol. 14, trans. J. Strachey (London: Hogarth Press, 1953–74), 75.

3. Freud, "Narcissism," 91.

4. Heinz Kohut, "Forms and Transformations of Narcissism," in *Essential Papers on Narcissism*, ed. Andrew Morrison (New York: New York University Press, 1986), 66.

5. Kohut, "Forms," 67.

6. See David Terman's "Structuralization and the Therapeutic Process" in *Learning from Kohut: Progress in Self Psychology*, vol. 4, ed. Arnold Goldberg (Hillsdale, NJ: Analytic Press, 1984).

7. Kohut, "Forms," 70.

8. Heinz Kohut, *The Restoration of the Self* (New York: International Universities Press, 1977), 177–78.

9. Kohut, *Restoration*, 177.

10. Joseph Lichtenberg, *Psychoanalysis and Motivation* (Hillsdale, NJ: Analytic Press, 1989).

11. The dynamic and multidimensional aspects of the nuclear self make me think that those, such as Robert Stolorow, Bernard Brandschaft, and George Atwood, who reject it as a reified notion are misguided (*Psychoanalytic Treatment: An Intersubjective Approach* [Hillsdale, NJ: Analytic Press, 1987]). The term "nuclear self" appears to point to an entity, but a careful reading of Kohut reveals that the self is anything but a stable, enduring thing that carries a set identity.

12. Kohut, *Restoration*, 180.

13. I will expand on the relation between Kohut and Hegel in the next chapter.

14. Heinz Kohut, *How Does Analysis Cure?* (Chicago: University of Chicago Press, 1984), 53.

15. Kohut, *How Does Analysis Cure?*, 53.

16. Jonathan Lear, *Freud* (New York: Routledge, 2005).

17. Kohut, *How Does Analysis Cure?*, 47.

18. Interestingly, Freud anticipates Kohut's selfobject theory in *On Narcissism* when he claims that full health can be attained only in reciprocated love relationships. His major solution to the problem of how to retain the self-love that is necessary for sustaining one's well-being while giving up one's primary narcissism to avoid pathology is to engage in reciprocal love relationships. When we send all of our libido into an object and that object loves us back, we retain the narcissistic sense of specialness without pathologically retaining our libido for ourselves. In its deepest sense a reciprocal love relation is a willingness of persons to be selfobjects for one another (see vol. 14 of the *Collected Works*, 99–100).

19. This is a central theme in *How Does Analysis Cure?*

20. See, for instance, Stephen Mitchell, *Relational Concepts in Psychoanalysis: An Integration* (Cambridge, MA: Harvard University Press, 1988), and George Atwood

and Robert Stolorow, *Contexts of Being: The Intersubjective Foundations of Psychological Life* (Hillsdale, NJ: Analytic Press, 1992).

   21. Kohut, "Forms," 82.
   22. Kohut, "Forms," 80.
   23. Kohut, "Forms," 81.
   24. Kohut, "Forms," 84.
   25. Kohut, "Forms," 82.
   26. Kohut, "Forms," 84.
   27. See Jonathan Lear, *Therapeutic Action* (New York: Other Press, 2003).

THREE

KOHUT AND THE PHILOSOPHIC TRADITION

The adequacy of Kohut's theory of the self depends not only on its effectiveness in therapeutic situations but also on its ability to subsume, organize, and extend the important theories of self that have preceded it. Kohut does not write about the philosophic tradition, nor does it appear that he knows it; yet, I believe that his concept of the bipolar nuclear self resonates with insights into the self that are found in the most profound philosophic theorists in the ancient, modern, and existentialist traditions.[1] Each of the poles of the nuclear self, along with their dynamic relationship, captures a significant theory of the self in philosophy. The idealized pole reverberates with the classical Greek tradition in its emphasis on defining the self through the organization of values. The grandiose pole connects to Nietzsche's will-to-power and Spinoza's conatus, while the playful, creative strand of narcissism captures Nietzsche's idea of the free spirit. Locating the self in the dynamic relation between the poles of the self and the person's predispositions and skills resonates with a number of the insights of the great dialectical thinkers: Heraclitus, Hegel, and Kierkegaard.

In addition, Kohut's theory of the self has significant connections to the most important philosophic concept of human nature in the twentieth century: Heidegger's phenomenological notion of Da-sein in *Being and Time*.[2] I hope to show that Kohut and Heidegger were trying to get to the same thing—how to live authentically—but that each was working with a very different set of problems, focusing on a different part of the psyche, and using very different languages. Rather than being contradictory, their theories complement one another. Kohut does not address the problem of how experience can be restricted and devitalized by our social existence, and Heidegger does not recognize the power of unconscious pathology to hinder our ability to be Da-sein—to be open to the world and our own indwelling possibilities. When these theories are melded, they form an extraordinarily powerful way of grasping the self and human experience.

47

THE IDEALIZED POLE OF THE SELF:
KOHUT AND THE GREEK PHILOSOPHERS

In claiming that a sector of the self must contain motivating ideals, Kohut finds himself in the good company of Socrates, Plato, Aristotle, and most of the theological thinkers of the religious era. All of these thinkers found that the essence of the soul is to produce meaning and that the most important arena of meaning is that which directs human activity—values. Plato held that without ideals to lead us, we would be hopelessly subjected to the tyranny of the impulses and desires, forced to do their bidding. Aristotle would add that without values we would not be able to "have a life," for having a life means having the ability to organize it.[3] Without ideals, there is no possibility for establishing a coherent life over which one has some control. For Plato, Aristotle, and the tradition that follows them, the most important problem in constructing an organized center to life—the self—is the ascertaining of ideals and making them the dominant power of motivation in the psyche.

Ideals, however, have an inherent problem. Unlike factual claims which can be supported by perception, they seem to lack validating grounds. For Socrates, the main work of philosophy was to question constructions of value as to their legitimacy and attempt to find a set of values that carried objective validity. If values could not be legitimated by local social traditions, perception, or personal desire, then he reasoned that only reason in and of itself could provide this ground. Without an objective ground ideals could not have the power to fend off the desires, provide a basis for social harmony, or establish psychic coherence. Hence, Plato sought to ground the truth of ideals in the objective world of the Forms and Aristotle tried to ground them in a teleological view of human nature.

Values that have a chance of achieving an objective justification are, by necessity, universal. Identifying with universal values was understood by the Greeks and others (especially Kant) as a way of overcoming our particularity and its social and biological entanglements. When we elevate ourselves to act on universal values, we shed our particular conditioning, our particular societies, and, for some, even our mortal particular bodies to act from values that supposedly hold true for all times and places. These thinkers hypothesized that when we transcend our particularity, we come to understand that our reality is more than just being mortal particulars doomed to rush around in our little spot of space and time and then die. In discovering our ability to act on universal values, we discover (supposedly) that we are of a like nature to those values: a spiritual, immortal substance.

The Sophists and other skeptics in the West doubted these equations, for they knew that life was not universal but inherently particular and embodied. Universal values can be seen as abstracting a set of experiences from the full range of human experiences and proclaiming that only these are worthy and that only those human beings who limit themselves to these experiences are praiseworthy. Persons who deviate from regnant ideals are typically seen as deviants and are persecuted for having the wrong kind of sexual orientation, religious beliefs, political position, and so forth. Such hideous intolerances reveal how distorting, confining, guilt-producing, and life-negating "universal" ideals can be. They not only limit the robust chaos of life but prejudice those who hold the ideal against those who do not fit it.

In sum, ideals are profoundly problematic. It seems we must have them in order to obtain any kind of organized life. However, no objective ground has ever been secured for them and they seem highly dangerous in their tendency to produce tight, rigid people trying to force their own and others' robust singularity into generalized cages of conformity. While Kohut did not directly engage this philosophical battle concerning the worth and dangers of ideals, his theory addresses it in a profound way.

First, the ideals which the philosophic tradition addresses are ones generated by a rational ego attempting to establish a universal code, while the values of the idealized pole of the self relate fundamentally to embodied, particular self-structure.[4] For Kohut, the self's ideals need to be in a concrete relation to the self's ambitions and the person's idiosyncratic abilities and predispositions. Since ambitions and traits are an essential part of a person's particularity, what Kohut is doing with self-ideals is immersing them in the embodied singularity of a person. In this way Kohut both removes ideals from the realm of abstract universality and redefines particularity in terms of self-activity. Our ideals must fit us—they must relate to who we actually are in a way that speaks to our individual personal history. Our ideals are not a lure to an abstract future that holds for everyone, but personal ideals for how our particular embodiments might extend beyond what they are now. Likewise, the justification for ideals is not through abstract rational deduction but by finding what ideals best fit my particularity. I justify my values not through a Socratic attempt to establish a universal meaning but through an examination of my particular being.

Obviously, while such a notion of ideals saves them from the critique that they box us into cages of conformity, it does not appear as though it can expand into ethical ideals, which are always universal. Yet, Kohut will need some of a person's ideals to be ethical; otherwise, his position of mature narcissism will be too self-centered for human beings needing to sustain themselves in a community of selfobject relatedness. I will argue in chapter 5 that one cannot generate optimal conditions for sustaining a nuclear self without some of her ideals being ethical ones. That is, when we fully establish what the best way is to organize our psyches, we find that the self and the ego must form an alliance. The self will ground our ideals in our particular experience, while the ego will critique and extend the values into an ethical realm.

In short, Kohut and the philosophers are dealing with very different problems when it comes to ideals. Kohut is asking why some people are able to have meaningful ideals and be motivated by them while others can't; the philosophers are inquiring into which ideals can claim to have validity. Both inquiries are needed. Valid ideals are of no use to someone who cannot psychologically be moved by ideals. For those human beings with strong enough idealized poles to be motivated by ideals, it is not enough just to have ideals. They need to critically examine and adjust their ideals to the real conditions of their lives.

THE GRANDIOSE POLE OF THE SELF: KOHUT AND NIETZSCHE

The philosophic tradition has been far less interested in understanding the self as a sheer particularity than as a participant in universality. For Plato, particularity was connected with a chaos of individuals clashing with one another, and chaos was seen as the ultimate enemy both of the soul (insanity) and the state (anarchy). Civilized social life is possible only when individuals are able either to identify with the universal or follow rulers who have formed such an identification. The Western tradition has largely followed Plato's lead in validating the essential transformation in life as one in which we change from a chaotic, undisciplined particularity to become a person governed by universal values and concerns. This transformational path has typically been understood as "the perfectibility of man."

In the nineteenth century, particularity finally got the heroic champion it had long needed: Friedrich Nietzsche. Nietzsche sees universal moral values as confining cages of social conformity that transform the richness of embodied particularity into the vapidness of generalized existence. With his luscious, sparkling prose he, like a siren, lures us to shatter our conceptual prisons and come out into the free vibrant air of lived particularity. He dims the bright light of Apollo so that we might once again be recalled to the dark chaotic energies of Dionysus.

Nietzsche's authentication of particularity carries with it a transformed relation to personal grandiosity. The idealistic tradition tends to denigrate grandiosity as ostentatious self-display or pride, while Nietzsche praises it. He commands us to kill God on the grounds that we could not extol ourselves as the highest authority if God exists. "If there were gods, how could I stand not to be one?"[5] Asserting one's grandiosity means proclaiming that no value, no being, no authority stands higher than the individual in her creative act. For Nietzsche, the will-to-power is the ultimate reality of the universe and it seeks no higher value other than the assertion of its own power. It is sheer primal energy.

If a particular individual holds herself accountable to a higher universal value, then that value must be achieved in order for life to be considered good. Living well will then be a serious business. When we relinquish the demand that life have an objective meaning, we can then play, for life can now be a game. Nietzsche often describes the free spirit as a child creating its world in play and then giving it up when the play starts to bore him. When we proclaim the expression of spontaneous particularity to be our highest goal, then we are not crushed by the weight of ideals or superego admonishments (to use Freud's terms). We are free to be who we are.

The greatest danger in life for Nietzsche is not the chaos feared by Plato or the lack of justified meaning but the enfeeblement of life caused by social forces strapping us into a collective straightjacket. These social forces are led by philosophers and theologians who proclaim that life must have meaning—just the meaning they find for it. For Nietzsche we must reject this approach to life—we must give up the need for objective meaning. To be alive, to feel exuberantly vital, to assert one's singular presence in the world and to be present to the presence of the world—this is the new goal that is no goal at all!

Kohut's concept of the grandiose pole of the self profoundly resonates with these magnetic insights of Nietzsche. The grandiose pole contains our ambitions (Kohut's term for the will-to-power). This side of the self seeks to express grandiosity—seeks to exhibit the specialness and greatness of the self. It wants to establish our singular presence in the world and to be active rather than passive.

Kohut also validates Nietzsche's sense that vitality is deeply connected to playfulness and creativity, for these are expressions of early narcissistic vivacity. He would like Nietzsche's metaphor of the free spirit as a child, for childhood (when it is nontraumatic) is the time when our narcissistic energy is allowed most freedom, presence, and exhibitionistic assertion. The great psychoanalytic champion of play is, of course, D. W. Winnicott, who asserted that all humans—children and adults alike—are most alive, most themselves, in play. Play occurs when we can enter a transitional psychological space between infantile merger and structured adult identity. As transitional, this space is not occupied by the overwhelming demands of infancy nor the repetitive responsibilities of adulthood. It is open to creativity and spontaneous thinking and feeling.

Kohut mirrors both Winnicott and Nietzsche in declaring the importance of this realm of narcissistic spontaneity, and reverberates profoundly with Nietzsche in postulating that grandiosity takes a double path—one that demands rigor, overcoming, and drive and another that is spontaneous, playful, and takes life to be a game. There is, obviously, a tension between these two paths of grandiosity that Nietzsche and Kohut describe, but both are necessary to a full life. Without playfulness, life becomes too driven, restless, and concerned with power and achievement. However, if grandiosity were only playful, the intensity of life that comes from ambitiously pushing one's life to more complex levels would lessen.

Hence, in his recognition of the grandiose pole of the nuclear self and his validation of playful narcissistic energy, I think that Kohut incorporates Nietzsche's profound insights and his enticement to assert the grandiosity of our selves. However, Kohut differs from Nietzsche in three significant ways, ways that I think reveal Kohut's more profound understanding of the multiple facets of human life.

First, Nietzsche's concept of the free spirit or the overman can appear infantile, for there is no process by which the spirit needs to mature. Nietzsche thinks that freeing individual narcissistic energy from its entrapment in structures of social conformity and religious repression is the major transformation that must occur, but in so doing misses the importance of the child's spirit needing to mature out of infantile grandiosity to more mature forms of self assertion. Kohut elaborates a path of optimal frustration and the transmuting internalization of mature objects that individuals need to follow in order to transform infantile grandiosity into mature narcissism. For Kohut we need to mature in order to be able to secure adult selfobject relationships. Since Nietzsche does not recognize the necessity for intimate caring relationships, he can find no necessary principle for maturation.

Second, for Nietzsche grandiosity is what life is all about. Enacting our particularity takes precedence over all else. Ideals are important only insofar as they are generated by a particularized grandiosity. In contrast, Kohut sees our ideals as constituting a separate realm. Although ideals go back to a common origin with grandiosity, they have a different developmental sequence and perform a different psychological function from grandiose energy. One might say that in Nietzsche's collapse of ideals into individual grandiosity, he fuses perfection with particularity, making his concept of the overman far too close to the description of someone suffering from megalomania. In Kohut's conception of the self, we need to keep our ideals apart from our particularity. We cannot fuse who we are with our ideals of perfection.

Third, Kohut would find Nietzsche's concept of the individual deficient in its anti-socialness. Nietzsche proclaims the primacy of the individual over the social (here he is aligned with a number of nineteenth-century thinkers, such as Thoreau and Emerson), while Kohut finds the individual to be inherently infused with the social. The social goes all the way down to the very soil in which the individual begins to take root and continues until death in our need for selfobject sustenance. Our grandiosity is not

Promethean, as Nietzsche would have it, but fragile and constantly dependent on selfobject support. Kohut would say that Nietzsche's fully independent overman is a philosophical fantasy not supported by empirical evidence. We always need others and they are an inherent part of everyone's self-structure. The difference between Nietzsche and Kohut is that when Nietzsche thought of the social, he envisioned mass society with its immense pressures to lure one into conformity, while when Kohut thought of the social, he thought of the tender care that is given by those closest to us—parents, siblings, and friends.

For Nietzsche, the social world is the great enemy of the individual, while for Kohut, it is not the social in general that is evil but the failure of very particular others to provide adequate selfobject functions when we need them. A strong healthy self can live with full vitality in the midst of the social world; someone with a severely fragmented self will not be able to live vitally in or out of society. The social for Kohut is not the problem; the lack of adequate selfobject responsiveness is.

Nietzsche is important because he, more than any other philosopher, validates the importance of grandiosity and playfulness. But he does so at the expense of understanding the need for ideals to stand over us and the need for connections with others, the lack of which destroys the self's ability to function adequately.

THE TENSIONS OF THE NUCLEAR SELF:
KOHUT, HEGEL, AND KIERKEGAARD

Like Hegel and Kierkegaard, Kohut sees the self as a set of tensions which must remain in a dynamic relationship rather than collapsing into a unity. In holding that the self is bipolar with the grandiose pole holding the strivings of the particular person and the idealized pole holding her cherished values, Kohut mirrors both Hegel and Kierkegaard, who claim that the fundamental opposition that humans must resolve to be whole is that between universality and particularity. Kohut knows that if ideals become too dominant, we lose the lusty vitality of particular life and that if grandiose singularity becomes too dominant, we can lose the sense of life's meaningfulness. He also knows that if we collapse the sense of perfection contained in ideals with our particularity, we fall into a narcissistic pathology. Ideals and grandiosity need to be aligned, not fused.

One could say that for all three the aim of the self is to find a "meaningful life"—one that asserts the liveliness of particular existence while organizing itself around values that give life a sense of importance. However, there is a tension. Ideals tend to weigh on us, take us out of spontaneity, and have us attend to what we should do rather than exuberantly doing what we feel like doing. Yet, without ideals, life's adventures have no genuine meaning. To be human is to dwell in the tension between these two sides of our selves.

Hegel, Kierkegaard, and Kohut also assert that the self is not a thing to be found but a subjective activity that comes into being through a developmental process. The self is an achievement, and as such can fail to come into being at all, or, what is more common, can fail to come into the fullness of being. There can be arrested development, highly circumscribed development, or optimal development into a fully actualized self. The Kohutian self is not a metaphysical being that retains a clear identity through eternity but a psychological self longing for wholeness and feeling inherently fragile.

Finally, we must take note that there are important dissimilarities between Kohut and the great nineteenth-century dialecticians. Because Hegel and Kierkegaard make the two poles of the self (universality vs. particularity) so opposed, they have to posit a heroic act of metaphysical reason realizing its oneness with the Absolute (Hegel) or a heroic leap of faith into the absurd (Kierkegaard) in order for the self to become unified with itself. Kohut depicts no such great drama for the soul. Rather, the psyche has a developmental history in which more or less integrity and vitality of functioning can be achieved. There is no final resolution, no telos, which, if achieved, will resolve all the psyche's tensions and bring development to an end. For psychoanalysis in general and self psychology in particular, there are no psychic structures that are invulnerable, none that cannot be traumatized or overwhelmed. There are no final goals that bring life's adventure to a completion. In this way, Kohut and the psychoanalytic tradition align with postmodernism and its claim that grand narratives are dead, for the grandest of all grand narratives is one which holds that a person can achieve a place beyond life's sufferings. We are vulnerable when we are born and remain vulnerable to the day we die. We never achieve self-sufficiency or immunity from psychological collapse. There is no secret gate leading out of our mortal and finite existences.

Kierkegaard's famous statement that the self is a relationship relating itself to itself[6] is similar to Kohut's notion that the self is a "tension arc" between ideals, ambitions, and traits. We are not our ideals, as Plato seems to indicate, nor our grandiose energy, as Nietzsche asserts, nor our idiosyncratic traits, talents, or character, as many of the novelists seem to think. We are all of these in relation to one another and in relation to the important selfobjects in our lives. When each of the sectors of the self is developed, moderately free of injury (or repaired from injury), and in a coherent alignment, and the selfobject relations are robust, then we feel the presence of a vital self. (When writing about Kohut, one finds oneself using a lot of "ands," for this is the nature of the self as relational, conditional, and multifaceted—it is never a simple self-sufficient identity.)

The difficult question for these dynamic theories of the self in which the self is not a thing but an ever shifting process is how the self can be the carrier of personal identity over time. One of the most remarkable of human experiences is the feeling that we continue to be the same person, even though almost everything about us changes over time. Kohut's answer is two-fold. First, he would say that there is a continuity in the changes that provides enough coherence to allow us to feel like the same person, and, second, that the "arc" itself has a quality to it that is what feels most like us. But the question then is raised about who or what is feeling this arc—is it the arc being aware of itself (which would make the arc a self-aware subjectivity) or another part of the psyche, such as the ego? This question points us toward the conundrum of self-awareness. The subjective self that is aware of the self as an object of awareness seems already to have transcended the self as object. If there were still another subjective moment in which awareness of self-awareness appeared, there would be a further transcendence, and so on ad infinitum. This leads us into the metaphysics of subjectivity, a speculation about whether there is some ontological "self" lying behind the psychological self. Engaging in metaphysical speculation about ultimate ontological selves is beyond the scope of this book. However, I can state that everything important about the self that we need to understand for living well is contained in the psychological self.

KOHUT AND ANCIENT WISDOM

As a set of ever shifting subjective relations, the self for Kohut never appears as a knowable object. To use Heraclitus' language, the self is not a thing but a process. A structure that is always processing never has an identity that can be captured and held but is always near, always present in its processing. Although it does not appear, the self can be known through its signs. The self is not unlike Heraclitus' description of the Delphic oracle: "The lord whose oracle is at Delphi neither speaks nor conceals, but gives signs."[7] When the self has been injured, it signals its fragmentation in symptoms, while when the self discovers an activity or object that significantly engages it, it signals its involvement by deepening the person's sense of vitality and zestfulness.

Like the signs that issued from the Delphic oracle, the signs that come from the self in terms of erotic attractions, symptoms, and dreams are not easily read, for like the pronouncements from the oracle, they are riddles. When someone feels a great erotic attraction for another person, it need not be seen literally as the self's signaling that it has found its true and only partner. The eros might be a repetition of an unresolved oedipal wish or an unconscious recognition that a relationship with the person will help her grow in a developmentally significant way and when the development is over, the relationship will disappear (much of teenage love is like this). Like an ancient sage, the person who would know her self must be adept at oracles and riddles.

There are further connections between oracles and the self. The Sphinx who confronts Oedipus is like an oracle in that she speaks in riddles. Oedipus enters a life and death struggle with her, for their engagement means one or the other must die. In grasping her riddle, Oedipus kills the Sphinx and seemingly ends a form of life in which riddles need to be confronted. Oedipus represents a new kind of human being, a kind that the philosophers were articulating—a person who uses his reason to organize and understand every facet of life. From now on it will not be a riddle-understanding, cunning intelligence (think of Odysseus) that reigns but a rational intelligence. Oedipus sets out to find the killer of Laius in the most rational of problem solving ways, not seeing the signs all along which indicate that he is the killer. Sophocles seems to be saying in this play, which stands with Hamlet as the most important ever written in the West, that we must beware of this new ability of reason which the Greek philosophers have just invented.[8] For all of its power, it might blind us to the core of who we are and what life is about. Understanding who one is, is not a matter for rational calculation but rests in the ability to read signs. One might say that the new priests of Apollo are the psychoanalysts and psychotherapists who learn how to listen for signs and interpret symptoms.

Let me draw one more connection between Kohut and Greek philosophy. The nuclear self also has a profound affinity with Aristotle's concept of "entelechy." Aristotle, the first biologist and natural scientist, hypothesized that living creatures develop from an immature state to being a mature member of their species because they have an entelechy—literally "an end (telos) inside." For Aristotle the most crucial fact about living things is that they develop. Indeed, this pattern of development is the essence of what it means to be a living member of a species.

For Kohut, the human organism has a natural impetus to develop a core self. If this self fails to develop, then the organism will fail to flourish. This is a radically different approach from other naturalists who want to eliminate any kind of teleological causation. Yet, for both Aristotle and Kohut a naturalistic approach to the human organism cannot deny the presence of an impetus toward the development and maturation of a self. This will be a crucial fact for ethics, for it establishes a value other than mere pleasure. It is good, by nature, to develop a self. However, unlike Aristotle who saw the development of reason as the final goal of human maturation, and, therefore, devalued irrational states in the psyche and lives that were less than philosophical, Kohut's nuclear self allows for all kinds of lives to be lived, with each one being able to be lived more fully the more a self is present.

Finally, I believe that there are strong parallels between Kohut's thought and that of Confucius. As I have already noted, both Kohut's and Confucius' theories of the self are relational as opposed to the regnant Western concept of the atomized individual. The self for them needs to exist in a matrix of established selfobject relationships, which for Confucius resides mainly in the extended family and secondarily in the rituals of the sustaining community. Both understood the extraordinary importance of family in the development and sustenance of the self.

Confucius was keenly aware of the difference between immature narcissism and mature narcissism and expresses them in his contrast between the "gentleman" and the "small man." The small man is the immature narcissist who is a pragmatic schemer, thinks about himself mainly in terms of wealth and gratifications, and does not understand how the self is sustained by its relation to family and ritual. The gentleman, on the other hand, respects his family (especially his father) and the organizing rituals of community life, identifies his personal well-being with the Tao (or in Kohut's terms "cosmic narcissism"), and realizes that his personal well-being is best served by working toward his full humanity. He is empathic to the needs of others and exhibits the mean in his appetites and actions.

> The gentleman understands what is moral. The small man understands what is "profitable."
> The gentleman helps others to realize what is good in them; he does not help them to realize what is bad in them. The small man does the opposite.
> The gentleman is at ease without being arrogant; the small man is arrogant without being at ease.[9]

As with Heraclitus, Confucius does not offer a conceptualization of the self but knows that when the self has been developed it is as apparent as the sun rising. The gentleman's wider sense of humanity radiates from his core self. The sage's acceptance of life, laughter, and wisdom make him stand out from others as being the supreme exemplification of self-actualization. The characteristics of empathy, laughter, acceptance, association with higher ideals, and wisdom are all characteristics that Kohut assigns to the fully mature narcissist.

HEIDEGGER'S NOTION OF DA-SEIN AND SELF PSYCHOLOGY

Martin Heidegger's *Being and Time* (1927) is the richest, most complex philosophical account of what it means to be human written in the twentieth century. His phenomenological method which examines lived experience without metaphysical presuppositions mirrors Kohut's demand that theory be experience-near. While their accounts are strikingly different, important intersections between Kohut's and Heidegger's work can be drawn.[10] What is most important for this enquiry into ethics is the way the two theories complement one another on what constitutes authentic living. Heidegger's account is brilliant in its analysis of what it means to live as a human being embedded in an everyday world of things and others but is psychologically naïve in holding that any- and everyone can achieve authenticity. Kohut's account, on the other hand, is ontologically naïve in that it imagines that once we develop a nuclear self, we will flourish so long as we can steer clear of psychologically traumatic situations and our wider social and political environments are not overly hostile. It does not recognize the power of social life to drag even psychologically healthy human beings into the alienation of everyday life. Together, however, these accounts provide a striking illumination of the complexities of individuals in their attempts to achieve a fullness of vitality. I will give a brief synopsis of Heidegger's account of Da-sein, concentrating on how we become inauthentic or authentic and then explore what the two theories together tell us about what is needed to live in the fullest way possible for humans.

Heidegger provides an ontological account of human experience, an account which he proclaims is prior to psychological, biological, and anthropological descriptions of what it means to be human, for it inquires into what it means to *be* a conscious being. Heidegger calls our ontological being *Da-sein*, or "being there," for Da-sein is that place in which Being discloses itself to itself, the place where Being enters into a relation with itself by being aware of itself. As that locus where the world is disclosed, Da-sein is inherently related to the world. Its being cannot be separated from the world that is disclosed to it. It is, in essence, a being-in-the-world. This is a stunning contradiction of Descartes' paradigmatic notion of the ego as a thinking substance with only a contingent relation to the world. For Heidegger the world is an essential part of our being.

As being-in-the-world, Da-sein finds itself immersed in things and having a fundamental caring attunement to those things. This caring attunement, which is not a choice but an ontological structure of consciousness, is both a concern for the world and a "taking care of business" kind of care—a making sure that our world is "ready-at-hand" for us. The world is not just an objective world of things but exists always and already for our use. The subjective and objective are fused in this account.

We are also always and already living in a world with other human beings with whom we are so connected that our existence cannot be conceived of without them. That is, we are Mitda-sein—beings whose essence it is to be with others. We are inherently social beings with no possibility of escaping infiltrations by the social world.

A third essential structure of Da-sein is that it must remain a mystery to itself. Humans are "thrown" into existence without reasons as to why we are here, why we are the way we are, why we have the particular worlds we do. This is another way of saying that Da-sein is irrevocably particular, for what is particular exists as absurd, exists beyond explanation. When we ask questions like "Why am I a boy?" "Why do I have my parents rather than Amy's?" "Why am I alive now rather than in the past or future?" there are no compelling answers. The concrete facts of our existence are inexplicable and our lives are essentially groundless. There is no necessity for our being the way we are. This discovery of our radical contingency—our understanding that we might not have been, our parents might not have been, the world might not have been—is so anxiety-provoking that we attempt to escape our thrownness by merging with others in a common social identity. This common social identity will prove to be the core of another ontological truth about Da-sein—its inescapable inauthenticity.

Heidegger asks who the subject of everyday experience is and surprisingly answers, "The who of everyday Da-sein is precisely not I myself."[11] Rather, the subject who experiences everyday life is "the They." That is, consciousness is unconsciously colonized by pervasive social codes to such an extent that the They becomes the subject of experience. "In [its] inconspicuousness and unascertainability, the They unfolds its true dictatorship. We enjoy ourselves and have fun the way *they* enjoy themselves. We read, see, and judge literature and art the way *they* see and judge. But we also withdraw from the 'great mass' the way *they* withdraw, we find 'shocking' what they find shocking."[12] Heidegger calls being captured by the They "falling prey" or "becoming entangled."

Subjectivity falling prey to the They is an unconscious process—we do not notice it happening. (To be clear: Heidegger does not call "falling prey" an unconscious process, but it happens without conscious awareness or consent.) The unconscious process by which subjectivity is colonized is not, however, the same kind of dynamic process that produces repressed or dissociated material. The colonization of subjectivity by the They is nontraumatic and hence involves no defensive dynamics. We can uncover this takeover merely by achieving an increased awareness of how we experience our world. The presence of the They in constructing and directing experience I will term "the social unconscious."

When Da-sein falls prey to the They, life sinks into an average everydayness. Language is reduced to "idle talk," in which a conversation is the They talking with itself in typical scripts. Knowledge is reduced to a shallow curiosity—poking into everything, exploring the "thises" and "thats" of life but never really trying to know their being. And our mood—we always are attuned to the world through a mood—is a kind of insipid knowingness that has ceased to wonder about anything. "Been there, done that." The aim of idle talk, shallow curiosity, and knowingness is to tranquilize ourselves. The essential form of this tranquilization is an incessant busyness, a busyness whose fundamental purpose is not action or genuine activity but an escape from our thrownness. Heidegger calls this way of living "inauthenticity."

In tranquilizing busyness, life ceases to flow forward; it "eddies." Much is happening, for sure, but inauthentic life is not our own. Its achievements are what the They want us to do. In the swirl of "shoulds," "musts," and the reduction of the world to a set of expectations, we become alienated from ourselves. This falling prey to the They is not something that might happen to us; it is a necessary structure of what it means to be human.

However, falling prey to the They is not the only way we can be present in the world. We can also be authentic, not to the exclusion of entanglement in the They but as a crucial modification of it. Authenticity is the ability to accept and acknowledge our thrownness, our incompleteness, our singular being without retreating into the tranquility of the They. When we are authentic we become aware of our particularity as a set of ownmost possibilities and act not simply as a variable in a set of social codes but as an agent that owns its own particular being.

As attractive as being authentic sounds, the path to authenticity is dark and difficult, for it involves falling into an anxiety—an angst—in which the foundations of familiarity and meaning dissolve. In angst we realize that our most inescapable ownmost possibility is our own nothingness. Dying is the one possibility that we will necessarily actualize, and we will actualize it as a singular being, for no one can die for us. To be Da-sein is to be a being-unto-death. It is not biological death that we fear, but existential death. Biological death is the breakdown of an organism, but existential death is the knowing that our very existence will become nonexistence. "*As the end of Da-sein death is the ownmost non-relational, certain, and, as such, indefinite and not to be bypassed possibility of Da-sein.*"[13] This is the deepest layer of our thrownness—we are thrown into an existence whose most certain possibility is our death. We do not choose to be mortal nor do we know why we are mortal. We are thrown into our mortality. However, in attending to it we discover our own particularity, for no one else can die our death. In the midst of nothingness we experience the being of our particular being and come to realize that "I am."

Heidegger's claim that the anticipation of death grants us the possibility of living authentically is a great shift in Western values. Death has typically been seen as the ultimate enemy that destroys life, while for Heidegger, death is that which makes us care about how we live our individual lives. Rather than ending our stay in time, death allows time to be a field in which we can realize our ownmost potentialities.

We can also come to our authenticity through what Heidegger calls the "call of conscience." Conscience silently summons to us when we are lost in the tranquilized busyness of the They. Although we attempt to feel fully at home in the coded existence of the They, something tells us, without words, that we have lost ourselves. Then we fill with "guilt" in which we come to know that we essentially are a "null *being* the ground of a nullity."[14] Individual persons are nullities because as particularities, there are no explanations for who they are or why they are the way they are. Nor is there a universal or social ideal that can legitimate them as singular. No individual can be understood or legitimated; rather, each is an openness—a nullity. That is, our "nullity" is our freedom. If there is no way I have to be or should be, then I can choose my being. In short, I can enact my ownmost possibilities rather than those possibilities that the They would have me become.

To live authentically for Heidegger means to resolutely be who one is. Rather than drifting on an open sea of possibility in which we can be and do almost anything, we resolutely choose to realize those possibilities which are most essentially *my possibilities,* and in so doing affirm our particular thrownnesses. Rather than drifting and eddying through life moving from this entertainment to that amusement, we rapturously inhabit our being.

> Nor does anticipatory resoluteness stem from "idealistic" expectations soaring above existence and its possibilities, but arises from the sober understanding of the basic factical possibilities of Da-sein. Together with the sober *Angst* that brings us before our individual potentiality-of-being, goes the unshakeable joy in this possibility. In it Da-sein becomes free of the entertaining "incidentals" that busy curiosity provides for itself, especially in terms of the events of the world.[15]

Heidegger's notion of resolutely and authentically living out of one's particularity stands in direct contrast both to the classical life of identifying with universal values and modern economic life which has us affirm every desire that arises. Heidegger sees both of these forms of life as being captured by different aspects of socialized existence and losing one's existential singularity.

To be authentic is to affirm the contradiction that we are both fated and free, that we have both a factical thrownness and an open set of inmost possibilities. We are concretely who we are as particulars and can change. If we emphasize our freedom in denial of our thrownness, we are tossed

into a vague realm of general possibilities and will likely fall prey to the
They's predilections. If we overly emphasize our factual thrownness (I am
male, middle-class, a professional, etc.), then we lose our sense of agency
and become trapped in repeating the doom that fate has granted us. We
must affirm both our thrownness and our openness.

One last Heideggerian point. When our subjectivity has fallen prey to
the They, the kind of care we tend to give others is a "leaping in"—we
leap into their problems and attempt to solve them. One might call this
"counseling." When we give authentic care, we "leap ahead"—we help
others by helping them discover their own resources to work through
their problems.[16]

HEIDEGGER AND KOHUT

Both Heidegger and Kohut offer visions of human nature that are decid-
edly anti-Cartesian, for both hold that we are embedded in the world with
no possibility of complete transcendence. For Heidegger we are always
in-the-world-with-others; for Kohut we develop through selfobject relationships and never outgrow our need for them. Subjectivity arises out of
intersubjectivity, not vice versa. This embeddedness of the individual in
the social has profound repercussions for the modernist projects of establishing freedom from authorities and achieving an independent individuality. For Heidegger, the most important kind of authority, the social order, is unavoidable. Without others there is no meaning and without
meaning there is no world. We might reject a religious authority, disagree
with a dominant political position, or rebel against our parents, but we
can never doubt all authorities, can never overthrow the entirety of the
social order, for the very act of overthrowing is an already scripted proce-
dure that has meaning in a social world. The achievement of authentic
individuality is not a release from our inauthentic social existence but a
modification of it. "[A]*uthentic* existence is nothing which hovers over
entangled everydayness, but is existentially only a modified grasp of
everydayness."[17] Modernity's overemphasis on individual freedom has
made it unmindful of our facticity, our embedded existence in this particular world.

Kohut would concur with Heidegger that we are social "all the way
down." He would emphasize, however, that it is not the generalized They
but those that play selfobject functions for us who are crucial in the construction of the self and its way of being in the world. He would agree
with Heidegger that without others there would be no world, but the
reason would be because neither a self nor organized experience could
form without selfobject care.

There is a further difference between Kohut and Heidegger in the way humans are social. While Heidegger accepts that a generalized other is inescapable in the existence of Da-sein, he finds this infiltration of the They as oppressive, leveling, and self-alienating. Kohut, on the other hand, finds the infiltration of others who are optimal selfobjects as giving vitality, sustaining meaning, and producing self-structure. Toxic others in the position of selfobjects, on the other hand, do not simply oppress experience, they have the power to pathologize it. Kohut focuses on particular others who play significant roles in the production of a self. Heidegger never mentions intimacy as a form of relating to others, while for Kohut intimacy is what generates self and gives meaning to life.

I believe that both Kohut's and Heidegger's accounts of human life are needed in order to understand fully the set of problems that living an authentic life must confront. What Kohut reveals is that there is a psychological ground for the possibility of organized consciousness—Da-sein. Heidegger treats conscious experience as an ontological realm onto itself, as though it had no psychological preconditions for its emergence. Kohut knows that without the development of a self through felicitous selfobject relations, the possibility of being Da-sein cannot appear. Yet, Kohut ignores the problem that Heidegger faces: selves being captured by an oppressive everydayness. Kohut tends to think that the production of a self is the ultimate task of psychological life and that when it is accomplished, then, except for the possibility of traumas, life has only its usual problems—realizing one's nuclear program, finding an intimate partner, and so on. But there is a genuine psychological problem that all selves face, namely, capture by the They and falling into devitalized, tranquilized, leveled lives. While having a coherent nuclear self is a necessary condition for dealing with the onslaught of social conformity, this is hardly sufficient. The path to full authenticity is paved not just with selfobjects but with philosophical tasks, such as facing one's death and hearing the call of conscience. These ideas are not in contradiction to Kohut—indeed, he says that one of the defining characteristics of mature narcissism is acceptance of one's mortality—but they do not receive the emphasis which they need in order for Kohut to have a complete theory of what it means to have an authentic self living vitally in the world.

Are Kohut's and Heidegger's conceptions of authenticity the same? I think so, but they use such different language and face such different problems that it is not easy to see. For Heidegger, authenticity occurs when one encounters her "ownmost possibilities" and resolutely follows them, resisting the temptation to get lost in the myriad possibilities for pleasure that modern life offers. These ownmost possibilities have the characteristics of not being simply values of the *They*, but *my* values. These values cannot be defined except to say that they are what appears when a person has allowed himself to be drawn into angst, courageously faced the inescapable possibility of not-being, and heard the silent inner call of that which is most herself. For Kohut, authenticity is finding a way to realize one's "nuclear program"—finding activities, persons, places, professions, and so on in which self can be fully engaged.

By "ownmost possibilities" Heidegger specifies two necessary traits of being authentic. The first is that authenticity always involves openness. What we discover is not who we actually are but a possibility of who we might be. Second, insofar as the possibilities we discover are our ownmost ones, they must dwell in our particular facticity. What Kohut would add to Heidegger's abstract language is that our facticity in relation to authenticity is the peculiar amalgam of ideals, ambitions, and traits of the nuclear self that each person has. I do not think that an adequate interpretation can be given to "ownmost possibilities" unless we interpret them as the possibilities of something like a Kohutian self. What could the "own" in "ownmost" refer to if not something like a self? It can't refer to our biological predispositions, for Heidegger distinguishes our being from merely biological accounts. Nor can it refer to those wants, desires, and goals we have because we belong to a particular society for these are part of inauthenticity. Referring possibilities merely to our "being" is not concrete enough to produce anything which looks like an "ownmost" possibility.

Heidegger eschewed advocating a notion of a self[18] because he thought such a notion was too entangled in the metaphysics of identity and not available for living one's existential particularity. Kohut's notion of a multi-faceted, dynamic self whose essence is to have possibilities both in terms of ideals and ambitions that are connected to our idiosyncratic traits seems to fit well with Heidegger's "ownmost possibilities."

Since for Heidegger we are always in danger of losing our authentic self because the They co-inhabits subjectivity along with the self, we must be resolute in our living. Authenticity is a problem that needs to be re-solved all the time; the authentic self is not a thing that comes into existence and is just there for the rest of our lives. We can lose it or have it severely compromised by social pressures. Kohut would agree about the fragility of the self's presence in experience but locate the dangers to the self not in social pressures but in selfobject failures and psychological traumas.

When we combine the notions of resoluteness and continual awareness of one's ownmost possibilities we realize that authenticity essentially involves the forming of commitments. To have a commitment, according to Jonathan Lear, means to be resolved to explore a field, activity, or relationship in which development is possible.[19] Commitment to an area in which development can occur is crucial, for development fuses Heidegger's notions of openness and facticity and incorporates Kohut's sense of a self as ideals and ambitions. A commitment must be fueled by vital energy that expresses the particularity of the person (ambitions) but which aims toward the realization of a meaningful goal (an ideal). In saying that the self is a set of commitments to areas in which it can develop is to emphasize that the self is not a thing (one cannot say this enough) but a process that is alive and vital, so long as it is in process. However, the process is not totally open and random but focused on specific ideals or ownmost possibilities. Our commitments—to a profession, a love relationship, a field of knowledge, the aliveness of the mind, a social cause, etc.—express the deepest values of the self but also its need to grow.

A life centered on commitments is very different from one organized around the pleasure principle. Indeed, the two constitute different ways of being in the world. When one defines one's life in terms of pleasure gratifications, then there seem to be endless possibilities to explore and weigh. Anything that looks as though it might give us pleasure is a possibility. Commitments constrain our possibilities. We cannot do just anything because we must tend to our commitments. Since commitments involve development, they, by necessity, involve frustration, suffering, difficult moments, and sacrifice. Life governed by a pleasure principle would have us run to easier pleasures when the pain gets difficult.

Of course, there is room for both commitment and pleasure. Just because life is centered on commitments does not mean that all of its events must occur as occasions within these commitments. Much of a well-lived life involves enjoyments and entertainments that have little to do with commitments. However, it does matter whether the strivings of a self in its commitments or a person's plethora of desires is the core of life. Commitments can allow for entertainments and pleasures, but a life devoted primarily to gratifications will have trouble locating and expressing the self.

The great enemy to the authentic self's developing and vitally growing through its commitments is, obviously, different for Kohut and Heidegger. For Heidegger, the great obstacle to our authenticity is our inauthenticity— our getting entangled in the social web and losing our original response to the world and ourselves. We can't be committed to our ownmost possibilities because we must always be concerned with what others expect of us. We lose ourselves in the social "oughts" and the "right" ways to appear, do things, and live. For Kohut the great enemy of the nuclear self's coming into being is inconsistent or toxic selfobject care. Certainly, both are right. A person with an injured nuclear self is likely to want to flee from her inner chaos to the stable structure of social life. That is, the person most likely to suffer severe capture by the They is one who has been psychologically injured.

Persons with strong vital selves have ballast with which to fend off social imposition, although everyone, even those with intact nuclear selves, are "Mitda-sein." Heidegger needs Kohut's psychology for finding who is best able to fend off the They; Kohut needs Heidegger's philosophy to understand what further tasks the nuclear self must accomplish in order to achieve a full vitality of functioning.

CONCLUSION

I have tried to show that Heinz Kohut's psychology of the self incorporates some of the most important insights into the nature of the self that have been offered during the rich and complex history of Western philosophy. The idealized pole of the self recognizes the essential need to ground and organize life around structures of meaning and value, an insight that is central to Plato's and Aristotle's conception of the human life. The grandiose pole of the self mirrors Nietzsche's concept of the free spirit exuberantly proclaiming the worth and specialness of the self's singularity. The concept of the nuclear self as a tension between ideals and ambitions/grandiosity captures the core of the dialectical conception of human experience found in Hegel and Kierkegaard. The concept of the self as an unconscious structured process that can only give signs of its nature finds profound reverberations with Heraclitus, Sophocles, and Confucius. The concept of the nuclear self is amplified by and expanded with Heidegger's notion of authenticity and gives substantial articulation to his notion of "ownmost possibilities."

This is not to say that we can now throw these great thinkers away and just read Kohut. He does not try to work out the problems of how ideals are to be justified, how the tension between individual and social ideals are to be negotiated, or how personal ideals are to be related to the realm of ethics. He also does not work out the ramifications of living as an individual in the social world or what conscious tasks must be undertaken to free one's self from the tentacles of society. While his nuclear self involves personal tensions between its sectors, it does not involve the great battles of consciousness as to whether a belief in God is necessary for full psychic vitality. Nor does Kohut explore the problem of how best to conceive of human freedom. Finally, he does not clearly distinguish between the subjectivity connected to the self and that connected to the ego. In short, Kohut's theory does not replace the rich philosophical history for thinking about the self.

Although Kohut does not replace the philosophical tradition, what he adds to it is immense. First, his insistence that the realm of meaning and ideals is essential for psychological health legitimates this realm within a naturalistic framework at a time when the pre-dominant naturalist theory tends to negate values and teleological motivation as real. Second, his compelling analysis of the centrality of a strong narcissistic component as necessary for a healthy psyche stands in the face of centuries of debilitating anti-narcissism (including Freud), which strangely has walked hand-in-hand with the West's emphasis on individualism. Third, his discovery that our narcissistic selves are inherently fragile and need to be bolstered by others throughout our lifetimes stands opposed to the value of self-sufficiency that has haunted the West's understanding of individualism from its very first statements in Plato and Aristotle to those of Thoreau and Nietzsche.

Finally, and most importantly, Kohut has uncovered the environmental conditions necessary for the development of strong and vital selves. His discovery that all children need empathic mirroring, merger with idealized others, and consistent optimal frustration in order to develop vital and coherent nuclear selves gives us not only the ground for childrearing but a ground upon which to base an entire social and ethical theory. While there have been other important accounts of human development, such as Aristotle's understanding of how the virtues develop and Erikson's theory of life's stages, Kohut's is the first theory that grasps the processes and stages that occur in the development of an unconscious core self, along with the necessary environmental conditions for that development to occur.

In the last three chapters of this book I will show how Kohut's concept of the nuclear self, bolstered with Heidegger's concept of authenticity, can offer novel and compelling answers to the problems of modernity, giving us a ground for being ethical, a path to self-realization, and a basis for making major shifts in social values. But before we can pick the ethical and social fruits of this theory, we need to construct a new understanding of the parts of the psyche and how they can optimally work together, fall into psychological pathologies, or become captured by the They.

NOTES

1. An earlier version of this chapter appeared as "The Philosophical Importance of Kohut's Bipolar Theory of the Self," in *Basic Ideas Reconsidered: Progress in Self Psychology*, vol. 12, ed. Arnold Goldberg (Hillsdale, NJ: Analytic Press, 1996).

2. Heidegger's philosophy has come under such severe attack for its possible underlying connections to Nazism that some statement needs to be made as to my relation to this contention. I believe that Heidegger's attempt to replace an ethical way of being human with a phenomenological ontology is highly dangerous and needs to be critically examined along with his dislike of the leveling forces at work in democracies. I think that the nonethical approach to human life in *Being and Time*, taken as a complete philosophy, is highly problematical but that Heidegger's brilliant analysis of human embeddedness in the world and how we might be able to attain a form of authenticity within that embeddedness can add a great deal to the understanding of human life offered by self psychology.

3. Jonathan Lear in *Happiness, Death, and the Remainder of Life* (Cambridge, MA: Harvard University Press, 2000) makes the simple but profound point that the revolutionary idea behind all of Greek ethics is the idea that persons can have lives.

4. I will fully develop the differences between the ego and the self in the following chapter. For now getting a sense of the difference between conscious ego experience organized by reason and an unconscious self that is immersed in a particular life history is enough.

5. Friedrich Nietzsche, *Thus Spoke Zarathustra*, trans. Walther Kaufmann (New York: Penguin Books, 1978), 86.

6. Kiekegaard, *The Sickness unto Death*, trans. H. Hong and E. Hong (Princeton, NJ: Princeton University Press, 1980), 13.

7. *The Presocratics*, ed. P. Wheelwright (New York: Odyssey Press, 1966), 70.

8. I am indebted to Marcia Dobson for these insights relating Kohut's notion of the self and Sophocles. See her paper "Freud, Kohut, Sophocles: Did Oedipus Do Wrong?" *International Journal of Psychoanalytic Self Psychology*, 2, no.1 (Feb. 2007): 53–76.

9. Confucius, *The Analects*, trans. D. C. Lau (New York: Penguin Books, 1979), 74, 115, 123.

10. See especially Arnold Goldberg's *Misunderstanding Freud* (New York: Other Press, 2004).

11. Martin Heidegger, *Being and Time*, trans. Joan Stambaugh (Albany, NY: SUNY Press, 1996), 108.

12. Heidegger, *Being and Time*, 119.

13. Heidegger, *Being and Time*, 239.

14. Heidegger, *Being and Time*, 282.

15. Heidegger, *Being and Time*, 286.

16. Heidegger, *Being and Time*, 114–15.

17. Heidegger, *Being and Time*, 167.

18. Heidegger, *Being and Time*, section 64.

19. Jonathan Lear, *Therapeutic Action* (New York: Other Press, 2003).

FOUR

A NEW METAPSYCHOLOGY
Freud, Aristotle, Heidegger, and Kohut

Heinz Kohut developed a remarkable new way of understanding the human psyche, one with the development of the self as its core. Although he makes numerous statements which indicate that he thinks the self is different from the ego (especially in *How Does Analysis Cure?*), he never develops a new metapyschology in which the functions of the ego and the self are clearly delineated. Are they different? How? Does the idealized pole of the nuclear self function more or less like a superego? How does an ambition differ from a drive? Kohut never worked out the answers to these questions, but I will try to do so in this chapter.

However, the matter is not as simple as attempting to map onto Freud a set of self-functions, for both Freud and Kohut ignored crucial parts of human experience that must be addressed in any adequate mapping of the psyche. First, the earliest psychologists in the West, Plato and Aristotle, said that a well-lived human life depended on the development of virtuous character traits. I believe they are right, for without the virtues we would not be able to moderate the power of the passions. Is character a part of the ego? The self? Or is it a different psychological set of functions from these two?

Second, Heidegger claims that the most debilitating (and inescapable) force in human life is the colonization of the individual psyche by generalized social existence. Experience organized around psychologically embedded social codes tends to be everydayish, flat, and without optimal vitality. These codes do not have the dynamic and harsh quality that Freud assigns superego values nor the teleological nature that Kohut gives the ideals of the self. Where are they to be located in psychic functionality?

Constructing a metapsychology that integrates Kohut's theory of the self, Freud's tripartite psyche, Aristotle's analysis of character, and Heidegger's phenomenological understanding of lived experience is, obviously, a Promethean task for both the author and reader, and good reasons must be given for undertaking it. I believe that a metapsychological map that delineates the parts of the psyche and the relations between them is of immense importance for a number of reasons. First, such a mapping gives us a powerful shorthand for grasping psychological dynamics whose full description would be too complex and dense to be useful. Freud's tripartite division of the psyche into the id, ego, and superego has, for example, been immensely effective in understanding a number of forms of psychopathology.

Further, I believe that Plato was right in thinking that the key to living well is the optimal arrangement of the parts of the soul. Plato's parts (reason, spirit, appetites) are all contained in the conscious ego while this inquiry will include unconscious parts, thus expanding Plato's crucial insights. I do not think that one can delineate what it means to be a person who can live well without describing what the optimal arrangement is between the parts of the psyche. That is, this metapsychological venture is the key to understanding ethical life.

Finally, I think that in ordinary living such a mapping is of immense importance. The key to living a self-aware life is to inquire into the source of one's motivations—asking from which part of the psyche the impetus for action is coming. It will make a great deal of difference if it is coming from the self, the ego, social pressures working through the unconscious, or defensive structures. Some motivations need to be fought, others ignored, and some others taken so seriously that one is willing to suffer for them, even die for them. The basic claim of this work is that a life organized around self-initiatives is far more vital that those organized around the ego's needs for legitimation and control, the persona's desires for social esteem and recognition, or the defenses' need to avoid any chaos that might re-stimulate a primary trauma.

The place that any new thinking about the parts of the psyche must begin is Freud's justly famous tripartite model. If we think of the id as those psychic forces present in us through our biological heritage and the superego as the repository of social forces, then we can see Freud's metapsychology as a variation on the widespread nineteenth-century theme that humans are caught in a tense struggle between the natural and the social. In this struggle the social is typically seen as a normalizing force that crushes our natural, vital selves, forcing their expression into generalized codes of behavior and reducing life to an arid artificiality. This theme occurs countless times in modern novels, from Goethe's *Werther* (perhaps the first great expression of the theme) through Hawthorne's *The Scarlet Letter* to Hemingway's stories and novels. The theme soars in American philosophy with Emerson, Thoreau, and Muir calling us to leave society and dwell in nature, for only there can we find our true selves. Who can forget Thoreau's mournful plaint that "most men live lives of quiet desperation" or his proclamation that "everything good is wild"?

From the middle of the nineteenth century to the present day, heroes and heroines have tended to exude a natural vitality and refuse to be co-opted into a standardized, de-individuating social order. Heathcliffe, Natty Bumppo, Paul Bunyan, Nietzsche's Zarathustra, Wagner's Sieg-fried, and any of Jane Austen's heroines exude a natural vitality and typically have overly socialized foils to play against. They are followed by John Wayne, Humphrey Bogart, Gary Cooper, Harrison Ford, and count-less other male heroes of the silver screen, along with the most cherished of the actresses, Katharine Hepburn.

Why has this theme of a war between our natural selves and the social order—more or less absent in the Greeks and Renaissance—become so powerful? I suspect it is responding to a number of social developments in the nineteenth century, especially the emergence of a mass urban soci-ety, the over-formality of Victorian culture, the moral strictness of a new middle class attempting to legitimate itself, the abstract rationalism of sci-ence, the industrial revolution, and the romance of the American wilder-ness. The new economic world required training, discipline, punctuality, exactitude, and efficiency—all traits that require the relinquishing of nat-ural spontaneity. The typical human work environment shifted from the small farm which grounded life in nature to the bureaucratic organization or factory which isolated persons from both nature and their families.

Freud's psychology is thoroughly conditioned by this way of conceptu-alizing modern life. Carlo Strenger writes that "Freud's structural model of the personality reflected the concerns of the middle class: the ego was supposed to keep the reins on all the instinctual demands that could ruin a middle class family."[1] Freud was wiser than most of the fanatical natu-ralists in that he realized that the social and natural were both necessary for human life. Yet, he still held that the satisfaction of the id is what gives us happiness and that the moral codes internalized as the superego, while necessary for the survival of the species, inhibited natural fulfillment and led to a kind of "permanent unhappiness."[2] As an amalgam of the natural and social, humans are doomed to be "discontent." What Freud added to the nineteenth-century conceptualization of the struggle between the natural and the social was that this conflict occurs mainly outside of con-scious awareness, in the seething dynamics of the unconscious.

For Freud, it is the heroic ego that must negotiate the conflict between our natural instincts and our social identity. The ego's task is immense, for it must attain real satisfactions in the world in order to survive, and to do this it has to deal with an external moral structure, an internalized moral structure (the superego) that could be far harsher than the public one, and imperious drives that seek their objects regardless of whether they are socially sanctioned. Worse, the ego has none of its own power with which to accomplish these functions but must borrow energy from the id through identifications with objects the id has loved. The ego does have the crucial tools of language, concept formation, and reasoning to help it with its tasks, along with a number of unconscious defenses it can use to keep conflicts out of consciousness if they generate too much anxiety.

For all of his brilliant work in mapping unconscious dynamics, I want to suggest that Freud was misled by the nature vs. society paradigm into oversimplifying the patterns of psychic conflict. He did not see that there was a source of motivation other than reality demands, social pressures, id drives, and superego reproaches—namely, the strivings of the self. Without this source of motivation, the human psyche does appear to be impossibly conflicted between natural impulses and social restrictions, dooming it to a kind of everyday unhappiness. Finally, he also did not grasp what I call the social unconscious—the values, norms, concepts, and so on that are unconsciously embedded in us in a nondynamic way—norms and concepts that typically can be uncovered without personal resistance needing to be overcome but can deaden experience as much as psychopathological blockages.

When we posit the central goal of psychological life as the development of a self, then the roles of both the natural and social change radically. While the social can impose its de-individuating norms, it can also act as a field of adventure in which we realize our nuclear goals and ambitions. The social can inhibit a person's drives, but without it in the form of selfobjects, there would be no self or organized experience at all. Moral norms can be seen as constrictions on natural expression but can also embody patterns by which selfobject experiences can best be secured. The social might constrict individual possibilities in the world, but without it, there would be no world of possibilities at all. In sum, if the self is "naturally" who we are (even more so than the id), then the natural and social are not at irrevocable odds with each other, for the self is necessarily a fusion of both.

Likewise, the "natural" energies in us need careful distinguishing, for the ambitions and ideals of our "natural" core selves are different from the biological urges and emotional reactions of the id. The kinds of fulfillments that come from satisfying these two kinds of natural energies are not only dissimilar but can be opposed. Life narratives organized around drive-satisfaction are quite different from those organized around self-realization. Hence, it makes a great deal of difference how we understand what constitutes the "natural" in us. If it is the id, then there is a great tension with the social and its restrictions on id aims and wishes, but if "being natural" is understood as acting from our essential selves, then there need be no fundamental stasis between the natural and social. In short, self psychology, unlike the naturalist or existentialist philosophies of the nineteenth and twentieth centuries, offers us a vision of human nature in which we are not required to be socially alienated in order to be most ourselves.

Because Freud did not distinguish the ego from the self, he saw the great difference in experience to be between the normal and the pathological (in which the id is overly repressed). He did not attempt to account for a kind of experience that is neither normalized nor pathological, a kind of experience that stands out as having a heightened sense of being and incommensurably more profound engagements with the world than the other two kinds of experience. He missed self experiences.

What follows is an attempt to work out a metapsychology that allows us to understand how we can have three general kinds of experiences: everyday normalized experience, experiences pathologically constricted by psychological defenses, and self experiences. Of course, almost all experiences have components of each. Most modern humans have some operative defenses, the social codes are always at work, and the self—even in a fragmented state—seems to be diffusely present. Thus, most experiences are a mixture of defensive, social, and self elements. However, it makes all the difference which factor predominates in experiences and which factors are secondary. Since all of these aspects qualify the experience of the ego, the key to understanding the parts of the psyche and how they operate is to grasp the nature of the ego. In the next section I will be making this inquiry's most important distinction—between the ego and the self. It is the confusion or fusion of the two which has made the self such a difficult notion to understand.

THE EGO AND ITS EXPERIENCE

As strange as it might at first seem, we must make a careful distinction between the "I" that we think of as ourselves and the self.[3] That there is this distinction is evident in the common locutions "I don't feel like myself today" or "I just haven't found myself." Indeed, some people claim that they have spent years—even decades—not being themselves; yet, all during this time there was an "I" that was having personal experiences and which wasn't missing or lost. If the "I" is the same as the self, then these sentences amount to the very strange statements of "I am not feeling like I am feeling today" and "I, who am here and present, am not able to find myself." Two of the most important statements that the "I" can make are "I have a self" and "I am being myself." How can the "I" "have a self" or "be a self" if the "I" is the same as the self? What all of these statements about "having a self," "losing oneself," "finding oneself," and "being true to oneself" indicate is that the "I" has a relation to the self. As such, it cannot simply be the self.

Other evidence for the distinction between the "I" and the self comes from persons who suffer from posttraumatic stress, who often feel as though they are not fully present or engaged in their own lives. When they have experiences, there is an "I" that has the experiences, but at the same time they feel as though those experiences are not really their experiences, for the experiences lack the full presence of a self. What this common occurrence points toward is that "I-experiences" need not be "self-experiences."

We will, like Kant, consider the "I" to be the ultimate transcendental condition for the possibility of conscious experience.[4] That is, for any and all experience, we can say that it is the experience of an "I." Whether the experience is one of average everydayness, a vital self experience, or one severely limited by psychopathology, it belongs to the "I." Again, since self experiences are only a subset of possible "I" experiences, the ego and the self must be different.

Another way of putting this crucial point is that the structure of the self can be in part empirically known, for it manifests itself in experience. One can determine not only what one's nuclear ideals and ambitions are but whether these poles of the self are functioning well or are injured. An injured self can engage in a therapeutic process that can heal injuries and transform self functioning. That is, the self is a psychological structure that comes into being through a recognizable developmental process that can be more or less adequate.

The "I" seems to be very different. No matter what characteristics we think might belong to the "I," the "I" can abstract itself from them and view them as contingent. I might now define my way of being in the world as "philosophically-minded" but my ego can say, "Enough philosophizing—I do not have to define myself that way!" That is, the "I" always has the feature of subjectivity—activity that cannot be reduced to objective conditions. The activity of consciousness always transcends any attempt to empirically or objectively know what it is. Eric Santner describes the "I" as a "non-symbolizable surplus within an otherwise intelligible reality."[5] There is no final scientific or discursive way to capture the "I"—it always is an excess or surplus of subjectivity that defies all attempts to understand it.

The self also has an ineffable singularity and subjectivity to it—a nonreducible remainder after the selfobject relations, ambitions, ideals, and traits have been analyzed. However, its subjective singularity is not that of the ego's inherently ungraspable subjectivity. The self—while it has qualities, ideals, ambitions, a style, a rhythm, idiosyncratic traits, selfobject support—is not equal to the sum of its parts. There is a remainder which has these traits. In contrast a psychological account of the "I" cannot be given, for it does not have a developmental history. Rather, conscious subjectivity seems to spring, like Athena, fully formed into the world.

While the ego can develop a mind and learn language, the presence of a transcendental subject seems to be a necessary condition for the possibility of experience rather than a structure of that experience. The self, on the other hand, is the precipitate of a developmental sequence.

Because the ego seems to transcend any psychological account of its origin or its structure, it also seems true to say that the ego cannot suffer psychological injuries the way the self does. The ego can remain uneducated and its powers remain dormant, but it does not seem capable of suffering the kind of traumas that fragment the self.

The "I" or ego is the subject of conscious experience. This sector of the psyche has a number of functions: it must act in the world to get the organism's needs met, communicate with the world to make sense of itself both to the world and itself, and gain knowledge of the world not only to act in and communicate with it but because we are the kind of being who seeks to know who we are and what the world is in which we live. In order to accomplish the tasks of action, communication, and knowledge, the ego is given immensely powerful tools by its culture: language, know how, concepts, and reasoning abilities. That is, the ego, with education and experience, can develop a mind. The more the ego's mind is developed, the more successful it is, all things being equal, in negotiating its tasks in the world.

Most philosophers and psychologists have been so impressed by the rational mind's ability to know and transform the world that they have identified the totality of psychological life with conscious mentality and proclaimed the development of the mind's rational powers as the solution to all the problems facing humanity, both individually and collectively. Indeed, from Socrates to the present day, philosophy and science have had as their primary aim the exploration of what the rational mind is, how it can attain knowledge, and how it can transform a seemingly irrational world into one of order and accountability. Hegel speaks for the whole tradition when he proclaims that "the real is the rational and the rational is the real." While the discovery of the unconscious has negated the identity of psychological life with consciousness, rational consciousness remains the most remarkable force in the history of the world. It has transformed a planet governed by natural processes to one increasingly dominated by human activities.

The conscious ego is also the seat of human agency and choice (not the unconscious self).[6] It consciously weighs options and directs the organized activity of the human organism. In order to accomplish its functions of negotiating the organism's interactions with its social and natural environments, the ego must accomplish another task—its primary task: it must establish and maintain coherence in the psyche. Complete psychological incoherence is psychosis and in this state the ego loses its ability to function at all. As Freud found, the major tools the ego has for dealing with trauma to the self are the psychological defensives, such as repression, dissociation, compensatory idealization, and intellectualization. These operate unconsciously and so we, along with Freud, acknowledge that the ego also has an unconscious part of its functioning.

When the ego uses its unconscious defenses to both protect the self from traumatic disintegration and to clear an anxiety-free space for conscious functioning, the psychodynamics that Freud and other psychoanalysts have so brilliantly described—symptom-formation, compensatory mechanisms, resistances, etc.—come into play. That these defense mechanisms can be utilized by very young babies leads me to believe that both self- and ego-functioning are present from the very beginning of psychological life. This means that the ego in its most primitive form exists before consciousness or directed thinking and is not, initially, a developmental achievement but part of the original furniture of the psyche. It can develop reasoning skills, language, memory, and so on in time, but its ability to use the defenses seems hard-wired and primordial.

That the ego is responsible for psychological coherence is another reason why it cannot have an objective identity. If it had such an identity, then it would also be another part of the psyche, and itself would have to be organized by another psychological agency whose function it was to provide an overall harmony. That is, whatever we conceive of as a coherence-making agency cannot itself be a "part" that needs to be brought into coherence. Jonathan Lear captures this essential point well when he says, "The core is not any determinate content in the psyche, nor is it any one of the psychic parts as opposed to the others. Rather, *the core is the elementary capacity of the psyche to hold itself together*"[7] (italics are Lear's). Thus, although for the sake of psychic mapping I am treating the ego as having specialized functions, and thus being a "part of the soul," in another way, it seems not to be a part at all but the presence of a coherence-generating subjectivity that pervades that entire psyche.

Along with its major functions of establishing psychological coherence and negotiating the organism's needs with the world, the ego has its own need: to establish its legitimacy. This need is inherently tied to the ego's essential subjectivity and self-consciousness. Since the conscious ego has no necessary ground for its choices and is aware that it has no ground, it feels the need to establish some basis that will legitimate its decisions. The remarkable power of the ego to be aware of its own activity means that it can raise questions about who the "I" is and what grants its existence worth.

Freud missed this need for legitimation when discussing the ego because he located the primary needs in the id. Kohut, in concentrating on the needs of the self for selfobject mirroring and idealization, also missed this ego need. But the great philosophers of the nineteenth and twentieth centuries—including Hegel, Kierkegaard, Nietzsche, Heidegger, and Sartre—found consciousness's need to establish a ground for itself to be the most pressing problem of human existence. It is this intense ego-need for a legitimating ground that lies behind the search for an objective reality on which to base human life, such as God, the Forms, or categorical imperatives. I believe it is why society cannot do without differential statuses, for there is a hope that one's life might be legitimated if one can achieve one of the exalted statuses. Many of my students seem to have as intense a need for the legitimation of high grades as they do for sex (id need) or friends (self need). The extraordinary drivenness for success in this country cannot be explained simply in terms of securing goods for survival or material comfort but must be correlated with the ego's need for legitimation.

As soon as literature appears in the West with Homer's *Iliad*, we find self-conscious human beings worrying about their legitimacy. The heroes of the *Iliad* are warriors attempting to prove themselves worthy on the battlefield and are almost insanely upset about slights to their statuses. The whole work revolves around the slight that Achilles receives from Agamemnon when Agamemnon declares he must give him his concubine to replace the one he had to send back to the priest of Apollo. Here we have the first full depiction of self-conscious human beings and their fundamental concern is about establishing their legitimacy.

This problem seems even more intensified in modernity when old structures of medieval legitimacy get replaced mainly with economic structures. The intensity with which modern persons are concerned with their socioeconomic status and constructing "important" life narratives are, to me, the driving force of contemporary life. The structure of legitimation is always the same—the ego must establish its meaning within the social codes and values of the person's society (or else it cannot make sense) but must always stand beyond them—not just be a token exemplification of a type.

As much as the ego longs for legitimation, it has an insuperable problem with establishing it. As Sartre puts it, consciousness is a "for itself" longing to become an "in-itself," but if it ever became an "in-itself" it would cease being conscious. No matter what objective principles the ego chooses as its ground, the ego's choosing of them already transcends the grounds chosen. That is, any choice of grounds by the ego itself requires a ground; hence, the ego's authorization of grounds must, in the end, be groundless. Given the need for legitimation and the impossibility of ever achieving one, Sartre says that the central emotion of consciousness is nausea, a claim which reverberates with Heidegger's assertion that angst is our essential experience and Kierkegaard's statement that despair is the defining condition of the "I." I believe that the ego's problem with legitimation cannot be solved if the ego and the self are seen as identical. It is only when we distinguish them that the ego can find a ground for its choices that both enables it to keep its openness and find an "authentic" source of action, for the self is the ground that can give the ego the sense of groundedness.

And this returns us to the problem of how to distinguish the "I" from the self. Since the "I" is capable of "self-consciousness" and is the central psychological agency of knowledge, action, understanding, and conscious meaning, it is easy to see why the ego has from the beginning of psychological theory been identified with the self and why Kohut's discovery of an unconscious self that is different from the ego is so revolutionary and so difficult to understand. Yet, unless the self is different from the ego, we fall into insoluble troubles. For one, we could not account for the experiences of losing ourselves, not feeling like ourselves, really feeling like ourselves, or being ourselves, all of which require the ego to have relationship to the self and not be identical with it. Two, it would not be possible to explain how persons can have highly functional, well-organized egos and be simultaneously devastated by feelings of inner depletion, fragmentation, and meaninglessness. We would not be able to explain why such consciously functional persons exhibit dissociated structures and are prone to such narcissistic symptoms as the addictive use of substances, cheating, entitlement behavior, and self-esteem fragility. The kind of person I have just described—one with a highly developed rational mind, keen conceptual skills, operating within a rich world of meanings, and actively pursuing goals while at the same time feeling an inner emptiness and exhibiting narcissistic symptoms—is not an oddity found here and there but someone who represents an increasingly common type in contemporary Western life. I think that unless the self and ego are separated, this kind of person cannot be understood.

Further, unless the self and ego are different, the problem of legitimation cannot be solved, for the self is the only possible ground that can legitimate ego choices. Kierkegaard and Heidegger would agree, as both say that despair/angst can be overcome if one can locate one's authentic self. However, we must specify that the self must give the ego a kind of ground that does not take away its openness, for without openness the ego would not be the ego. The self must be a contingent ground for the ego.

This, in fact, is just what happens when the self and ego form a strong axis of relatedness. That the self leaves the ego free is clear, for the ego can always lose the self, misinterpret the self, or choose against the self. However, if the ego chooses to align with the self, it feels joyfully grounded, as though it had found its proper marriage partner. It is as though one had been searching for someone to love and then found just the right person. As the search for a lover ceases when one finds the special other, so the ego's search for legitimation ceases when it aligns with the self. The partnership can never be certain of stability, for all psychological structure is tenuous, but this seems to be the one ground that can calm the ego's quest for legitimation. It is not that the ego has found some self-justifying principle (as Kant sought) or some absolute ground (a Platonic form, God), for these are rational discoveries and the ego's reason can also undermine them. There is something about the self's presence in conscious experience that simply makes the ego feel grounded.

So, why doesn't the ego easily find the self, form the essential alliance needed for healthy psychological functioning, and have the wonderful experience of feeling like a someone living a worthy, grounded, meaningful life? There are three obstacles to the development of this alignment. The first is that the self is the sector of the psyche that will harbor any and all psychological injuries. Insofar as the self is wounded or traumatized, it constitutes a source of incoherence and the ego's relating to it is dangerous and anxiety-provoking. The more modern life tends to traumatize the psyche, the more modern persons will be unable to establish a strong self/ego alliance at the heart of psychological functioning.

Second, there is a structural tension between the values of the ego and those of the self. The ego, as most of the Western philosophers have proclaimed, is the source of freedom and has as its highest value the expression of this freedom, which, in Aristotle's terms, is complete "self-sufficiency," while the self needs to be located in a stable realm of connectedness. The ego's valuing freedom and independence above all other values is nothing other than the proclamation that it values itself. The essence of consciousness is, in Sartre's terms, freedom. It is this value which lies behind postmodernism's overarching values of openness and possibility and why a psychology of the self is understood as problematic to this philosophical orientation.[8]

When freedom and the need for legitimacy are put together, they produce the central motivating value of the ego: power. This is what Nietzsche saw most clearly. The ego seeks power not only to achieve independence from the limiting conditions of the world and the difficulty of survival but seeks it to be in full control of the psyche. If trauma can throw the psyche into a chaotic and even psychotic fragmentation and the ego has the task of residing over the coherence of the psyche, then above all the ego wants control both of the outer world and of its inner world. Hence, Plato, our first systematic philosopher, had as the center of his ethical philosophy the achievement of self-mastery and the center of his epistemological/metaphysical philosophy the forms—concepts by which we could organize experience and gain power over the world.[9]

However, the ego's values of freedom and power are, in essence, antithetical to the self's need for selfobjects. Since the self arises and develops out of acts of love and needs these acts of love to continue flourishing, its values must revolve around love. But love typically limits independence, takes away self-sufficiency, and is opposed by power. When power enters human relations, it tends to turn them into situations of control, situations in which Hegel's famous master/slave dialectic plays itself out. But as Hegel so brilliantly said, a slave cannot be a genuine selfobject for a master nor a master for a slave. When relationships descend into power struggles for control, the self and its need for love and affirmation, along with its need to love, go wanting.

Freud was right, the psyche is inherently dynamic because it is inherently conflictual. He first identified the conflict as fundamentally between the drives and later as between the ego, id, and superego. The metapsychology presented here is a variation on this scheme but finds the crucial dynamic conflict between the ego with its values of freedom and power and the self with its need to exist within a dependent matrix of love. We will follow the ramifications of this tension between the values of the self and those of the ego as they occur in modern life in chapter 7.

UNCONSCIOUS ORGANIZING STRUCTURES

What kind of thing is the self? First, it is no thing at all but a dynamic system which, when present in experience, infuses it with singular meaning, vitality, and presence. That is, the self is a psychological system that unconsciously organizes, colors, and motivates the ego's experiences. It is, in short, an unconscious motivating structure. In order to understand what in general unconscious motivating structures are, we must turn, once again, to Kant.

Kant's Copernican revolution in philosophy is that the world is not simply given to experience but that the mind (unconsciously) takes the received data of sensation and organizes it into a world. In order for the mind to do this, it must have unconscious organizing structures, structures which Kant called the categories. In more contemporary terms, the mind uses language and social concepts to transform whatever appears into a meaningful world. Most of this happens outside the realm of conscious choice.

Our worlds, then, come into being through the unconscious organizing structures of subjectivity. If, for instance, we have paranoid structures, then no matter what the objects of the world actually are, they will be experienced as having some danger lurking in them. If we are being driven by the need to merge with an idealized selfobject, then experience will have a sense of emptiness until such an object appears. We then become riveted on that object and all the other objects of the world recede into the background.

Every unconscious structure that organizes experience both gives us a world and sets a limitation on what we can experience. As limitations, structuring conditions are often maligned as blockages to the supreme value of modernity, freedom. We wish to rid ourselves of all such structures. But without organizing conditions there would not be a world at all; there would only be chaos. There is no possibility of freeing ourselves from all conditions that subjectively organize a world to arrive at some kind of real or noumenal world.

Every world also excludes other possible worlds. If I live in a world which is experienced primarily through a serious philosophical attitude, then I cannot live in the world of a happy-go-lucky person. If I live in a world given through middle-class economic structures, then different sets of material objects will appear than appear to those who are fabulously wealthy or extremely poor. If a person is driven by a lack of self-structure to be morbidly dependent on relationships, then the world will by necessity be riveted on these relationships and all their impossibilities.

While we cannot live without unconscious organizing structures to give us a world, we can evaluate which conditions give us better or worse worlds. Not all worlds are equally worthy. Some organizing structures, according to Heidegger, give us an average expectable world in which we live without authentic engagement. Freud showed that the organizing structures of a neurotic will arbitrarily limit possibilities, including possibilities for intimacy, self-assertion, and psychic vitality. I want to say that when experience is organized by a strong self/ego alliance, it opens up an optimal world of meaningfulness, flexibility, and adventure.

Since different worlds are produced by different dynamics of the unconscious organizing structures, it is necessary to turn to these structures and their dynamics in order to understand what kind of psychological functioning produces what kinds of experiences for the ego. I must, of course, qualify what follows with the statement that while the categories and schemes of psychic dynamics that I propose are clear and, I believe, helpful in both understanding and treating the psyche, all psychological functioning is complex, messy, and multiply-determined.

The unconscious organizing structures that are primarily responsible for producing action are the id, character, self, and the social unconscious (centered on the persona). These parts of the psyche thrust themselves into ego consciousness, giving impetus and/or structure to our motivations.

The Id

I will use the term "id" to designate any drive, desire, emotion, wish, or need that appears to have some kind of biological origin, such as the desire to fall asleep. While I hold that all humans have a complex set of basic needs and emotions, what these are and how they operate is not important here.[10] What is important is to see that desires, needs, and emotions can act as structuring conditions for our experience of the world. The world seen through hunger has a different focus and mood than the one seen when sexual desire is foremost. Lovers are known to forget food; the starving typically overlook a luscious sexual opportunity for a meal, even if it's gruel. The world looks quite different when we are angry than when we are calmly interested. Desires, needs, and emotions are typically not chosen but simply appear in experience. They unconsciously arise to color, shape, focus, and direct our conscious experience and actions. In short, I use the concept of "id" much like Freud did as that set of motivators which seem to be biologically wired and which can move us regardless of whether self-structure is in place or social conventions have been learned. The infant does not yet have a self nor is she attuned to social values, but organizes her world around her id needs for milk, security, sleep, etc. Where I am in disagreement with Freud is in his finding the id to be the sole primary psychological bedrock. Id needs, narcissistic grandiosity, and ego functions all seem structurally primary. Psychological bedrock is not a force or drive but an ecosystem of different processes and structures.

Character

The greatest psychologists of the ancient world—Plato and Aristotle—thought that the key to living well was establishing a strong alliance between virtuous character traits and ego-rationality. They were very close to hitting the mark, but character, as important as it is, is not the same as self, for its unconscious organizing functions differ from those of the self. This is fortunate, for it means that people with injured selves can still moderate the power of the passions without having to resort to excessive repression. Our character determines how we characteristically respond to typical human situations and the emotions/desires/needs they arouse, such as situations of food consumption, danger, exchange of gifts and services, and the id states of hunger, fear, envy, and so on.

Character traits are "characteristic" ways one has of responding to the world—ways that develop through habits and which become habitual. If I develop the character trait of justice, then I will be in the habit of trying to be fair in my dealings, and can remain just—or moderate, courageous, kind, etc.—even if I am unable to access my self. The kind of character traits that best meliorate the power of the passions and give them the possibility of becoming my wants, needs, and emotions rather than blind impulsive forces was brilliantly elaborated by Aristotle. Character traits that represent the mean between the extremes allow for the needs and emotions to appear in experience but not be overwhelming. The virtues (courage, generosity, moderation in food consumption, cheerfulness of disposition, etc.) allow us to block the immediate power of the id without repressing it, thereby providing a space for us to think about what best to do. As such, virtuous character has both conscious and unconscious aspects to it. Virtuous character traits unconsciously moderate the drives and desires such that when they come to consciousness, they do not overwhelm it. We can then consciously and freely decide how best to respond. In choosing what to do, the virtuous person will try to find an action which is not excessive or deficient, thereby doing both what is good and reinforcing the virtuous character trait.

Character has often been confused with the self (I think this is true of Aristotle) in that both offer a familiar response to common situations in the inner and outer worlds. But character is less dynamic and less subjectively active (unconsciously) than the self. Character, as Aristotle said, is a set of habits which give psychic stability and the possibility for delayed response, while the self actively holds ideals and contains grandiose energy that vitalizes activity. The self has to continually develop through time, while character can remain stable. The self and character also have different developmental patterns. The self is developed through empathic mirroring, idealization, transmuting internalization, and optimal frustration. Character, according to Aristotle, is built primarily through techniques of reinforcement and mimicking. It is learned behavior that can involve moments of optimal frustration and internalization, but these happen at a much more conscious level than they do in the development of the self, as when a child consciously tries to be just like Mom or Dad, mimics their behavior, and in so doing starts developing a habitual response. Most importantly, while character deeply influences what appears in subjective experience it does not itself appear to be a form of subjectivity, while the self is. Character doesn't experience the world or suffer trauma; the self does.

Virtuous character traits have a saving power to them. In persons whose selves have been ravaged, there is still the possibility of living a good life through character. Character modulates the power of the passions without excessive indulgence or repression. It enables us to live as good persons even when the unconscious is full of rage, destructive impulse, and revenge. The destructiveness might come out in hidden ways, but this is very different from its directly exploding into the world with all its fury. It is also true that even persons with intact selves need the virtuous character traits. The self harbors vitality, ideals, and ambitions, but these do not necessarily mean that people with selves will be temperate, just, courageous, or generous. Those who champion having a strong self as the final goal of psychic life usually fail to acknowledge the necessity of virtuous character, while character without self cannot provide the vitality and sense of singular presence that having a self produces.

The Social Unconscious

The social unconscious includes all the social concepts, values, mores, and codes that have become unconsciously embedded in our way of being in the world because we are members of a culture. As Heidegger says, our social existence gives us the world, for it gives us criteria of importance, names the most useful objects, designates what kind of life is best, and tells us how to be who we are—a boy or girl, man or woman, young or mature, rich or poor, a professional or worker. It even scripts how to be a scoundrel, a rebel, and a social outcast. When we attempt to be "natural"— that is, to locate ourselves outside of social codes—we are already enact- ing the codes that validate "naturalness" as a good way to be and that also script how to look and act naturally. We are all embedded in our cultures and while we might be able to alter or overcome some of our social situ- atedness, we can never throw all of it off. Indeed, the very value of freeing ourselves from social codes is itself one of the strongest of the coded val- ues of modern Western culture.

The social unconscious differs from the personal unconscious in that in a healthy state it is not dynamic. That is, there are not personal defenses and resistances that prevent us from uncovering the social codes through which we construct our worlds. There might be strong penalties in terms of social alienation in becoming aware of and challenging our cultural norms, but we do not have to face repressed trauma in such a confronta- tion. Because of the undynamic character of the social unconscious, it is available for conscious intervention and readjustment. The most impor- tant province for readjustment is that part of ourselves that carries our social identity: the *persona*.

One's persona is who one appears to be both to himself and others. It is the part of ourselves that carries a name and is recognized through social statuses (the child of x and y, student, middle-aged, beautiful, talented, natural guy, etc.). We can think of the persona as the objectified subject— the subject taken as object. Since our personae represent our objectified subjectivities, they are typically the cause for much personal scrutiny, re- flexivity, and design by the "I." Indeed, most of what counts as self-care is concerned with designing the objective traits of one's personal life, such as the choice of lifestyle, appearance, profession, and other statuses. Be- cause of these conscious constructions, it appears that one's persona works at a conscious level, but this is not so, for once persona choices are made, they tend to become unconscious structuring conditions for con- scious experience.

Persons who do not suffer from significant psychopathology can con- sciously change and adjust their personae without overdetermined anxi- ety and stress. The case is otherwise for persons who suffer from a fragmented or enfeebled self. For these people the persona often needs to work in a defensive way, helping to provide coherence for psychic functioning that the injured self cannot. When the self is intact, it acts like an inner force organizing and holding the psyche together; when it is fragmented, a defensive exoderm is needed to impose order on an inner chaos. Threats to the persona or social failures carry with them far more devastation for these people than for those who have coherent nuclear selves. If the persona is acting as a substitute for the self, then this part of the social unconscious does become dynamic, engages in the defenses and resistance, and becomes more rigid.

It is in this defensive state that the social unconscious takes on the characteristics Freud ascribed to the superego. People in general seem to need some kind of social rules and prohibitions that operate in them to confront the most serious of the emotional impulses (anger causing a predisposition to physically attack, sudden sexual desire, etc.). These rules seem to be a backup system to the virtues, an extra mechanism for coping with difficult temptations and emotions that can't be easily contained by character. We might say that the superego is that part of the social unconscious that centers on prohibitions that inhibit our most antisocial impulses. It acts with the force of command and is instilled with a fear of social consequences. In its normal form, it does not have as its primary motivating force the death drive and does not significantly make us fall into a "permanent unhappiness" or crush the vital life of the soul.

However, when the self is injured and the superego comes to play a strong role in psychological dynamics, then it can become harsh and self-negating, consciously and unconsciously judging the ego and/or self to be inadequate, bad, or a failure. Under these conditions the narcissistic rage from a trauma can be used to fuel a dynamic of self-negation. There can be a number of reasons for such a dynamic, any or all of which can apply in particular cases: the need to make sense of the world's neglectful or abusive actions toward oneself by locating the source of the traumatic suffering in one's "badness," the attempt to control the narcissistic rage caused by trauma by directing it against the self, and/or the attempt to use moral control over oneself to fight off the disorganizing effects of trauma. In all of these cases the superego activity is pathologized and the psyche suffers constrictions of its ability to live with full vitality.

The persona is often held to be the "false self," but this is only true when it is acting defensively and as a substitute for genuine self functioning. If the unconscious nuclear self is coherent and expresses itself through the persona, the persona is not false but can be a genuine vehicle of self activity.

When the social unconscious is the major organizing structure of the "I," experience takes on the quality of "average everydayness." It has neither the sparkle of authentic self-experience nor the anxiety and rigidity of pathological experience. Rather than feeling fully alive, one is simply busy, occupied with the daily routines of living and carrying out the tasks of her social roles.

The Self

Self-experiences are those that mobilize our deepest ambitions, ideals, idiosyncratic abilities, and spontaneous playfulness. When we find activities in which we can realize our nuclear selves, we feel alive, are erotically engaged with the world, and experience our lives as meaningful. In highly felicitous situations, the self realizes its nuclear program through the persona, making social roles vehicles for self-expression. This provides further coherence and synthesis for the psyche, and life feels especially vital and meaningful. When the self is at the center of psychic life, the persona does not carry a sense of "phoniness" (to evoke the inimitable Holden Caulfield from *Catcher in the Rye*), for it can be an integral expression of the self.

The id is also transformed when its needs, wishes, and emotions pass through the self on the way to consciousness, for they become integrated with nuclear ideals and ambitions. For instance, a sexual urge from the id might unite with the self's ideal to partake of an intimate relationship and fuse with the self's grandiosity to sustain such a special relation. The self making love to a cherished partner is very different from a genital discharge with an accommodating partner and also different from love making that is overly governed by social codes of how best to make love. The id sex experience is likely to be deficient in meaning; persona sex feels somewhat contrived and performed. When the self is present in a sexual experience, it feels profoundly personal and singular, embodying the deepest core of what makes life meaningful for the person.

We might say that there are four senses in which human beings think of themselves as "selves," and it has been the confusion of these four senses that has led, I believe, to so much unnecessary suffering for modern people. The id, self, ego, and persona are all aspects of who we are and are often said to be "the self." When we feel strong emotions or desires, we are likely to feel as though this is really who we are, for they feel so much more individuated than desires that have been processed through the social unconscious. Freud and a number of other nineteenth-century "naturalists" seem to claim that the id—our passions—is who we most naturally are. Others—especially the social scientists—have been so impressed with the social construction of human nature that they locate who we are in our personal identity—our social statuses, personal narratives, social relationships, and so on. For still others (including almost all the philosophers) the conscious ego—the "I"—is who we most are. And, finally, there is Kohut's claim that who we most are is a self that is a psychological transformation of original narcissistic grandiosity.

All are right. We are biological, social, psychological creatures who participate in the mystery of subjectivity. Yet, the id, ego, self, and persona play very different roles in psychic life and if we try to have one substitute for the functions of the other, the psyche falls into nonoptimal functioning. Without id impulses, we would not have clues about when to sleep, wake, eat, rest, run from danger, love, mourn, and reproduce. But the id does not give us essential structures of meaning nor is it capable of forming ideals that can teleologically lead us into the future. The ego negotiates our interactions with the world and protects psychological coherence, but, aside from its quest for legitimation, it cannot provide the motivations for action that the self, id, or persona can. In the modern world, the ego also tends to operate with a high degree of rationality and impersonal decision-making, causing experience to feel overly general and artificially constructed. The persona is our passport for interactions with society, but it is bought at the price of social acceptability and adaptability. The self, as Kohut attempted to show, is the *axis mundi* around which all these psychic components revolve. When it is vital and coherent, it can integrate the id and persona, ground ego consciousness, and make us feel at home in the wider world.

THE AIMS OF PSYCHIC LIFE

Before proceeding to show how the different parts of the psyche interrelate to produce average everyday experience, self experience, or pathologized experience, we need to state what the final aims of psychic life are. I believe the psyche has two fundamental ends: to optimize its sense of liveliness and to sustain a sense of coherent meaning. Of these two, I believe that the psyche most seeks to achieve its greatest intensity of life and is quite willing to disrupt a stable structure of meaning if that structure is too life-limiting. On the other hand, if the striving for the intensity of life leads to too much chaos or psychic disorganization, the need for stable and consistent meaning will reassert its balancing power. In cases in which traumas severely disrupt the structure of meaning, the ego will use its defenses to limit the disorganizing elements of the trauma and reinstate a meaningful order, even if that new order involves a limitation on vitality.

Some of the most intense of human experiences occur during times of struggle, pain, darkness, and despair. When we change our view about what the psyche seeks from pleasure to intensity, we then do not automatically think of pain as evil or pleasure as good. Many pleasures dull experience and lead us away from the self, while the pain that occurs in struggling to realize an ideal of the self can often make us feel alive. Pain which is pointless (such as when we injure ourselves) can be very intense but in its meaninglessness it does not satisfy the psyche. On the other hand, struggle, pain, despair, and suffering for the sake of a commitment enlivens us, perhaps, even most enlivens us. Goethe thought so, as did Nietzsche.

In two of the most profound contemporary works on the life of the soul, Jonathan Lear's *Happiness, Death, and the Remainder of Life* and Eric Santner's *The Psychotheology of the Everyday Life*, the authors echo Freud in proclaiming that life essentially involves excess—an excess of pressure, an excess of encountering otherness in ourselves and the world. The ego's rationality wants to bind this chaotic excess and organize it into some kind of system, but this will have the tendency to kill life. While life might be seeking increasingly complex forms of order to enhance intensity, there can be no final end or structure that represents the highest amount of intensity. In Nietzsche's words, life always seeks to exceed itself, to overcome itself. For Alfred North Whitehead, life is adventure—it is change, exploration, creativity. This is what gives life its liveliness.

But life must also take place in a framework of meaningfulness. Adventures cannot be experienced as senseless or the world totally without structure or meaning, for this is a psychotic state. Jonathan Lear says, "Humans are inherently makers and interpreters of meaning. . . . People make more meaning than they know what to do with. This is what Freud meant by the unconscious."[11] Since the psyche creates more meaning than it can use or that can exist without conflict or tension, it is in a constant state of readjusting its scheme of meanings to incorporate new experiences, new abilities, new maturity, new friends, and so on. This exploration of the realm of meaning—bringing together disparate elements into a consistency or finding new ways of interpreting the world and oneself—constitutes the essence of the life of the soul. The problem with psychopathology is that it (unconsciously) demands repetition of structures of meaning and cannot creatively respond to changing circumstances. Sometimes this blockage happens in only one sector of life, such as love or work, and sometimes only at a very hidden level of engagement in this sector, but always there is an arbitrary barrier that limits the creative possibilities of life.

We might think of the psyche's seeking life as the energy of the psychic system and its system of meanings as the organization of this energy. We can then see that the fundamental tension that generates psychic life is the opposition between life forces always seeking to go beyond what has been achieved (what Lear calls the essential restlessness of the soul) and structures of meaning that we need to keep the psyche and world coherent. Life disorganizes; meaning organizes. Life is adventure, but the adventure needs a purpose. Chaos can be tolerated and even cherished when it opens a space for richer meanings to emerge; otherwise, it is a momentary disruption, signifying nothing, or, worse, a catastrophic trauma that profoundly compromises the soul's ability to live fully.

The fundamental claim of this work is that nothing gives the soul more vitality and meaningfulness than the presence and activation of a self, for the self is that unconscious process that transforms external meanings into its own protein and actively engages the world from a viewpoint of personal singularity rather than one of social conformity, rational suitability, or blind id impulse. When a need or desire from either the id or social unconscious is satisfied, we feel pleasure; but when the self realizes its values or ambitions, we experience a kind of erotic joy.

PSYCHOLOGICAL DYNAMICS

Usual experiences have elements from all the parts of the psyche in them—id impulses as transformed by character, social constructions, self strivings, defensive limitations, and ego needs and structures. However, it is useful to take three major forms of experience as pure types and analyze them for what arrangement of the psychic parts produces them: normalized experiences, self experiences, and pathologically restricted experiences. This division differs radically from the binary or dialectical kind of division that has characterized Western thinking: authentic vs. inauthentic, healthy vs. pathological, free vs. determined, individualized vs. socialized. It is only when we expand the general categories of experience to three that we can become clear about how the structure of self experiences differs from the psychic configurations that produce normalized experiences on the one hand and pathologically limited experiences on the other.

Normalized Experience

Normalized experiences are the kind of experiences Heidegger designates as captured by "the They" and which Foucault terms "docile."[12] In this kind of experience life feels everydayish—a bit flat, mechanical, and organized according to external pressures. This kind of experience is usually produced by a strong ego/persona axis, where the social unconscious is the primary organizing structure for determining experience. Life feels everydayish because it is governed by social codes rather than being produced by an originary singular self. Id urges can be and often are present in these kinds of experience, but they typically pass not only through character but also the persona, further socializing them. The id might produce a desire for food, but what we consciously feel is the need for a hamburger or Japanese sushi, depending upon what is the socially proper thing for us to eat at this particular time of the day, given who we are with, how socially acceptable our weight is, and so on.

In this psychological configuration, the self is not central. This might be because it has been traumatized or because we have formed psychological habits to pay attention to our socialized desires. In this latter configuration the self is forgotten in the rush of everyday life. In this normalized psychic configuration, we find ourselves always and already paying attention to the dailyness of life. We get up, shower, groom, dress, eat breakfast, organize what needs to get done, and start doing it. Our mood is already in place: another day, as usual. At the end of the day, we seek relief from the daily routines by enjoying some form of benign entertainment or soothing elixirs, but these, too, are haunted with dailyness. We look forward to the weekend when we hope that excitement will relieve the lack of liveliness that infects the week days, but, with this kind of psychological organization, the weekend will probably be socially encoded as well—we will have fun the way "they" have fun.

In short, insofar as our fundamental source of motivation comes from the social unconscious rather than the self, experience feels as though it is not quite ours. And this is because it isn't quite ours, for there is something generalized and un-individuated about experience when its main organizing axis is the ego/social unconscious. As Heidegger says, it is not the "I" but the "They" which is the subject of everyday experience.

The key verb form of this psychological configuration is "ought" or "should." In Kant's language, experience is directed by hypothetical imperatives: if we want good teeth and breath, we ought to brush our teeth; if we want good health, we ought to exercise, eat well, drink moderately, and never smoke. Everywhere we turn there are "oughts" commanding us: we ought to get to work early to miss rush hour; we ought to wear these clothes to impress those people; we ought to be nice to the secretary; and so on for the entirety of the day. Even id motivations typically get taken over by ought-structures. We want sex with our partner but think we ought to have it in just this way, with just the right amount of animal passion combined with the right amount of care and concern for our partner. The constant pounding of the "ought" is what Freud described as pressure from the superego.

We can use Foucault's term "docility" to describe the psyche in its state of ordinary experiencing. It is docile because it follows the social prescriptions that it has painlessly internalized. Docility does not mean being inactive, for persons whose experience is fundamentally structured through the social unconscious can be highly motivated, fabulously successful people. They can be driven toward excellence in their fields or feel a deep need to be caring parents or exciting love partners. But persons whose major experiential configuration is governed by the social unconscious feel that their life is not quite their own, or that something continues to be missing, despite all they are doing. Life is almost completely taken up with events in which something "has to" get done, even if what "has to" get done is pleasant, such as improving a golf game or learning new dance steps. Life lived through norms is normalized.

Self Experience

When the nuclear self is both intact and the major unconscious organizing structure determining ego experience, life transforms. Experiences now feel as though they are mine and carry a sense of vitality, coherence, and meaningfulness. The world does not appear as an oppositional place from which our pleasures must be won through work or luck but as a field in which we can realize our ownmost possibilities. A crucial difference between motivations that stem from a self and those that come from either id or persona desires is that desires typically represent only a part of who we are. The part might be a basic need, such as the need for social recognition, but it is always only a part. Hence, all desires that do not pass through the self—even healthy, normal desires—are to some degree fragmenting. It is otherwise with motivation that comes from the self or passes through the self. The ambitions and values of the self represent the energetic core of who we are and when we enact them, our whole selves feel erotically alive. Our being feels engaged and energized in our activity, be it work, love, or recreation. We seem to be tireless in self activities—the more we do them, the more we seem to fill with vitality rather than fatigue.

The self does not function only in joyous activities but is that part of ourselves that can feel triumphant even in moments of tragedy. Kohut writes of a couple who stood up to the Nazis, were incarcerated and eventually executed. From their notebooks, we find not dismay and depression over their ill fortune of being good people done in by evil forces but a tone of triumph and greatness. The ideals harbored in the self stood fast and while their personal organisms were to be eliminated, their selves did not disintegrate but remained intact.[13]

When the ego forms a strong alliance with a coherent self, the other parts of the psyche also transform. The id forces, especially the emotions, can become more robust. With the self grounding the ego, the ego feels less anxious in the presence of strong emotions and needs. Greater peaks of intensity can be reached—both in the positive and negative emotions, with the result that we feel more alive, present to ourselves, and engaged with the world. Likewise, the presence of the self transforms the ego's relation to the persona. Rather than being the source of "They" commands and social pressures, the persona can be used as a vehicle to realize the ideals and ambitions of the self. The social structure is experienced not as an arbitrary imposition on the "I" that constricts experience but constitutes a realm that opens up possibilities for self-realization. Marriage roles, for instance, can be felt as a joyous realm of ever expanding expressions of the self rather than a socially demanded constriction of sexual drives from the id.

When the self is present, the anxiety about losing oneself in one's social roles is lessened. This anxiety, which I find to be very powerful in the college students I teach, can produce profound ambivalence in one's social roles, such that one both occupies these roles and simultaneously rebels against them. Ambivalence always has the tendency to lessen the intensity of experience, so it is important to be able to occupy one's roles without being immobilized by ambivalence. Confucius speaks of the importance of the rectification of names—that fathers should be fathers, rulers rulers, and professors professors. If one takes on a role, one should wholeheartedly be that role. Of course, a role is only an aspect of who anyone is, and so one must both identify with the role while knowing that the role is not the same as the self. I think that this is much more likely to occur if one has a self that is secure in its worth beyond social roles.

The ego, of course, must pay a price for the great benefits that come from aligning with the self, a price that many modern persons might find too high, for it involves a significant loss of freedom and flexibility. When the ego is not connected to the self's ambitions and ideals, it has maximum freedom to adjust to situations, to try out new experiences, to design whatever life feels best under shifting conditions. It need not be a martyr to its own cause, because it has no grounding cause. When the ego chooses to align itself with the self, life is not so flexible. Ideals need to be enacted; ambitions, realized. We can be defeated or thwarted. Our selves can go unrealized or our lives can become failures. With the pleasures of the id/ego/persona constellation, such failure is easy to avoid or refuse to acknowledge. If we miss some pleasures here or there, what does it matter? We can always find ways to get our pleasures and minimize our pains. Sometimes the world is unkind and defeats us with disease or accidents. But these are unfortunate; they are not tragic. Making the self the center of life rather than the pursuit of pleasure opens up the possibilities of both authenticity and tragedy.

Further, when the self is strongly connected to the "I," a new need comes to the forefront: the need for selfobject relationships. We seek to have friends or lovers whom we can trust will perform our self functions when narcissistic blows disable us. With Kohut's realization that the self is always vulnerable and therefore in need of a network of selfobjects, our relation to the world of others changes from what it is in normalized experience. Others cannot be treated as objects to be used by the self, for they are essential to the well-being of the self. What I will try to show in the next chapter is that adult selfobject needs cannot be met unless one is willing to engage in ethical reciprocity. We might say that when desire encounters an other, it wants to use it for its satisfaction; but when self encounters an other, it wants to find its worth mirrored, and this cannot happen unless the other is found to have worth. When one experiences herself as a self, then others can be respected as independent centers of agency, feeling, and selfhood, too.

When the "I" is able to consistently align itself with the self, life becomes dynamic. The self, in itself, is the most dynamic sector of the unconscious psyche since ideals and ambitions constitute its core, and both need constant revision as they are reached and surpassed. An ego that can depend upon a vibrant, organized self can creatively play with its persona or personal identity. Changes can be made in status, new ventures undertaken, and lifestyles redesigned because the persona is not carrying structural responsibility for holding the psyche together. With a self, I don't have to be the model professor but can imaginatively alter this persona to fit my idiosyncratic traits, thereby becoming a singular professor.

Many of the critiques of a self-based psychology see the self as too concerned with identity and repetitive to be valued as the heart of vital creative experiences. I believe these critiques confuse self with both the ego and the persona. It is quite true that when the persona carries the responsibility for psychic stability, it becomes rigid and un-dynamic. Likewise, the ego cannot take on a singular (or any) identity without losing its openness. But the self is neither the ego nor the persona. It is a psychological structure which, when organized and free of pathology, can ground a life of flexibility and dynamic creativity. That is, the optimal life of the soul depends upon a mixture of organization and disorganization at both conscious and unconscious levels of experience, but extensive disorganization at the unconscious level, especially in the coherence of the self, can cause rigidity and over-organization at the level of conscious experience.

It is important to understand that the "self" way of being in the world is a shorthand for the "self/character/ego" axis. The self needs the virtues of character to integrate the id emotions and it needs the ego powers of mind to direct its ambitions and ideals. The development of character is crucial if narcissism is going to achieve maturity, for without the virtues we could not engage in selfobject reciprocity nor fully overcome the natural bent toward selfishness. If a person has developed somewhat of a self without the virtues, there is a likelihood of spoilage—the self is there, but the person remains immoderate in desires, unfair and/or ungenerous in dealings with others, and afraid to face difficult situations. Likewise, if a person has developed a self but not developed the linguistic and rational powers of the ego, she will not be able to explore fully the possibilities for self-expression available in her environment. The best kind of life is one in which the self is coherent and vital, the ego well developed in its mental capacities, and the virtues strong in relation to the difficult situations that life presents.

Pathologically Limited Experience

Self structure becomes pathologically disorganized when it suffers trauma, where trauma is defined as any event or experience in which the structure of the self is shattered by overwhelming emotional flooding or stimuli (such as unbearable pain) and/or a shattering of the coherence of a meaningful world. Traumatic events are not just overwhelmingly intrusive stimuli, such as in cases of sexual abuse, but any significant loss of an expectable environment, such as an intolerably long absence of the mother or a consistent lack of empathic mirroring. Kohut notes that single traumas are not, for the most part, devastating and can be repaired. What appears most injurious is a chronic state of trauma—the state of living with an inconsistent alcoholic parent or a parent suffering from a narcissistic disorder which prevents them from attending to the self-needs of the child.

Traumatic injuries to the self typically evoke narcissistic rage and disintegration anxiety and are often accompanied by overwhelming grief at the loss of a once cherished world. The emotional chaos is so disorganizing and destabilizing that the ego must institute defensive measures both to protect the core of the self and to restore some form of ego functionality. These defenses no longer allow an easy flow from the id to the ego (since the id now harbors traumatic rage and/or grief) or from the self to the ego (since the self is fragmented and the site of trauma). As the self and the id are the primary sources of spontaneity in the psyche, the ego now has difficulty spontaneously initiating activity or responding to events. It must rely on the "oughts" of the social unconscious or the plans and dictums of rational consciousness.

With the diminished ability of the self to center and organize psychic life, the psyche takes on the conflictual structure that Freud so brilliantly described. The id forces constantly threaten the ego, for they contain traumatic emotions, narcissistic rage, and driven energy, while the social unconscious is more likely to become a punishing superego as it attempts to defend against the dangerous forces of the id and the annihilating injuries in the self. One might say that the psyche organized around the self is a libidinal one—one full of love for itself and the world—while the traumatized psyche is a culture of the death drive—one full of outraged aggression and aggressive defenses against that aggression.

Insofar as the ego is denied the support of a coherent self, it suffers from a constant low-level anxiety that psychic functioning could genuinely fall apart at any moment. As such disintegration anxiety is noxiously debilitating, it, too, must be defended against, and the whole conflictual dynamic is eliminated from consciousness and thrown into an unconscious dungeon from where it will symptomatize the organism as the price for its being eliminated from experience.

This inner dynamic of conflict, repression, defense, resistance, and symptom-formation involves a loss of available energy for the world, and depression begins to color experience. This depressiveness is often too noxious to be tolerated and it too becomes hidden by a kind of manic energy. This manic energy, which acts as a great counter to depressive inertia, can seem to be enlivening, but the vitality is not grounded in the self and, hence, its products do not carry meaning for the self. Instead, the manic energy often connects to the persona or goals determined by a rational decision-making process. As such it can help motivate one to live a very successful life, where success can act as a great compensation to deficits in the self. But in the end success in the realm of ego/persona life is not the same as self-realization. Successful lives organized around ego/persona pathologized structures usually have the sense of being driven or compelled. They involve not just achievement but defense; their strivings for grandiosity are also attempts to escape from deficits, trauma, and inner pain. I believe that this description of the manically driven person organized around the ego/persona grid fits many modern persons.

In short, when the self is injured and must be replaced with a defensive organization of experience, we lose vitality, an ability to connect to others, a sense of psychic cohesion, and the ability to react creatively and flexibly to situations. The pathology need not be totally debilitating, for there often appear pockets in life where the pathology goes into abeyance and the self can un-cocoon itself. It is also true that the defensive organization need not excessively get in the way of ordinary experience. Indeed, ordinary experience will feel like a relief for it does not remind the ego of the self's injuries.

Given this structural analysis of psychic pathology, we can see why and how different psychotherapeutic techniques are called for. Since psychopathology involves trauma, injuries to the self, and defensive ego dynamics, the healing of the psyche will be multidimensional. Resistances and defenses need to be loosened, disintegration anxiety and narcissistic rage released, and the self restored—all in a complex process that can involve conflicting elements. The resistances and defenses belong to the unconscious side of the ego and, since the ego participates in language, can be reached through "the talking cure." Hence, the best tool for working with the defenses and resistances seems to be linguistic interpretation. The self, on the other hand, develops out of and is repaired by empathic mirroring or the ability to merge with an idealized other. These processes are not essentially linguistic but a matter of attuned presence. They are, in the words of contemporary theory, intersubjective or relational. Overcoming trauma relates to the patient's feeling of safety and consistency in the therapeutic office. Insofar as interpretations—even brilliant and insightful interpretations—can be experienced as unempathic or as aggressively attacking, they can re-traumatize a patient and send the self more deeply into a cocooned state.

Two conclusions follow from the above analysis: first, it is the self and the injuries it suffers that is the core of psychopathology, not the conflicts between the drives or between the drives and the superego. Thus, care for the self in its traumatized state must be the first concern of an analysis or therapy. Second, enhancing the knowledge and extension of the ego is important both because the defenses need to be dismantled as healthy self-structure comes into being and because a person's vital functioning depends not just on the self but upon the development of a strong self/ego/character alliance. However, interpretations cannot be abstracted from the matrix of selfobject transferences or the presence of internalized trauma. They carry not just understanding but empathy or the lack of it, a safe adventure or an attack, a caring presence or a narcissistic need to show off brilliance.

CONCLUSION

I have attempted to make a crucial distinction between the ego and the self, with the ego being the subject of conscious experience whose functions are to interact with the world, communicate meanings to itself and others, seek legitimation, and provide coherence to the psyche, while the self is the key unconscious organizing structure on whose well-being depends the vitality, sense of meaningfulness, psychological coherence, and strength of agency of the person. The ego is the "I" we experience as the subject of conscious experience. The self is one of the key unconscious motivating structures, along with the id, character, and the social unconscious. In terms of practical life, these are the crucial parts of the soul.

I hold that the psychological arrangement of these parts that produces the most alive kind of life is one which is organized around a self/character/ego axis, with the self being the central motivating agency, virtuous character personalizing and moderating the power of the passions, and the ego providing thoughtful direction and critical acumen for the ambitions, ideals, and spontaneous impulses of the self.

I have analyzed human experience into three general types: everyday experiences, self experiences, and experiences constricted by psychopathology. Most experiences are a combination of all three; however, it makes a great deal of difference what the proportion of each is in experience. The more the self is present, the more enlivened and meaningful experience becomes. Even when one is submerged in the mire of every-day tasks, the penumbral presence of a self can make these seem meaningful as they are part of a life that has a genuine purpose.

I believe that rather than having a strong self/character/ego axis, modern persons tend to have an ego/id/persona axis as their defining psychological constellations. As such, modern persons tend to lose track of what is meaningful to their selves and devote their lives to processes of legitimation and desire-gratification. To transform modernity into a more self-oriented world, persons must learn to rethink about their individual lives, and modern society needs to radically shift some of its most ingrained practices. The final two chapters take up each of these issues in turn.

NOTES

1. Carlos Strenger, *The Designed Self* (Hillsdale, NJ: Analytic Press, 2005), 44.

2. See "Civilization and Its Discontents," *Standard Edition*, vol. 21, 128.

3. I am, obviously, not the first to attempt to make this distinction. It is an operational distinction in Kohut and Winnicott (they use the distinction) but one that is not conceptually elaborated. C. G. Jung makes the distinction between the ego and the self one of the fulcrums of his analytical psychology. Like the distinction I will be making, Jung sees the ego as conscious and rational, while the self is an unconscious structure. However, for Jung the self does not come into being through a developmental process but is an archetypal presence giving identity to the person. Kohut's unconscious self is the precipitate of a developmental process and not in any way a metaphysical archetype. See *The Essential Jung*, ed. Anthony Storr (Princeton, NJ: Princeton University Press, 1983), 230–309.

4. Immanuel Kant, *Critique of Pure Reason*, trans. Norman Kemp Smith (New York: MacMillan Press, 1929).

5. Strenger, *The Designed Self*, 74.

6. Kohut speaks of the self as a source of independent agency, but I agree with the critique of Stolorow, Brandshaft, and Atwood in their *Psychoanalytic Treatment: An Intersubjective Approach* (Hillsdale, NJ: Analytic Press, 1987) that the Kohutian self lacks the kind of tools it takes to be an agent. It must align with the conscious ego in order to act in the world with deliberation, knowledge, and care. The self might provide a strong impetus toward action, but the ego tools must come into play for action to take place.

7. Jonathan Lear, *Therapeutic Action* (New York: Other Press, 2003), 118.

8. See Judith Teicholz's *Kohut, Loewald, and the Postmoderns* (Hillsdale, NJ: Analytic Press, 1999) for an excellent discussion of the relation between Kohut's theory and that of postmodernism.

9. Heidegger's "The Question Concerning Technology," in *Basic Writings*, ed. David Krell (New York: Harper & Row, 1977), elaborates brilliantly on the point of how conceptualization is a way of capturing the world and making it useful for us. That is, it is a way of gaining power over the world.

FIVE

WHY IT IS GOOD TO BE GOOD

What I propose to do in this chapter constitutes, I believe, a genuinely important conceptual revolution: I will attempt to show that the only adequate ground for moral life is narcissism, so long as the self is understood in a Kohutian way. If by narcissism we mean making one's particular, embodied self the central concern of life, then what I am positing goes against almost all previous ethical theories, which have claimed that ethical life comes into existence only when we are able to transcend the particular narcissistic self by identifying ourselves with universal values (ancient and medieval philosophy), limiting our narcissistic pursuits by obeying general moral laws (Kant), being selflessly altruistic (Christianity), or having a concern for the general welfare (utilitarianism). All of these ways of being ethical assert that the narcissistic individual person, in her particularity, must be overcome.

When we shift to self psychology's understanding of psychological life, we see that establishing and maintaining a core self is the essence of living well, and that the self is fragile and subject to fragmentation and trauma. Therefore, we must always be engaged in bolstering and restoring the self. The essential element of the restoration process is the use of selfobjects. From this basic understanding of the psychology of the self, we can find four important reasons why any individual would want to be a good human being, whereby "good" is meant someone who is characterized by the moral virtues, concerned for the welfare of others, and willing to be just and fair in his interactions with other human beings. Self psychology can show us that it is good to be ethical because we have (1) a need for integrity, (2) a need to engage in empathic reciprocity with others, (3) a need to develop the moral virtues, and (4) a need to expand our ideals into ethical universals. The first three reasons are fairly straightforward and come from our need to have a coherent self at the core of experience and the dependence of that self on selfobjects. The fourth reason—the extension of our ideals to the realm of universality—is the hardest to establish for it asks us to be good even when there is no anticipation of selfobject reciprocity.

THE NEED FOR INTEGRITY

In chapter 1 we found that many persons can engage in immoral acts only if they engage in vertical splitting. Everyone has a self-image that needs to remain affirmative in order for the self to be vibrant and assertive. To violate one's sense of goodness threatens the loss of the feeling of self-worth on which rests the general sense of psychic well-being. However, there are times when a person wants something that he cannot get except by acting against what he knows to be right. The only way such a person can both retain a sense of self-worth and engage in the immoral activity is to split off the part of himself that carries his self-image from the part that is performing the action. When persons engage in vertical splitting they are conscious of what they are doing but disavow its reality or its wrongness.[1] The "person who cheats" is split off from "the good person that I am" in such a way that one's self-image is not affected by the wrongdoing. That is, we act in such a way as to hide from ourselves. Goldberg sees vertical splitting as the primary psychological mechanism used by perverts who are often upstanding citizens in most of their lives but who have such perverse habits as flashing their genitals to children and being peeping toms.

Although vertical splitting allows one to get away with a disavowed act, the psychological costs are high. The ego might cheat and simultaneously disown that cheating is occurring, but the unconscious self knows what the person has done and suffers. When a person cheats, the self seems less able to be self-affirming. Vertical splitting not only lowers the self's spirit but splits the psyche. It breaks down flows of communication and energy, making the psyche into a kind of cold war spying game in which one part seeks to hide from another what it is doing while the other always kind of knows and suspects.

The opposite of splitting is integrity. Integrity implies an integration of parts into an integral whole that, like an integer, is one with itself. Integrity can be applied to many aspects of psychological functioning. A person can be said to have integrity if she acts on the values she avows, really believes what she says she believes, or has values that are consistent with themselves. But most of all, having integrity implies that someone is capable of being true to herself. That is, a person with integrity has a core nature and acts from it rather than out of social pressures to conform, immediate impulses for gratification, or hastily thought-up plans for quick gain. A person with integrity does not have major split-off parts of her psyche that operate independently of each other.

The question now arises as to why splitting is bad and integrity good. Why not cheat, get ahead, and engage in vertical splitting to protect one's self-image? Why try to achieve integrity if self-consistency implies the inability to have a full range of adaptable responses to any situation? Doesn't integrity get in the way of satisfaction?

These are difficult questions for psychologies that posit pleasure as the final aim of human life. It might very well be that cheating and vertical splitting produce more pleasure than either not cheating or not splitting. Indeed, integrity often seems to get in the way of pleasure optimization. The reigning psychologies that valorize pleasure and psychic multiplicity not only cannot offer reasons as to why integrity is a value but seem to side against it. In the world of the pleasure-seeking individual in the market ungoverned by a set of objective values, it seems best to be fully flexible and adaptable rather than limited by the notion that one needs to be consistent with oneself.

Self psychology offers a different story. Self psychology holds that life is not fundamentally about the production of pleasure but about the development of self. It recognizes that people with fragmented or injured selves can have many pleasures but still exist in a state of unhappiness. It recognizes that people can attain a high level of success within the market system with which they can satisfy almost any fantasy and still feel empty because they do not have vital selves. On the other hand, people with strong selves can suffer great amounts of pain and endure sacrifice while remaining deeply happy, especially if the suffering they are undergoing is in order to realize an ideal or ambition of the self.

For self psychology, integrity must be a key value, for integrity is the value that proclaims the importance of an integrated self occupying a central place within psychic functioning. Having a self and having integrity go hand in hand, for it is the self and only the self that can ground an integrated psyche. Of course, full integration is a fantasy, for the psyche is far too complex and multidimensional to bring every impulse, social pressure, ego scheme, or character response into a single unified system. Nor would we want to. Yet, it makes a great deal of difference if the psyche is organized around a coherent integrated self, for this will go a long way in establishing a core basis from which to act. We can be true to ourselves because we have a self to be true to.

Self psychology's emphasis on integrity and developing a self strong enough to avoid vertical splits goes a long way toward solving the problem of the cheater. Indeed, it will eliminate all cheating which depends on vertical splitting to be tolerable, and I think that this accounts for most of the cheating that happens. If being an ethical person is also being a person who has integrity, then self psychology can offer us one good reason for being good; having a self and having integrity go hand in hand.

THE NEED FOR RECIPROCITY

Self psychology can offer further, even more compelling, reasons for being ethical. Kohut held that the self can come into existence only if early caretakers are able to perform the essential functions of the baby's self—sustaining its perfection and worth through empathic mirroring and allowing themselves to be idealized and merged with. Even if a strong nuclear self comes into existence, a person still needs others both to help it perform its essential self functions in times of narcissistic injuries and to give it a general safety net so that it can adventure into the world. That is, Kohut's concept of the self is not the invulnerable ego proclaimed by Socrates and most of the philosophic tradition as the achievable goal of self-development but a vulnerable self that needs lifelong responsive others to sustain itself. If Socrates' drinking the hemlock without an iota of suffering grounds the image of the imperturbable substantial self that sustained the West for most of its history, Kohut's self is aligned with the one given to us in a number of feminist and ethnic philosophies—a self vulnerable to loss, fragile in its structural grounding, and needing others to help nourish and sustain it for a lifetime.

Socrates' kind of self becomes both invulnerable and ethical in the act of identifying itself with a set of universal meanings that are impervious to change or deformation. It is the invulnerability to change and possible fragmentation that gives such a person a sense of self-sufficient well-being. However, the cost of achieving this kind of self is high—it is the loss of one's concrete particularity, one's situatedness in the world, and the wealth of emotional life. The Socratic self (and its myriad variations in the West, from Stoicism to American rugged individualism) cannot allow itself to be dependent on others or the environment, and, hence, achieves its integrity at the cost of losing immersion in life itself. And, Kohut might add, this kind of self is an illusion, a set of intellectualizing defenses that refuses to live in this world with full emotional intensity.

Kohut's self becomes ethical not by identifying with universal values but by acknowledging its vulnerability and dependence. Since we need others who can perform selfobject functions for us throughout our lives, it is crucial for the development and maintenance of the self that it surround itself with such people. Persons who don't have such friends and decide they are strong enough to go it alone typically pay the price of having to live through defenses or other non-self structures, for the self, according to Kohut, has only two choices—allow itself to be helped by others or live with other centers of initiative motivating life. The cost of the latter is high, for it reduces our sense of aliveness, limits our developmental growth, and isolates us from the joy of shared existence with others.

Given the inescapable vulnerability of the self, it becomes essential for a person to be able to make and sustain friendships and/or intimacies. It is important to emphasize that while everyone has situational selfobject needs, they can typically only be met by someone with whom one has established a long-term relationship and whom one can trust. That is, we cannot sustain the self through the ups and downs of life without belonging to committed selfobject relationships. While one of these relationships might be with a therapist, for the most part they are with friends and family.

If we ask what kind of person is able to make and sustain friendships, the answer is, obviously, someone able to engage in selfobject reciprocity—someone who is willing to empathically care for others as she expects them to empathically care for her. Persons best able to offer reciprocal friendship to others are those who have developed the character traits of being empathic, caring, and genuinely concerned about the well-being of another. Since we usually associate the traits of empathy, care, and reciprocity with people who are ethical, I think Kohut's claim that all selves need to be in selfobject relationships entails that it is personally good to become an ethically good person.

The key ethical trait needed to engage in selfobject reciprocity is empathy. Empathy is an extraordinary trait which provides us with the capacity for experiencing the internal states of other human beings. While Kohut at first thought of empathy as a mere tool for gathering data about the subjectivity of others through "vicarious introspection," he realized toward the end of his career that empathic knowing and presence was part of the curative effect of psychoanalysis. When we unempathically use empathy as a tool to gather knowledge about other persons it need neither be curative nor ethical, for when it is paired with other traits, such as a tendency to control human beings, it can be used for unethical purposes.

To empathically use empathy as a way of experiencing or knowing the inner feelings of another, one must not just grasp these feelings but resonate with them in a kind of sensitive mirroring way. When I am with a friend whom I experience as sad, I can resonate with this sadness by mirroring it in a lowered quiet demeanor which is vicariously sad rather than being actually sad. When empathy is fully present, it is the experience of one subject subjectively responding to the subjectivity of another subject. In all other modes of experiencing, there appears to be objectification—the experiencing the other as an object, or even the objectively experiencing of the other as an object. It is only in empathy that we affirm the subjectivity of the other in the most profound way possible—by mirroring it in our own subjectivity. This mirroring is experienced by the other as a profound affirmation—an affirmation far beyond anything that might be said in words.

The difference between an infantile or immature use of selfobjects and a mature one is the presence of reciprocity. The baby expects the mother to empathically mirror and sustain it with her greatness; it does not feel the need to do the same for her. As we grow older, infantile narcissism ought to transform into mature narcissism. We still want and need selfobject support, but we are willing to engage in reciprocity in order to get it. If we remain infantile and expect to get selfobject support without reciprocating, then we will have to pay for it in some way, or else we will not get it. But, with the exception of psychotherapy, all nonreciprocal payments for selfobject support (such as flattery, monetary payment, sexual favors, etc.) will involve the internal knowledge that one is manipulating love and care, and care achieved through manipulation typically turns out to be deficient care. That is, what the self needs to sustain itself is to feel loved and affirmed. If it buys love or affirmation, then it is not getting love or affirmation. Rather, one's ability to pay is being affirmed.

Reciprocity of care is the essence of what many people think of as the quintessential moral maxim: "Do unto others as you would have them do unto you." Underlying this principle is another one, without which it makes little sense: "Love thyself fully and desire loving things to be done to one." Unless one narcissistically loves oneself, the command to love others as oneself makes no sense. The combination of self-love and care for others is even clearer in the biblical command to "Love your neighbor as yourself." If one does not love oneself, one cannot love the neighbor, and, from a self psychological viewpoint, if one does really love oneself, one will love the neighbor.

To engage in reciprocity we must treat others as independent centers of initiative, as persons who can suffer or flourish, and as beings who have intrinsic value. If we do not do this, we cannot reap full selfobject support from them when we need it, for that support cannot be experienced as worthy if it comes from someone whom we do not value or do not think is acting as an independent agent. Engaging in selfobject reciprocity demands that one treat others with moral respect, treat them as ends in themselves. It is what it means to engage in what Buber calls an "I-Thou" relationship.

I think that reciprocity also entails that one develop a keen sense of fairness. Indeed, one can hardly imagine what reciprocity would look like without fairness. Fairness, however, is what John Rawls found to be the essence of the notion of justice. Thus, we can now say that in order for persons to sustain their selves they need not simply to be caring, empathic, and concerned with others, but also they must be just—at least in their friendships. Since Rawls and many other modern theorists have found justice to be the essential notion of morality, we have a further reason from self psychology as to why it is good to be good.

However, before I sound too much like a Kantian proclaiming the intrinsic worth of justice, fairness, and treating others as ends in themselves, let me clarify where I fully differ from Kant and the ethical tradition he spawned. Kant held that the only true moral motive is respect for the moral law without any expectation of reward for one's moral actions. The moral person must not be moved by concerns for personal happiness. A number of other thinkers (typically religious) locate morality within altruism—doing good for others without any expectation that they will do good for you. I think that this approach of searching for a non–self-serving motive has been more or less disastrous, as it has separated ethics from personal development and left us with no possible answer as to why it is good to be good.

The motive of someone helping a friend in a mutual selfobject relationship is concern for the well-being of the friend. If it were anything other than that, it would not be a genuine friendship. Just because this concern for the other arises out of a friendship which we engage in, in part to get our selfobject needs met, ought not to lessen the goodness of the person acting out of concern for the other. The person helping someone in a reciprocal selfobject relationship has a caring motive and the act stems from a permanent character trait rather than a momentary impulse.

This theory locates ethical activity not in a realm of pure reason or abstract generalized love but in the robust matrix of friendships in which there is lived mutuality of respect and care. I think that this kind of reciprocity is the natural breeding ground for people to become fully ethical. Without it a person falls into the dangers of becoming a harsh moral legalist requiring strict obedience to the law or becoming a moral spiritualist who hopes and prays for the good but does not know how to help restore the self functioning of those closest to him. It is the hearty world of self-selfobject friendships and love relationships that gives birth to an embodied, sensitive, caring person—the essence of what it means to be ethical.

THE NEED TO DEVELOP THE MORAL VIRTUES

My claim that only people capable of empathic, caring reciprocity can engage fully in mature selfobject relationships is consonant with Aristotle's contention that only good people can participate fully in the practice of friendship.[2] By "good person" Aristotle means someone who has developed the moral virtues such as courage, justice, moderation, and generosity. It is fairly easy to understand why a person who lacked such virtues could not sustain a friendship. Very few psychologically healthy people will put up with unbalanced reciprocities, excessive consumption of shared resources, cowardice in the face of challenges (especially the challenges of sustaining love and friendship), and a tightness of giving. The only kind of person who would remain friends with such an un-virtuous person is one who is either a saint or suffers from such significant psychopathology that they will take any kind of friend they can get, or worse, be driven by repetitive structures to seek out friends who would injure them. I do not believe that such injured people can provide free, genuinely caring selfobject functions, for their nourishment will always have a toxic residue—a need to control, to take revenge, to keep the other in a state of dependency so they won't be abandoned, and so on. That is, such "friends" do not seek to promote the development of a genuine self but wish to keep it in a state of pathological neediness. People in such relationships do not practice friendship but morbid dependency.

The Aristotelian virtues are necessary not only for friendship but also for the development of a nuclear self capable of living in reality. Kohut says that for infantile grandiosity to transform into mature ambitions, the child must undergo events of optimal frustration. I contend that the process of optimal frustration is very close to what Aristotle describes as the development of the moral and intellectual virtues. For Aristotle the moral virtues are character traits that represent the mean between the extremes in relation to situations that arouse basic human emotions and desires. The mean allows the emotions or desires to be experienced without either overwhelming or underwhelming us. In allowing an emotion or desire to appear, the virtues provide motivation for action, while in not allowing an agent to be overwhelmed, they provide the calm necessary for thinking about what to do.

Optimal frustration generates a similar kind of character structure. It occurs in situations in which we cannot simply opt for immediate gratification or feel nothing at all—rather, we are presented with a problem that demands we hold our responses in abeyance until we can figure out how best to solve the problem. We will not be able to tolerate the delay in satisfaction unless we have begun to develop the virtues, for the virtues constitute the kind of character we must have in order to tolerate frustration in any particular kind of situation. For instance, courage is what allows us to tolerate the presence of fear rather than denying it (rashness) or running away (cowardice). Not only are the moral virtues needed to block the demand for immediate gratification, but the intellectual virtues are also required to solve the problems. A solution based on immediate desire or emotional discharge fails to constitute an experience of optimal frustration.

The difference between Kohut and Aristotle is that Kohut uses optimal frustration in a general application to all developmental problems while Aristotle is careful in specifying the crucial kinds of situations that require virtuous responses. Thus, he can name the virtues while Kohut has no similar characterlogical inventory. I believe that Kohut's general theory of development through optimal frustration entails Aristotle's specific virtues. In essence, optimal frustration creates the same character structure as the Aristotelian virtues.

Another way of saying this is that if a person has insufficient optimal frustrations, they will tend to remain infantile (spoiled) in their demand for instant gratification, while if they have been overwhelmed rather than optimally frustrated, they will be traumatized, become defensive, and have a lessened ability to feel their emotions and desires. The Kohutian self and Aristotle's ethical person appear to be very close—I would even say one and the same.

The virtues for Aristotle are not an end in themselves but a means by which we are able to best accomplish our human function of self-directing our lives in a rational, thoughtful way.[3] What Aristotelian virtues give a human being is the possibility of choosing a life. What a successful developmental pattern of optimal frustration gives a person is ambitious vitality for achievement in life. Aristotle knew that to have a life, a person needs to moderate the power of the passions (the id); Kohut knew that in order to have a life, one's grandiose energy had to be transformed and organized. Infantile grandiosity has no impetus to action, for it is already perfect; injured grandiosity has no impetus for action for the spirit of the person has been crushed. Only grandiosity that has been optimally frustrated can ground the possibility of someone becoming a mature agent.

Thus, the goal of both the virtues and optimal frustration is the same: the possibility of agency. Action requires the presence of the moral and intellectual virtues because in order for someone to choose between alternative possibilities, the power of immediate responses must be moderated and the ability to think about the consequences and meanings of different courses of action developed. Agency is crucial for the possibility of becoming an ethical person, for with it comes the possibility of responsibility.

We can see from this analysis that agency is not a function of the self per se but of the self as supplemented by the ego and character formation. Without character and the development of the ego, a person will have little possibility of choosing those paths in the world that will realize the self. It is crucial to see that the rational ego and character are allies of the self, not, as many Romantics proclaimed, enemies of the self that destroy its vital energy by moderating it and cramming it into normalized schemas. The philosophy advocated here is a fusion of the spontaneous/irrational vitality of the grandiose self with the moral virtues and rational abilities advocated by the Greeks. One might say that spontaneous irrationality without character and reason is blind and nondevelopmental, while moderate rationality without the grandiose self is only tepidly alive. The Romantics are right to rail against the production of a modern kind of person who develops the moral and intellectual virtues for use by a persona/ego alliance in forgetfulness of the creative originality of the self but wrong in thinking that moderation and reason are the problems.

If we accept self psychology's primary tenet that the most important psychological task is developing a nuclear self, then we have good reasons for wanting to be a person with integrity, empathy, care, a sense of fairness, the moral and intellectual virtues, and a sense of responsibility. But these are exactly the terms we associate with being an ethical person. If we want to have a self, then we need to develop the traits of an ethical person. If asked why developing a self is so important, self psychology can show that a psyche grounded in a coherent self is capable of more liveliness, joy, and agency than any other kind of psychic arrangement. Without an intact self, experience is not even fully experienced. Experiences happen, have meaning and intensity, but lack the crucial quality of being fully "my" experiences. Rather, they are experiences that happen in me or to me. They float in psychic space like an untethered raft in the midst of a wide ocean. The self is the harbor, the place where experience can be anchored and find a home or, to shift metaphors, a place where experiences can take root, grow, and develop.

Thus, self psychology offers to our culture an immeasurable gift, for it provides an answer as to why we should be moral that does not involve improvable metaphysical claims about God or a demand that we transcend our particularity. For those who try to be good and act with integrity, it offers the great solace that they are not being dupes but are living the only kind of lives that offer genuine happiness. For those who are tempted to be cheaters, it offers a great caution. What cheaters think their cheating will get them only appears to be in their best interest, for by cheating a person is making himself into the kind of person who is lessening his chances of developing and sustaining a self.

However, a problem remains. Just because someone has the moral virtues and empathy does not mean that he will think it right to apply them to all people at all times. That is, we can be ethically caring with those close to us or seen as belonging to the same group as us and vicious with those who are not in the chosen group. Some of the most loving family and community men have been Nazis, racists, and Mafiosi. That is, the exercise of virtues and reciprocity tends to be group or context dependent. To be fully ethical is to be predisposed to treat all people ethically. Why would someone who believes that the fundamental psychological task in life is the development and realization of a self want to be a universalist in the scope of his values rather than someone who reserves them just for friends? In order to explore this—the most difficult problem for my undertaking of grounding ethics in self psychology—we need first to turn to the nature of ideals and how they function in life.

THE NEED FOR IDEALS

For Kohut, the idealized pole is that part of the self that carries teleological values. It is extraordinarily important that self psychology finds that teleological motivation—being moved by ideals—is essential to having a healthy self. For self psychology ideals are not cages that repress the drives, self-expression, or the erotic body but vehicles for giving life meaning and making the future a source of dynamic interest. Ideals open up time and extend the self into time. Yet, Freud and Nietzsche are not wrong in being wary of ideals, for they can be imposed punitively on the self by a harsh superego and/or a rigid society. Whether ideals generate liveliness and meaningful systems for the organization of life or function as sources of repression depends upon whether the ideals represent the internal strivings of the self or derive from a defensive and over-controlling social unconscious (in Freud's terms, the superego). Ideals imposed by society or a repressive superego are cages; those structuring the self are beacons pointing toward new possibilities of enhanced life. Note that it is not the content of the ideals by which we can say whether they are self-ideals or defensive ideals; it is how they function in the psyche. Someone might have as a part of a self-ideal to become a lawyer, while another person might be using the same ideal to hold himself together defensively or make himself amenable to society.

I cannot emphasize enough the importance of Kohut's legitimizing of ideals as part of the core self. A number of forces combined in the late nineteenth and early twentieth centuries to throw values and ideals into question. First, science became the predominant source of truth for the culture, but science can have knowledge only about facts, not values. When science looked for motivators it looked to drives, forces, or anything that worked in a causal way. In an entirely different vein, Nietzsche exposed moral ideals as limiting life by contracting its possibilities and confining us to socialized pens. The Romantics added that the true self was found in emotional, spontaneous creativity—a singularity of expression, a lived particularity. Since ideals are always structured and tinged with commonness, they are antithetical to this individuality. As soon as one expresses a value, any value—"I want to be a professor; I want to help others; I want to be filthy rich"—one states what can be valued by any and everybody. Values seem to negate individuality.

These criticisms of values as de-individualizing generalized structures strongly influenced two of the most important existentialist ethicists of the twentieth century: Martin Buber and Emmanuel Levinas. Both retreated from ethics as a form of experience mediated by moral laws, the production of general welfare, or any such principle. They claimed that ethical experience occurred when a human being in his singularity faced another human being in her singularity and recognized her singular worth without the mediation of principles or concepts that reduced the other to a type or categorized them (the suffering ones, the needy ones, the ones who need to be told the truth, etc.).

Since Romanticism, existentialism (and its offspring, postmodernism), and science all find ideals problematical, the very process of establishing and believing in values has become one of the compelling problems for sensitive thoughtful people in modernity. In contrast, self psychology is a breath of spring air, offering new life for the value of values.

What Kohut realized from his psychoanalytic work is that the ability to have strong meaningful ideals is crucial in establishing a self and releasing the full life of the soul. Without meaningful ideals to structure the self and open up our ownmost possibilities in the future, there is a feeling of being lost on an open sea with no directions for how to find land.

Part of the trouble that Nietzsche, Heidegger, and many postmodern thinkers have had with ideals is the result of taking one aspect of idealization and making it the whole truth of ideals. Ideals do offer a universal structure, something that seems to de-individualize and which can be used to limit and control the creative variables of life, but they can also offer possibilities for creative individual expression. Thousands of human beings have been moved by the ideal of keeping the philosophic tradition alive in our culture, but no one teaches it quite like I do. Thousands have been moved by the ideal of psychological well-being to practice psychoanalysis and psychotherapy, but each practitioner worth his salt will put a creative individuating mark on the process. In short, nonrigid ideals give us the possibility of connecting to wider, more universal meanings while concomitantly offering us the opportunity to creatively individuate them. Indeed, I think that creative, spontaneous acts outside of the structure of ideals tend to be ephemeral, shallow, and unable to give much meaning. A happening is only that—just a happening; it cannot sustain us or open up a future. In a world without the teleological impetus of ideals, time can become an endless repetition of meaningless moments. Ideals, believed in and beloved, can sustain us through suffering, keep hope alive, and allow us to live in the fullness of time.

But this clarion call for reestablishing the worth of ideals does not answer the question as to why people with strong selves would want to have ethical ideals rather than just personal goals or limited social ideals such as Nazism, in which they need not bring empathy, care, and virtues to others outside their group identity. Kohut did not address whether a meaningful ideal had to have an objective justification or a certain content to be acceptable. Psychologically, it is unimportant whether one is vitalized by the ideal of being a creative artist or a punk rocker, a Nazi or a liberal democrat. But in philosophy and cultural life it makes all the difference what the content of one's ideal is and whether it has a claim to validity.

Kohut gives as a reason to go beyond merely personal ideals the need of the mature narcissist to identify with wider, more permanent ideals. Acknowledging mortality is a devastating blow to one's narcissism, for it means that the center of all worth will, necessarily, come to an end. This realization is so difficult that it is experienced as a traumatic injury to the self and sends many people into a low-level depression for decades, if not their entire lives. One of the ways we can overcome this blow is to adopt universal values, values that transcend the vicissitudes of time. When we identify a portion of the self's idealized pole with some general ideal, we expand ourselves and feel connected, once again, to a kind of greatness and perfection.

But we are still stuck, for these wider values can have as their content some kind of limited cultural norm that not only allows for the nonethical treatment of others but requires it (such as militant religious movements, white supremacy, etc). The full ethical position demands that we extend our empathic concern to others with whom we are not in a reciprocal relationship, that we give respect to all human beings and maybe even all sentient creatures. What would lead a narcissist to this position?

THE UNIVERSAL EXTENSION OF ETHICAL CONCERN

The argument from the viewpoint of self psychology for the universal extension of moral concern rests on the notion that the choice not to extend empathic, respectful care to all human beings (and, perhaps, all sentient creatures) involves a fragmentation of ourselves, a loss of agency, and a replacement of the self as the center of experience by the ego.

Let us start with what we have previously determined. We have found that we need to develop certain character traits and predispositions to engage fully in selfobject relationships, namely, the moral virtues, the ability to empathize with others, and the predisposition to care for and respect others. However, as Aristotle says, we exercise these traits in relation to situations. For instance, we exercise the trait of generosity more fully in our families than we do with friends, and more fully with friends than acquaintances. But how about when we are in situations with those we do not know or those trying to harm us? If we do not extend some empathic generosity and care to such people, can we say that we are really caring, empathic, and generous people? Are we injuring our abilities to be the kind of people able to get selfobject supplies if we do not exhibit at least some range of the virtues in these difficult situations? Are the ethical traits of self and character so context-dependent that they can entirely disappear if certain contextual variables are absent?

To say that we will exhibit our virtues and empathic sympathies in some situations and not in others entails that a decision must be made as what distinguishes the situations. This kind of distinction is the kind of thing that the ego does, and, as such, it puts the ego in charge of the life of the soul. The ego has, as we discovered, the extraordinary power to abstract itself from everything, including a person's character. However, while a psyche organized around the rational ego (the Platonic psyche) might give one the most control over life, it is not the most alive way to live. When the self is at the center of experience, such abstraction is not as easy. The ego distances itself from the self in order to freely make optimal decisions, but the self is immersed in life, immersed in selfobject relations, immersed in friendships, tied to cherished ideals and devoted to accomplishment in chosen arenas of endeavor. It cannot so easily distance itself from the character traits or ideals with which it engages life. We have seen that part of any self's set of ideals ought to be the ideal of being an empathic, caring, virtuous human being, for only when this ideal infuses our lives do we become optimally able to engage in what strengthens the self more than anything else—selfobject relationships. Other parts of a self's ideals are optional, but not these ethical traits for they are the traits necessary for any self to sustain itself. The self cannot, like the ego, just turn these traits on and off depending on the context. In short, the ego can live a kind of disembodied, un-situated kind of existence; the self is inherently embodied and situated.

Another way to make this psychological argument is from the value of psychological integrity. We have seen that integrity must be a value to a psyche centered on a self, for it is the value that essentially supports the self's being the fulcrum of the psyche. This does not mean that we must have one highest value or that our lives cannot have multiple dimensions. It means that when a person with an integrated psyche engages in the manifold dimensions of life, she is fully present, active, and alive in them. The parts do not war against one another in an integrated psyche but work together to produce a focused meaningful life.

Integrity means being who you are, regardless of situation. If one is an empathic caring person, then one remains empathic and caring, even in difficult situations. This does not mean that we cannot be aggressive. If I need aggression to protect myself or what is precious to me or if I need aggression where it is legitimately called for—on playing fields or combat—then it is right (and natural) to be aggressive. But one can be aggressive in a just, caring, and empathic way. Indeed, on the sporting fields this is precisely what is called for—aggression without loss of virtue or humanity. Empathically caring for one's enemies makes life much more difficult than being able to aggress against them without counter-feelings, but this might be the price for being an integrated human being living from a core self.

Finally, I believe that keeping one's character and empathic predisposition in all situations leads to more aliveness of the soul, for it makes one active and assertive rather than dependent upon circumstances to determine who one is. If I have to change my character depending on who I am with or what circumstances I am facing, then who I am is contextually determined, and this is a passive way of being human rather than active. When I retain the essence of myself—in Aristotle's terms, my "goodness"—regardless of circumstance, then I actively assert my being in the world. This, I believe, is the power of both Socrates' and Jesus' deaths. They retained their essential natures when the world demanded on the price of death that they change.

CONCLUSION

I have attempted to show in this chapter why, if one accepts Kohut's theory of the self, a person would want to become an ethical human being, whereby "ethical human being" I mean someone who is empathic and caring of others, shows others respect and treats others fairly, engages in reciprocity, and is willing to extend these traits to all human beings and, perhaps, all sentient creatures. The reason for developing empathy, care, the virtues, and a sense of fair reciprocity is that these characteristics most insure the ability to establish and maintain selfobject relationships. The reasons to extend our care and respect to others with whom we are not in reciprocal selfobject relationships are that to refuse such extension means that the ego rather than the self is the center of psychological life, that we lose a sense of integrity, and that we declare ourselves to be determined by the variables of situations rather than our own core nature. It is because the self both is a core psychological structure of a person and needs selfobject support to sustain itself that it must become ethical. If the self were capable of being self-sufficient, it would not need others. If the self were only a set of communal relationships it would lose its particularity and there would be no way of extending values beyond those of the parochial community. It is only a particularized but fragile self that needs to be ethical. But this is just the kind of self that humans have.

NOTES

1. See Arnold Goldberg's *Being of Two Minds* (Hillsdale, NJ: Analytic Press, 1999) for a detailed analysis of vertical splitting.
2. See Aristotle's *Nichomachean Ethics*, Book VIII.

Six

A Self Psychological
Vision of Ethical Life

REVIEW OF THE ARGUMENT

The primary reason why Western thought has missed the profound inter-connection between doing what is best for oneself and being a morally good person is that it has misconceived the self to be a kind of independent substance whose fundamental goal is to seek self-sufficiency. The achievement of self-sufficiency involves the transcendence of particularity (which is always needy), either by identifying with universal values or merging with a universal substance (God). As such, its highest moment does not involve friendship, love, or care for the other, for all of these involve dependence and interrelations with finite changeable particulars.

Everything changes when we conceive of the self as fragile, interdependent, and needing a trustworthy matrix of selfobjects. The self needs others in ways that are genuinely supportive of mature narcissism, ways that do not indulge immature forms of gratification or bind the person in morbid forms of dependency. One can get this kind of support only through reciprocity that involves empathy, care, and the practice of the virtues. We need these moral traits not just to block the power of the passions or open up the possibility of rational life but to generate and sustain a self. Moderating the passions and establishing reason as a dominant psychological agency are questionable as final ends, for they can make life less intense and keep us from the richness of embodied particularity. However, they are worthy aims when balanced with the need to establish the centrality of the self. The life of the soul is not the same as the life of the mind (the ego). The ethic here aligns the optimal life of the soul with its having a self at its fulcrum. It is this alignment that demands that we become ethical persons in a way which was not conceivable in earlier forms of ethics.

Why is it good to be good? Because it is only by being good people that we can fully develop or sustain our selves and without a developed and sustained self we cannot be as intensely alive as possible. Here is a return to one of the most profound insights of Greek philosophy but without the transcendence of particularity that Greek thought entailed: the person who is able to reap the most personal happiness is the good person. Bad people cannot be fully happy for they have unjust souls that are anarchically controlled by whims, can't be empathic with themselves or others, and can't engage in the kind of friendships that supply necessary selfobject support. Note that there is no reason why bad persons cannot have highly functioning egos capable of crafty, even brilliant reasoning and action. What bad persons can't fully have are selves, for it is the self—not the ego—that needs human connectedness.

I have tried to show why it is personally good to be morally good; but it can also be shown that it is morally good to have a narcissistically healthy self. When we inquire into what kind of human being creates the most human misery and suffering, I think we will find that it is those humans who have suffered severe trauma to the self and harbor an unremitting narcissistic rage. Narcissistic rage differs radically from ordinary anger and aggression. Ordinary anger is typically caused by a specific injury or obstacle, has a specific target, and once discharged it disappears. Narcissistic rage, on the other hand, can fester forever, seek revenge on any and all persons who might get unconsciously associated with the cause of the trauma, and wills their annihilation. It is never satisfied, regardless of how many victories of revenge and acts of destruction it commits. I believe the harboring of unconscious rage due to injuries to the self forms the core motivational structure of evil persons—persons who seek to harm others for seemingly no reason other than seeing them suffer. The great antidote to evil is the development of persons with healthy nuclear selves.

THE JUSTIFICATION OF A SELF PSYCHOLOGICAL ETHICS

Kant held that for a value to be a moral value it must be universalizable. I believe this principle to be correct but think that Western thought has, for the most part, tried to universalize the wrong kind of thing: general principles that designate certain kinds of actions as always being right or wrong. No such unconditional principles have ever been found. What needs to be universalized is a way of being human. If asked whether I would be willing to live in a world that was populated by people who had integral vital selves, who were empathic and caring, who exhibited the moral and intellectual virtues, and who were willing to extend ethical concern to all other human beings, my answer is "Yes, Amen, let such a world come into being! These are just the kind of human beings with whom I want to live, for they will have little need to cause gratuitous violence and will be available for selfobject support."

Such individuals will add richness and diversity to the human community by pursuing their singular ideals and ambitions but will limit their pursuits not by obeying external moral rules or authorities but by naturally developing the virtues, a sense of empathic care, and integrity. These qualities do not transform the individuals into a normalized devitalized type; rather, they humanize them.

Thus the self psychological ethical vision has both personal and moral justifications. The personal justification for living as an ethical person is that it gives one more vitality of experience than any other way of being human, while the ethical justification is that we can universalize the kind of person organized around a self. It is not only personally good to have a self; it is morally good to have a self. It is not only personally good to be morally good but morally good to be a narcissistically healthy person.

Since I am proposing a naturalistic ethics—one which finds the liveliness of life and the optimal functioning of the psyche to be the highest goods, I need to face directly the claim that I might be committing the "naturalistic fallacy." Since Hume and G. E. Moore, the naturalistic fallacy has played almost as important a role in systems of justification as the principle of universalization. The naturalistic fallacy holds that any attempt to define a moral term with a factual property must always fail, for we can ask in any situation which exhibits the natural property whether or not it is "good" or "right." The most famous example of this is G. E. Moore's critique of the utilitarian identification of good with pleasure. We might meaningfully ask of any situation that produces an optimum amount of pleasure whether or not it is good, and, since the question makes sense, "good" and "pleasure" cannot mean the same thing. All ethical terms seem indefinable by natural properties, for we can meaningfully ask about a person or situation that exhibits the natural property (such as a soul's having vitality or optimal functionality) whether it is good.

Is it true by definition that personal vitality, meaningfulness of experience, and the optimal functioning of the psyche are good? Of course not. Can it be argued for? Not really. What kind of argument could be given for saying that having a soul that feels robustly alive, self-confident, and actively pursuing meaningful goals is better than one that is somewhat depressed, self-negating, and purposeless? While one can without self-contradiction hold that it is better to be a depressed, self-negating human being who cannot self-assertively act without shame or guilt than a person who is vitalized, living a meaningful life, and helping others to do so, too, I cannot imagine who could say this meaningfully or under what conditions. I am sure that we can imaginatively invent a situation in which more good might be capable of being experienced or done in a depressed state, but such examples always think the way the ego thinks—in abstractions. A person acts not just in a situation but has a life that is embodied and which persists through time. I would never say that my ideal self-psychologically developed person will do what is morally best in every situation, but that in general and over the course of a lifetime, such persons produce the most good both for themselves and for others.

Another reason why the naturalistic fallacy does not apply to this ethics is that its first principle is not a principle at all. It is an urge from the psyche to seek life, an urge which we affirm, as Nietzsche says, with a "Yes!" A "Yes" to life! That is the ground of ethics, not a proposition or a judgment, which are ego-productions. It is the self that must first say "Yes!" and then the ego can formulate the principle that the aim of the soul is to seek aliveness. The justification for this first principle is not that it is true by definition or that it has an a priori certainty, but that at the center of every psyche is a felt urge to be as alive as possible.

Finally, we need to raise the issue of metaphysics. My account of the self has stayed within what I take to be an empirical psychology—one that is derived from clinical evidence and which is subject to falsification if future data from psychoanalysis and child development studies can be better accounted for by other theories. The self of self psychology is not the self of religions or of many metaphysical theories—an immortal soul which carries an identity through all of time. Might there be such a self that lies behind this psychological self or behind the subjectivity of the ego? The answer is, yes, there might be. This work is an inquiry into moral psychology, not ontology. The "I" of the ego remains a mystery. Where does it come from? What account of nature can explain its possibility? Is there a core ontological self that actualizes itself in terms of a psychological self of the kind Kohut describes? I inquire into none of these questions.

As such this theory neither destroys a religious person's belief in an immortal soul nor aids it. What it does destroy is the supposed need to have a God in order to have a ground for moral life. Indeed, it destroys the need to do metaphysics in order to have a coherent concept of ethical life. All we need to live well is what is available to us in terms of our psychological self. If we do happen to have immortal souls that have some kind of inconceivable afterlives, that is fine, but it has no bearing on living as ethical human beings in this life. I am in agreement with Kant in thinking that the belief in immortal souls and God is beyond the realm of knowledge and available only for faith. If faith in God and immortal souls is calming and supportive of the self, then it is (all other things being equal) a good; if it involves that one engage in acts of self-mortification or self-negation, then the faith is an evil—both to the person holding the faith and to those whom his life touches.

The battles about what metaphysical beliefs in fact make one feel more alive need not be engaged, for it is not the having or failing to have certain metaphysical beliefs that grounds the life of the soul, but the self. It is the fundamental claim of this work that when a person's psyche is organized around a coherent, vitalized self, then it is optimally alive regardless of whether the person is a practicing Buddhist, secular atheist, Platonist, or anything else—so long as the person is not practicing in a fundamentalist way—a way which is defensive, rigid, and exclusive. The goal of ethics is to determine how to live the best of human lives. The claim of this work is that that happens when one develops a coherent, vital self that expands its empathic concern to all human beings. It requires no particular metaphysics and counts against none.

THE PARTS OF THE SOUL AND ETHICS

There is another way to think about ethical life from the structure of the soul that I have elaborated, and this is to look at ethics from the viewpoint of each of the parts of the soul. The id seeks satisfaction and pleasure and is the source for hedonistic ethics. The social unconscious is the embodiment of the mores of one's society and locates morality in obedience to local custom. The ego tends to be governed by reason and pushes us toward a universal ethics of laws and principles. Character gives us virtue ethics, while the self is most concerned with existing in a matrix of love, care, and empathic support. Seeking pleasure, being located in a particular community (rather than the idea of a universal community), governing oneself and critiquing one's community by universal values, developing the virtues, and having empathic concern for other human beings are all part of the moral structure of human existence. Each makes sense because it derives from an essential part of the psyche; each in abstraction from the others is an ethics that represents only a part of who we are as humans.

All of these ethical perspectives and various combinations of them have had strong supporters throughout Western history. Hedonistic ethical theories which emphasize that life is about attaining personal pleasure presume that the id is the center of human life. Utilitarianism takes the id imperative for pleasure and combines it with the ego's need for universal extension. De-ontological ethics which emphasize law and principle derive from a highly developed rational ego. Moral principles originate from a kind of thinking in which we abstract ourselves from our particular circumstances, are not overly swayed by local ties and personal biases, and act from a sense of rightness rather than one of embodied love or care. Virtue ethics, obviously, holds that the development of character is crucial to living well both as an individual and in a community. An ethics which fully emphasizes the cohesion of the community rather than privileging the individual (such as Confucian ethics) derives from the social unconscious. Lastly, ethical theories that emphasize love, reciprocity, empathy, and concern seem to derive from the self and its selfobject relations.

Each of these kinds of ethics captures a truth about the soul and human life. Seeing that different ethics originate from different parts of the soul helps explain why ethical life is so complicated and unable to be reduced to a simple system of a few basic moral laws, a set of virtues, loving kindness, community cohesion, or pleasure-seeking. Human life involves all of these dimensions because the soul has an id, a character, a self, a social unconscious, and an ego. To leave out any of these aspects of ethical life is to leave out or repress a part of the soul. Life involves seeking pleasure for ourselves and others, belonging to a community, developing character by which to face the difficulties of life, finding ways to realize and sustain the self, and rationally thinking about life, including having the rational abilities to critique our communities, our desires, our self imperatives, and even our own rational moral laws.

Since moral life has these five components and each can conflict with the other, how are we to organize ethical life? I do not think that a simple hierarchical arrangement of imperatives works, such as having the concerns of the self always coming first, followed by virtue, reason, the community, and then the desires (such a scheme is a project of the ego). Nor is there a kind of moral algorithm which can be applied to all cases. Rather, an ecological webbing of ethical perspectives with the self as the central fulcrum seems to be best. That is, what I am claiming is that people who have strong self/ego/character centers will tend to the community, listen to advice of reason, be supported by virtuous character, and know when to delight in satisfying desires. When the id gets too much of the upper hand, it tends to use others for its satisfactions. When we act too much as members of a localized community, we tend to act blindly with the embedded prejudices that characterize such communities. When reason abstracts itself from the rest of the psyche and attempts to produce moral life from itself, it will tend to be overly general and fail to recognize the concrete particularity of persons in situations. Hence, the imperative I have been arguing for—that we construct human beings with a strong self/character/ego axis—remains intact.

In the end Aristotle was right when he claimed that one has to become a person of practical wisdom and have a sensitive feel for what is best in each situation. Obviously, a life in which a person is realizing her self in commitments, has developed the moral and intellectual virtues, has a vital set of friendships that sustain the self, is capable of a rich satisfaction of the desires, and lives in a sustaining community fulfills all of the needs of the psyche. I believe that the key to living fully and wisely is not, as Aristotle said, simply the development of the virtues, but the maturation of the self. The importance of the moral and intellectual virtues is that the self cannot fully develop or sustain itself without the virtues. What I have attempted to do is to develop more fully what the nature of a person of practical wisdom is—to add to Aristotle's vision the complexity of modern life, a psyche with an unconscious, and a self that is the ground of healthy psychological existence.

TRANSFORMATIONS OF ETHICS

While self psychology gives us good reasons for being good, it does not mean that traditional notions of what it means to be good are left unchanged. Three dramatic shifts need to occur if ethics is to incorporate the psychology of self articulated here: (1) we need to reconceive the structure of the ethical experience away from the simple notion that ethics involves the application of a principle to a situation, (2) the ethical point of view must relinquish its hostility to narcissism, and (3) the ethical point of view must recognize and affirm the existence of unconscious mentality.

First, while there have been in the West a number of ways of thinking about what constitutes the structure of moral experience, the one which understands ethics to be the application of a moral principle to a situation has seemed to predominate. Ethics is a matter of finding and applying the correct moral principles, be they moral laws of the Kantian type or something like the principle of utility. In this way morality appears to be a mirror of science in which individual events are understood as falling under general laws of nature. This way of understanding ethical life has been severely critiqued by both analytic philosophers who cannot find any laws that hold for all situations and by the great continental ethicists Buber and Levinas who find that such a notion of ethics tends to reduce others to objects who fall under general categories—those who need help, their pleasure enhanced, honest communication, and so on. Ethics for these thinkers is about encountering other subjects in the richness of their subjectivity and not reducing them to objects. They want us to have a direct relation to the subjectivity of the other, not a relation mediated by a set of general laws. Ethics for Buber is to treat the other as a "Thou," and for Levinas to be able to be present face-to-face with the other.

The self psychological ethics presented here finds that the ethical situation is best understood as a multidimensional, complex experience which centers on the empathic apprehension of the subjectivity of another (and, hence, agrees with Levinas and Buber), but also involves the predisposition to act virtuously in relation to others, attentiveness to the well-being of the selves of others, an attentiveness to what delights others and causes them pain, an awareness of how acts weave or unravel the complex fabric of a local community, and a willingness to extend empathic care and respect to those beyond one's immediate community of selfobjects. This last dimension might best be conceived of as the application of general principles to situations. It is an important part of the ethical experience, but only a dimension and not the essence. For a self psychological ethics, it is more important who is doing the acting rather than what principle they are acting under. In this way it is an Aristotelian perspective rather than a Kantian one, but an Aristotelian position that significantly complexifies the notion of what it means to be a moral agent, a complexification which includes a Kantian dimension.[1]

Second, traditional morality needs to relinquish its hostility toward narcissism. The moral point of view has traditionally denigrated self-oriented intentions as selfish, demanded that we comply with some general ideal of what a good person ought to be in order to have worth, or minimally held that we need to restrain our individual pursuits by obeying moral laws or attending to the general welfare. In opposition to this traditional stance, self psychology has us empathically affirm the particularity of ourselves and others as our prima facie first duty. It is legitimate to want the needs of one's self to get met, including the need to feel special, so long as we do not use others as a mere means in our interactions.

What needs ethical censure is not mature narcissism but infantile or pathological narcissism which typically involves unwarranted aggression against others, entitlement demands, and failures to recognize others as independent sources of agency and feeling. Infantile narcissistic demands need to be confronted, but a mature person asserting the grandeur of oneself in the world is not only not a sin, but a signal to others that they may do the same—that they can delight in themselves.

Narcissism is also highly problematical when the self is identified the way it has been in modernity—as a set of desires located in an atomized individual. Affirming the self is not identical with affirming the desires, needs, and wants of ourselves and others. Many parents think they must gratify their children in order to affirm them, where in fact, affirming isolated aspects of behavior or atomized desires is often experienced by children as fragmenting. Indeed, denying many of one's or others' desires is necessary in order for commitments to self activities to establish themselves.

The third great shift a self psychological ethics requires is the recognition of unconscious mentality as central to human existence. The self and the psychological dynamics surrounding it are, for the most part, unconscious, and so if the self is the center of moral life, then to be fully moral persons, we must become better at knowing how to access our unconscious predispositions and processes.[2]

The recognition of the unconscious has been highly problematic for ethics, for it raises the question of whether we are responsible for our unconscious intentions—intentions that we do not choose to have, do not, in general, know that we have, and whose effects are often hidden from us. From Plato through the present day, it has been a fundamental tenet of the moral point of view that we are responsible only for our consciously intended acts. If we can show that an act we committed was not consciously intended, we do not have to assume moral responsibility for it. This attitude toward unconscious or unintended actions has meant that traditional morality has not been able to locate a primary source of evil and has proven impotent in overcoming the suffering that comes from unconscious intentions, especially what ensues from narcissistic rage. The inability to understand unconscious motivations has also meant that morality itself could be the bearer of unconscious rage, as Nietzsche so brilliantly revealed.

Recent ethical theory has tended to focus on monumental moral catastrophes such as the Holocaust, while losing track of the small, hardly noticeable tragedies of everyday life that arise from unconscious forces— a mother projecting her own inadequacies into her daughter and then shaming her; an Oedipally obsessed young man seducing a woman and then devastating her by immediately losing interest in her; a spouse destroying the independence of his mate in order to control her in a way he couldn't his mother; a teacher who transforms his narcissistic rage into punitively difficult exams that shatter many of his students' hopes. These and countless other incidents like them lower the ability of persons to feel alive, have worth, and proceed as agents with life. They are acts of evil and they happen countless times in every community every day.

The most common kind of unconscious motivation that overdetermines conscious actions is transference. Transferences occur when an unconscious organizing principle gets developed—typically in childhood—and is then used to interpret all like experiences, ignoring crucial factors that differentiate a current situation from the past. If a mother has been smothering in her care, there will be a tendency to experience women in general as smothering. The transference can even make one relate only to smothering women, for all the others do not show up on one's radar screen as having worth or interest. One's organizing principle is then constantly confirmed as being correct.

All transferences, whether positive or negative, involve injustices, for in transferences some people get more than they deserve and others less. In love relationships, the positive transferences uniting a current love object with a past source of life-sustaining love are part of what romantic love is about and why we don't think of justice as the foundation for love relations. But it is different in the workplace. When one person gets less than what he deserves because his boss unconsciously transfers onto him the hatred he felt for a punitive father or another gets promotions unwarranted by her productivity because there is a positive transference connecting her with the beloved Aunt Abigail of childhood, then wrong is committed and un-necessary suffering is perpetrated. Oedipal transferences bring unwar-ranted ambivalence into love relationships and usually undermine them. Most of the suffering that I have seen in marriages and broken families re-sults from unresolved transferences tearing them apart.

Addictive activity also has an essential unconscious component—typi-cally, a severe inner emptiness in the self that a person is trying to fill with a substance or activity (compulsive gambling, sex, etc.). When we look at all the individual lives and families ruined by addicted gamblers, alcoholics, and drug addicts, the misery is untold. It is estimated that a great deal of identity crime and property crime is committed by persons needing to sup-port their drug habits. Every two years more Americans are killed by drunk drivers (whom I assume to have a drinking problem in part motivated by unconscious suffering) than were killed in Vietnam. Few addicted people have the conscious intentions of ruining theirs and their beloveds' lives, but they cannot consciously control or even admit that they have a problem, because a key component of the addiction lies in the unconscious.

Unconscious motivations also seem to be a necessary component in group prejudices and group aggression, including aggressions that result in genocide. In cases of prejudice one can usually find persons or groups unconsciously projecting their disavowed negative traits onto others and then aggressing against them. White persons in America have seen Afri-can Americans as "over-sexed" or "animalistic," Hispanics as "lazy and dumb." Group paranoia and narcissistic rage combine to be lethal ingre-dients in the group hatred that spawns so much social evil.

In sum, when we add together the unnecessary suffering caused by the transferences, paranoia, projection, narcissistic rage, and addictive com-pulsions, it is overwhelming. I would say that the unconscious motiva-tions are a decisive factor in almost all of what is evil in the human world. Despite the massive evil caused by unconscious motivations, traditional ethics has little to say about them, for it holds us responsible only for our consciously intended actions. If we can possibly show that we did not intend the negative consequences of our actions—did not intend to be late to the important meeting, did not intend to hit our little brother, did not intend to forget our anniversary, then we are not responsible for the con-sequences of our deeds, do not have to suffer guilt for what we did or even inquire into why we did it. Since a lack of conscious intentionality lets us off the hook for any deed, we have become a culture of excuses. "I didn't mean to be late—the traffic was awful." "I didn't mean to hit Bob-by—I didn't see him behind me." "I didn't mean to forget our anniversa-ry—life has been so hectic lately, that I just didn't even know what day it was." Meanwhile, we reap the satisfaction of proving our superiority over those who showed up to the meeting on time, aggressed violently against our little brother, and communicated to our spouses that we rue the day we married them.

Unconscious motivations present a terrible dilemma: if we don't take responsibility for them, then the major source of evil in ourselves goes unchecked, but if we do take responsibility for them, then it seems that we must be held accountable for the consequences of motivations that we do not choose to have and which operate in us beyond the realm of conscious awareness. This feels too much like being held responsible for who one has been fated to be.

The key to solving this dilemma is to tease apart the notion of responsibility from those of accountability and guilt. We can make this separation if we differentiate between *accepting responsibility* for what we do and *taking responsibility* for what we do.[3] When I take responsibility for an action, I imply that I had a choice and could have done otherwise than I did. If what I did was wrong, then I am guilty of a wrongdoing. Accepting responsibility does not have the implications that I could have done otherwise than I did or that I am guilty of a wrongdoing. For example, say that I unintentionally take a top coat from a rack at a restaurant that is identical to mine except for a hidden name on the inside pocket that I do not see. I later discover my mistake, accept responsibility for the misdeed, and make reparations to the proper owner (find where he lives, return the coat with apologies). I need suffer no guilt, for I did not intend to steal the coat. I am remorseful for the pain I have caused the man, accept the responsibility for the coat's safe return, but do not think I am a bad person or guilty of a misdeed.

While accepting responsibility for one's destructive unconscious motivations does not entail accountability or guilt, it does commit one to discover who he is and attempt to change himself so that the negative consequences will not occur again. The change from being a person who denies unconscious motivations and offers endless excuses in order to avoid guilt to one who accepts responsibility for unconscious intentions, feels remorse for the harm she has unintentionally caused others, and commits herself to a journey of self discovery might be the most important transformation that a human being can make. It is a transformation that humanizes us, gives us depth, and helps cure us from being an involuntary carrier of pain and suffering for ourselves and others.

A SELF PSYCHOLOGICAL VISION OF ETHICAL LIFE

The essence of an ethics base in self psychology is neither the Old Testament/Kantian dictum to place oneself under the law nor the modern maxim to generate pleasure for oneself and the general populace. Rather, it is aligned with the ancient Greek principle "Know thyself." However, the self that one is commanded to know is not the conscious ego or the social persona but an unconscious self webbed in a dark net of irrational dynamics. One can satisfy the basic moral command only by probing into what is unfamiliar and not readily knowable in oneself. The person who would be moral must set out to explore her own unconscious territory and be willing to encounter the other that dwells so closely to her as to not be seen. If a self is fundamentally actualized in a person's commitments, one of those commitments that all persons need to make is to know themselves.

How does one come to know her unconscious? And who is the "I" who is doing the knowing of the self? The "I" has been traditionally seen as the ego and its knowledge has been seen as a kind of objective fact-gathering about who one is. But this is just the kind of knowledge that Freud said was a kind of knowing that was not knowing. Freud gave up hypnosis not simply because he was not terribly good at it but because he found it produced a kind of knowledge that had no transforming force. He might hypnotize a patient, learn repressed and forgotten truths about her life, tell her, and have her accept what he said as the truth of her life without anything of significance happening. Knowledge of the self, while it looks like other forms of knowledge, is not like them at all. It is very common for persons in psychoanalysis or psychotherapy to cognitively discover a neurotic pattern quite quickly and then spend years attempting to "know" what it really means to be oedipal, paranoid or depleted. This knowing involves avowing a truth of oneself as a subject subjectively experiencing oneself rather than knowing a truth about an object who happens to be oneself.

What Freud developed in his psychoanalytic practice was a whole different way of coming to know oneself, where "knowing" and "owning" intertwine to form a new way of being in the world, a way of integrity. In the act of knowing oneself, one becomes who one genuinely is. "Knowing oneself" becomes identical with "being oneself." This kind of knowing is what makes a human being a complex, content-filled subject rather than an abstract ego knowing objective truths about the person, truths which it can choose to change at any moment. I believe that this kind of knowing is what Hegel's *Phenomenology of the Spirit* concerns itself with—a kind of knowing that simultaneously constitutes the being of the self. It is the becoming of a subject rather than an ego using objective methodologies to determine the facts about who one is.

In the state of self-knowledge, the psyche seems to lose its divisions of the id, ego, self, and persona and become whole. There is an "I" that does not feel like the abstracted subject of ego experience but a full, richly textured subject that weaves together threads of the ego, self, id, and persona. This subject has the conscious critical abilities of the ego, the nourishing presence of the self, and the vitality of emotional responsiveness. Desires now feel like they are mine rather than internal pressures on me, and my social roles, if they are attuned with the self, feel like gifts from society for the possibility of self-expression rather than imposed structures limiting a natural spontaneity. I believe a person with this kind of rich subjectivity naturally chooses to be ethical—to dwell as a person embedded in a culture with others about whom she cares and whom she needs.

It is very difficult to describe the fullness of the psychoanalytic state of knowing oneself. Our lives expand and start to incorporate what was previously eliminated from our owned experiences—the extraordinary wishes and thinking that occurs in dreams and daydreams, disavowed behavior for which we always had a ready excuse, and spontaneous images or compulsions that arise. Our day selves and night selves begin to discover one another and become one self. In the act of becoming known, disavowed wishes and hostile aims that resulted in symptoms, depressive moods, and self-destructive acting out cease being independent parts of the psyche, draining and diverting its energy and unconsciously overdetermining actions. With this kind of self knowledge we attain integrity and cease being a vehicle by which split-off parts act independently with their own agendas.

If the heart of moral life is self knowledge and attaining this knowledge involves an immersion in one's unconscious, then taking ethical life seriously means learning how to understand the unconscious. This is no easy matter, for it involves an ability to work with the symbols and images of dreams and symptoms, a general knowledge of how the unconscious works, and a particular understanding of oneself. These are the skills of a poet, a rigorous theorist, and an experimental scientist analyzing a very strange particular specimen. The humanities and sciences might be radically split in their orientations toward the world, but both kinds of mind are needed to attain knowledge of the self. Yet, there is something other than skills involved in self knowledge that cannot be named—the ability of the psyche to integrate into its identity that which it had excluded through the various defenses. The difficulty of this integration is why the main human virtue is courage.

Thus, with self psychology and the psychoanalytic tradition we not only get good reasons for why it is good to be good, we get a new paradigm for what constitutes living well as a human being. The paradigm of the "psychoanalytic person" is not the wise philosopher of the Greeks whose reason seemed able to reach into eternal realms of truth and whose calm rationality kept him safe from being overwhelmed by life's vicissitudes. It is not the paradigm of the Renaissance man who learns many skills and enjoys many facets of life, for such a person need not have a core self or an inwardly directed focus. Nor is this paradigm the Romantic one of the Dionysian artist spontaneously creating his life, living with a full intensity of emotion, and celebrating the dynamic chaos of existence. It is none of these but has elements of each. The moral virtues of the philosopher are retained along with the rational powers of the ego, but the virtues and reason are for the sake of the self and not the goal of becoming a self-sufficient sage. Like the Renaissance man the psychoanalytic person is engaged in the multiple facets of human existence, but these facets are more psychological than worldly. If the self requires an intense concentrated exploration of one facet of life, then the value of being as multitalented as DaVinci is foregone. Like the Romantic, the psychoanalytic person seeks a height of intensity but finds this not so much in spontaneous gesture as in commitments to self-realizing activities and relationships. Unlike any of them, however, is the focus on exploring and knowing what is unconscious in oneself.

Freud discovered a new territory whose importance far exceeds that of the New World discovered by Columbus, for it is an inner world that all humans have. He gave us our first detailed maps by which to explore this territory, maps that became more accurate with Kohut's work and which continue to be refined in the psychoanalytic tradition. Although many commentators have lamented the loss of a spiritual dimension of the self in modernity, the psychoanalytic tradition has opened up an inner world that is so rich, textured, and decisive in determining who we are that we should be celebrating the discovery of a vast treasure. Of course, like all good adventures, adventure into the unconscious must involve encounters with dragons and highwaymen, sirens and forbidden fruit, traumatic disappointments, invasive intrusions, devastated dreams, and fragile hopes. It is an adventure the end of which is becoming a full human being rather than one who lives out of the narrowly constricted limits of rational consciousness.

With self psychology we not only learn why it is good to be good but achieve a much more profound sense of what that goodness might be. Do we now have an answer to the question of how it is best to live as a human being? Yes—it is best to live with the self as the core factor in one's motivations and to live in such a way as to support the vitality and coherence of the self. This primarily involves developing and sustaining close relations with other human beings, something which in turn requires the presence of the moral virtues, empathic responsiveness, respect for others, and the ability to engage in reciprocity. It also involves achieving an integrity by which we extend our care, respect, and empathy to all human beings and, perhaps, all creatures with whom we can empathically resonate.

Does having such an answer to the great ethical question of human life mean that this inquiry is at an end? No! Since everyone's self is singular and in process, the inquiry into one's own self and life can never be completed. Since the self lies in the unconscious, we can never be sure of its contours and shapes. Since the self is intersubjective, we need always be relating to and inquiring about the selves of others, others who are themselves changing, shifting, and unconscious. Hence, these ethical inquiries cannot be completed. Further, while I have tried to explore the relationships between self psychology and ethics, I have not tackled the great mysteries of human existence: What is consciousness? How and why did nature produce a being that must generate meanings to live? Does the universe itself have a field of objective meanings that can be accessed? The inquiry into the nature of human existence is hardly at an end.

Socrates, in the first formulation of what it means to live an ethical life, had two crucial intuitions about that life. First, a well-lived life must be a life of inquiry, and second, the best personal life is the life of an ethically good person. This treatise confirms these intuitions. It is good to be good, but being good is not the application of a moral formula to diverse events of life but a commitment to inquiring into who one is and what human life is all about.

NOTES

1. See Nancy Sherman's *Making a Necessity of Virtue: Aristotle and Kant on Virtue* (Cambridge: Cambridge University Press, 1997).

2. Integrating the unconscious into ethical life is the major theme of my book *Ethics and the Discovery of the Unconscious* (Albany, NY: SUNY Press, 1997). I will only briefly sketch that argument here.

3. Jonathan Lear makes this crucial distinction in *Love and Its Place in Nature* (New York: Farrar, Straus, and Giroux, 1990) and I use it in *Ethics and the Discovery of the Unconscious.*

Seven

Self Psychology and Modernity
Actualizing the Self in an Era of Desire

With our new metapsychology we can gain a clearer insight into the psycho/social problems of modern persons, including their propensity toward cheating, for all of them relate to the underlying problem of the ego's inability to ground itself in the self. This disappearance of the self from modern experience is due neither to chance nor random trauma but is the result of modernity's systematically establishing conditions that traumatize the self or make us inattentive to its presence and needs. These conditions are both material and conceptual. The material conditions revolve around how modernity methodically destabilizes selfobject relationships, while the conceptual conditions involve confusing the ego with the self, seeing difference and independence as decisive signs of a strong self, and thinking of freedom as the maximization of opportunity.

THE MARKET AND THE DESTABILIZATION
OF SELFOBJECT RELATIONS

As many commentators have noted, the advent of an industrialized market economy in the nineteenth century brought with it a radical division of life into public and private sectors. Each sphere developed its own set of values with the market favoring competitiveness, aggression, chance-taking, rule-following, efficiency, productivity, power, wealth, and a problem-solving kind of intelligence, while the home esteems love, care, empathy, and security. The workplace needs driving energy, the display of talent, and the proof of one's worth; the home provides relaxation, renewal, and acceptance. The workplace requires one to be ready to change location, friends, and local attachments if advancement or better opportunities open elsewhere. It is a place (at least in the professional classes) of adventure, danger, and high stakes whose goal is success. The home is supposed to be stable, consistent, warm, and safe. Its goal is to sustain

131

and support the members of the family by providing a secure source of selfobject supplies.

On the surface, this social arrangement is terrific for the self. The public world offers more possibilities for self-realization than any previous society, while the home is able to offer the sustenance and nourishment the self needs to remain vital. However, whenever there is a strong division of values, there is bound to be tension and conflict between them. At first, this division was solved (for the middle classes) by dividing the responsibility for realizing the values in each sphere between the genders. In general, men occupied the public world of work and politics, while women were "the homemakers."[1] The values of the public sphere came to be associated with male values and those of the home with female values. For the past half century, this gendered solution for how to negotiate the different value spheres has more or less disappeared, as both men and women have adopted the workplace as the source of income, personal identity, and self-expression. With both genders fully engaged in the workplace, the values of love and intimacy started to seep into this arena, often with disastrous consequences. The public sphere has more or less solved this problem by intensifying the reign of public and impersonal values. Values of the home—sexual love, favoring those you like (rather than those who deserve it)—and empathic concern (rather than objective evaluation) are being excised from the office, classroom, and playing fields. As the public world makes selfobject experiences increasingly less available, the need for them in home life becomes ever more important.

And this is where the difficulty lies, for modernity is destabilizing the home, as pressures from the market make it increasingly difficult to maintain a relaxing, empathic, secure place where selves can be nurtured and sustained.[2] This destabilization takes a number of forms. First, the home is simply empty a lot of the time—it is more a place of loneliness than love. The parents are at work for increasingly long hours and the children are occupied with extracurricular activities, biding their time at childcare centers, or just being alone at home. The parents often assuage their guilt for being absent by buying things for their children, thus producing a kind of understimulated, overindulged child who feels both empty and entitled.

Second, many professional people have difficulty turning off the stress and strain of the work world when they do come home. The competitive tensions and little narcissistic injuries parents suffer on a daily basis make it hard for them to be present to and caring for one another or their families. Often the tensions and aggravations of the day are soothed by a martini or glass of wine, but this strategy, too, makes one less available as a selfobject for others. Hence, whether one is irritably aggressive or serenely high makes little difference when it comes to the ability to be present, caring, and empathic—the kind of person that everyone in the family needs, especially young children.

Third, the fatigue from work and commuting makes an evening in front of the television almost mandatory (the average household has 2.9 TVs and the average American watches four hours of TV daily—40 percent of his or her free time).[3] While family television watching probably has some residual selfobject effectiveness in that it can be a communitarian event, it is not a situation that calls forth empathy, strong idealization, or even much of a twinship bond. It is not an occasion in which younger children can see their parents as active centers of a dynamic life. Instead, they observe them as passive recipients of the standard fare of the society. They exhibit and enact, to the children's dismay, Heidegger's claim that the They is the subject of everyday experience. It is no wonder that the primary value of youth culture is to never grow up.

Fourth, one cannot watch television without being bombarded by images and narratives that are meant to stimulate desire and proclaim the ego world of success as the only normative reality. What is being sold through advertising in general is not this product or that but a way of life that centers on desire and the attainment of wealth and power needed to satisfy desire. In short, with the television at the heart of home life, the values of the home are being infiltrated, undermined, and replaced by the values of the market. The home becomes so bereft of selfobject supplies that dangerous substitutes for soothing, such as salty or sugary foods, are being consumed at rates that have turned America into the land of the obese.

Television, of course, now has to compete with cell phones, the Internet, and personal devices that can hold more music than one could listen to in a year. Indeed, if there has been any dramatic change in everyday life, it is how much it has become electronified. When I asked several classes of college students to estimate how much of their days were spent engaged with electronic experience—how many hours they were talking on phones of one kind or another, texting, working or playing on computers, watching television, or listening electronically to music, the general answer was eight to ten hours—more than half of each of their waking time per day. What this electronification of experience means is not fully clear, but it clearly deprives experience of a face to face quality. One of the great ethicists of the twentieth century, Emmanuel Levinas, has emphasized that it is the encounter with the face that humanizes us and grounds ethical life. When we do not have to look into another's eyes or see their facial expressions, we do not have the primary experience that calls forth our empathic concern.[4] Our fundamental interactions are now with machines and non-present others. Whatever else is involved in the electronification of life, it entails a decrease in the availability of empathic selfobject experiences.

The above is a benign assessment of the electronification of experience. A harsher and probably more accurate appraisal is that it involves a radical privatization of experience, a collapsing of experience into each person's own little world. Family television watching is largely a thing of the past; now many households have televisions for every member and each watches his own program. One of the effects of this arrangement is that the negotiations that used to occur in dividing up TV time—how do we decide who gets to see what—have been lost and with them occasions in which fairness could be learned. The electronic privatization of life takes other forms, including the erosion of the liveliness of public spaces. What used to be a fairly exciting hustle and bustle of airports, school hallways, or the downtowns in large cities in which strangers looked at one another with some intensity is now a set of individuals lost in conversations on cell phones, listening to iPods, or playing video games on private devices. It seems as though America has become the land of the Cyclops in which each person lives alone in his own cave.

The growing dominance of the values of the economic sphere is transforming the basic ways we think about ourselves and the world. It is, as Max Weber said, shifting from organizing life around activities that have intrinsic worth to organizing life with instrumental or functional values. When instrumental value becomes dominant, then everything in life—including spouses, family, and ourselves—becomes commodities, or what Heidegger calls "standing reserve."[5] The world is disclosed as one of standing reserve when everything is experienced in its readiness to do work for us. The tree is not simply a tree but a possible source of shade, firewood, fruit, a place to hang a swing, a thing that would fit our aesthetic delight more if it were trimmed, an obstacle to be cut down, and so on. What we lose is the tree as tree or, in Heidegger's words, the being of the tree. We even convert ourselves into standing reserve. We identify which of our skills and talents has the most value in the market, develop these, and sell it to the highest bidder. We transform ourselves from unique centers of perception and initiative into productive, efficient workers—standing reserve—who sell our skills to the highest bidders.

This "standing reserve" way of being imposes its values so innocuously that we do not even notice that a great horror has occurred. The actuality of the world has been transformed into a realm of possibility. Nothing is what it is but only what it can do for us. It cannot be experienced as having being or value in itself but only as having use-value.

When the imposition "to be useful" enters the home, those who ought to have intrinsic worth and individual being are unnoticeably transformed into standing reserve. "What have you done for me lately?" becomes the essential question. When spouses must constantly prove their worth to each other in terms of being sexually exciting, income-producing, service-rendering, and so on, then marriage is always on the verge of failure, for each of the partners might at any time find the other to be suboptimal or replaceable with someone who pleases them more. Hence, rather than being the relation that can supply the most secure selfobject support, contemporary marriage often turns out to be a source of sustained anxiety, as each partner continually questions whether the other is optimally satisfying them and worries about whether they are optimally satisfying their partner.

When the value of standing reserve falls on children, they feel the need to establish their worth—their use-value—rather than feeling that they are valued in themselves. This orientation typically leads to a premature relinquishing of childhood needs for attention and care and attending to the parents' needs, especially their need to have their children be special and great—a sports hero or the smartest kid in the class—in order to make the parents feel great. The pressure to be exceptional makes children feel anxious. "Will I be loved if I am not successful?" "What happens if others are more talented than I am in the next round and I fall behind?" There might be lovely assurances from the parents that, of course, they are loved for who they are, but the children can feel their parents' desperation to have special children as a compensation for their inner deficiencies.

Middle-class children are often raised with a strong anticipation that their most important achievement in life will be to have a successful position in the socioeconomic world. Since success is predicated on talent, skill, or special traits such as exceptional beauty or strength, these success-indicating traits are strongly re-enforced by the parents to the neglect of the self. The beauty of the little girl is affirmed, not the little girl who is beautiful; the athletic gifts of the young boy are applauded, not the boy who is athletically gifted. This kind of re-enforcement of traits leads to a fragmentation and depletion of the nuclear self. When these children grow up, they will have little ability to affirm or assert themselves but will tend to identify with their successful parts. When people suffering from this kind of background are not triumphing or using their talents to attain the admiration of others, they often feel empty, chaotic, and anxious.

Add to these sources of anxiety that the home is not a sacred place from which anxiety-free exploration of the world can occur but a house with a use-function that can be replaced by a better one at any time. When nothing has value in itself and everything is subject to market valuation, then life becomes abstract. We can abstract ourselves from spouses, families, friends, institutions, natural settings, homes, and so on if more useful—satisfying—alternatives come along. While the destabilized modern home is disastrous for the development and sustenance of selves, it does produce the kind of persons who can flourish in the public world of market interactions. They are driven by emptiness and since they distrust that their emptiness can ever be filled with love, they seek to fill the inner void with material goods, esteemed statuses, or successes of any kind. They are willing to sacrifice their self-needs and even their id-needs in order to achieve legitimation in the public economic world. That is, they compensate for a sense of inner emptiness by establishing grandiosity in the socioeconomic world. But this compensatory greatness never fully satisfies, for it never can repair the original injuries to the self, so ever greater successes, homes, spouses, vacations must be sought, and ever greater time must be put into work in order for these greater things to come into being. But profound contentment is never found, for this only comes when the self feels a deep inner sense of worth.

In short, the power of the economic system is completely colonizing the home space, making it difficult for persons to attain selfobject support there. When one adds to the depleted home the fact that professional ethics has forced empathy, care, and affection out of the workplace, we can see how hostile the modern world has become for the development and sustenance of selves.

I believe the seminal conceptual confusion that leads to the undermining of the selfobject world in modernity is the mistaking of the ego for the self. The "I" that is present in all ego experiences has as its fundamental goals legitimation, control, and power, while the self's needs are for love, relation, care, and expression. When the self is absent from conscious experience, the ego focuses on id demands and persona identifications, fusing them with its goals for power and success. This psychological constellation then generates the modern lifestyle of centering lives on professional work that grants legitimating persona statuses and generates income for the satisfaction of endless desires. The more this constellation takes hold, the more the self is ignored and lost from experience.

This conflict between the ego and the self is remarkably portrayed in the largest, and, some would claim, most compelling piece of music in the Western tradition, Richard Wagner's Ring Cycle. In the Ring, one set of characters—Alberich, Wotan, and Hagan—forswear love and seek wealth, domination, and legitimation. They want, above all else, the cursed ring of the stolen Rhine gold. For the Rhine maidens the gold is a thing of natural delight, shimmering in the sunlit water. But if someone forswears love and turns the gold into a ring, then it will grant world domination. This is just what Niebelungen Alberich does, and in so doing attracts the chief deity, Wotan, to the ring's power. It is not hard for the power of the ring to seduce Wotan, for he has already offered the goddess of love, Freia, to the giants for building the biggest and best mansion around—Valhalla. Another set of characters—Sigmund, Sieglinda, Brunnhilda, and Siegfried—seek love, union, wholeness, and the natural expression of themselves. The various leitmotifs associated with them—love, heroism, springtime, the sword—all stem from the basic nature motif which begins the work. What is natural for humans is to engage in reciprocal empathy, erotic excitement, and care. But this kind of being is being driven out of existence by a new kind of legitimation-focused creature. This creature so identifies with ego consciousness that it is haunted by profound emptiness and feelings of pervasive insecurity (especially Wotan). In the end, no one gets the ring, the gods go up in flames, and Alberich is defeated. These deaths do not, however, mean that love triumphs. Siegmund, Sieglinda, and Siegfried have already died or been killed. Supposedly, Brunnhilda's suicide at the end redeems the world for love, but there is no comedic resolution, no final victory of goodness. The world of love is forever vulnerable to the world governed by those who thoroughly identify themselves with the conscious ego.

BEING AN INDIVIDUAL VS. BEING A SELF

An essential reason why the self has been lost in the modern world is modernity's misconception of what it means to be an individual. It is true that having a self individuates one—makes one original and unique rather than one more variation of a socially coded way of life. Hence, the modern emphasis on individuality appears to favor a society of selves. However, modernity defines individuality as establishing one's difference from others and one's ability to be independent. It turns out that both values, while expressing aspects of the self, diminish our ability to develop and nourish our selves. They are not evil values but values which if not balanced by values of connectedness lead to a kind of ferocious ego-dominance of experience.

"Being different" is an attempt to capture a genuine aspect of the self—its singularity and specialness. However, since differentiation always concerns properties, characteristics, or statuses, it occurs within the realm of the general, and, as such, can never establish or express singularity. Since anyone can, in principle, have spiked purple hair along with a nose ring and tongue piercing, these properties—or any properties like them—can never express the singularity and specialness of the self. The self-sustaining feeling of being special comes only with the presence of the nuclear self. When a person's self is intact, it retains traces of its initial grandiosity and perfection and the person feels naturally special. Living with a sense of a singular specialness has three extraordinary consequences: it supports self confidence, diminishes the need for entitlement (since specialness is already present), and allows one to be loved and acclaimed without fear that infantile narcissism will be stimulated. These three benefits all enhance the sense of agency, of one's ability to assert oneself in the world without guilt or shame.

Establishing one's difference from others, on the other hand, does not increase self-confidence, decrease entitlement needs, make one feel more loveable, or augment the sense of agency. What being different does produce is the feeling that one is different, and this always carries with it a sense of alienation. Feeling like an alien increases one's sense of separation and isolation, a state that typically decreases a person's abilities to feel self-worth and to ask for selfobject support. Also, asserting difference almost always carries the sense of superiority with it. One is being different because those who follow the norm are not good enough for one. Feeling superior always seems to carry with it a residue of undeveloped infantile narcissism, while feeling special, when it comes from the presence of a self, need not involve either feeling superior or feeling alienated. In short, equating "having a self" with "being an individual who expresses difference" is psychologically disastrous. It cuts one off from selfobject supplies and reinforces an infantile expression of grandiosity.

The second defining characteristic of modern individuality—independence—might be even more detrimental to the self than the value of difference, for it causes persons to either reject or minimize selfobject support. The prominence given to the value of independence prematurely pulls children out of their families, makes fragile eighteen-year-olds think that they must go away to college far from their set of friends and family, and even causes many to avoid intimate love relationships. There are some European cities in which the households of single persons are almost half of the total households of the city, while in Chicago the number of single households is over a third. In *Bowling Alone* Robert Putnam documents how groups which have been supportive for years suddenly in the 1990s crumbled and disappeared.[6] It could be that the escalating economic pressures have forced people into more privatized spheres or that the values of independence have finally completely won over those of connectedness. Most likely, it was a combination of both these factors that did in the connectiveness of group associations. In terms of the value of independence, nothing much is lost in the disintegration of community activities, but from the viewpoint of self psychology, it is a catastrophic turn.

To explore an example I am most familiar with, look at the phenomenon of the young going away to college from the viewpoint of self psychology. Every year several million eighteen-year-olds will leave their homes and home towns to go away to college. There are a number of reasons why they do this, including the market reason that you are supposed to go to the best college or university that you can get into and a sense of youthful adventurousness, but the dominant conceptual framework for going away to college revolves around the need to establish oneself as independent from one's family and one's past.

In self psychological terms, what going away to college involves is a loss of the selfobject framework that has supported one for her entire life. This typically involves leaving one's family, close set of friends, favorite pets, favorite places that she knows can help restore her core, and the soothing world of the familiar. The only thing students can really bring with them is their music, and it is not by chance that college students are incredibly attached to the machines that play their favorite music. They are the only easily transportable selfobjects that can help soothe and restore them.[7]

This sudden loss of the sphere of selfobjects is traumatic for a number of students. The symptoms of this trauma can be seen everywhere during the first days of college—binge drinking, instantaneous love relationships, empty sexual forays, desperate phone calls back home, isolation, and intense clumping together into larger sustaining entities (the dorm wings). For some students the trauma will subside and they will have normal college lives, but for many others, the patterns of alcohol and drug misuse, shallow friendships, isolation, and mechanical work will keep them from full development during the college years.

The value of independence leads to further problems. It demands that we make our decisions by ourselves, despite the fact that we rarely have the experience, wisdom, and foresight to choose well, especially when we are young. Without others or some kind of tradition to rely on, we can depend only on the rational powers of the ego to guide us. As powerful and clearsighted as reason might be (its powers are, indeed, extraordinary), it has two intractable problems when it comes to realizing our selves. First, rational methodologies are supposed to work for all persons, and, hence, feel impersonal, for they fail to capture what is unique and special about one's self. Second, decisions achieved through these processes can feel manipulated and fake, for the weight put on variables is often simply arbitrary. How can a person attempting to decide whether to accept a job offer in a different city objectively weigh the importance of such variables as moving to a less desirable climate, moving away from good friends, disrupting the lives of one's children, going on new adventures, getting a higher salary, and so on?

It is Nietzsche's concept of the overman that most fully expresses modernity's notion of the differentiated independent individual. The overman will have no authorities over him and, thus, kills his religious impulse to believe in God. He will not follow anyone else's command or philosophy. He eschews the common and ordinary and, hence, flees from the marketplace to dwell in his solitude. He even despises reason as a ground for life, for reason fails to differentiate and individuate. The only ground for the free spirit is the creative pronouncement of "And so I will it." There is a kind of Kantian demand for purity in Nietzsche—the self must free itself of all foreign elements, as though every social input were defiling, negating, and confusing. The overman must even free himself from past decisions, for the past is what was chosen and as such constitutes a limitation on the spontaneous choice of the present. The overman is the individual ceaselessly creating his own world.

The contemporary version of this Nietzschean doctrine is that individuals are supposed to creatively "design" themselves. Carlo Strenger's *The Designed Self* details how young persons feel the pressure to create lives that have the marks of great art—originality, genius, beauty, and awe—and the psychological problems they encounter by holding this kind of ethic. The first problem of young persons who want to create their lives without reference to social codes or family hopes is that such self-designed lives teeter on the brink of meaninglessness. If one can make herself into anything, then what does it matter what she creates? Why is any one kind of designed life better than any other?

The second problem is that if I am free to create my own life, then how can I choose anything other than the most stupendous of lives, a life that is a monumental achievement. Great lives must both attain a generous amount of social goods (status, wealth, etc.) and also be rich with personal meaningfulness. "While they (GenXers) do not have to fight established authorities, they need to live up to the demand to create a life that combines financial, professional, and social success, together with having loads of fun and a sexy persona. . . . Particularly those gifted enough to have many options live with the constant anxiety that they might fail to live sufficiently spectacular lives."[8]

There is one other problem with the self-designed life that Strenger doesn't inquire into: who is doing the creating? If we do not yet have a self—for this is what is to be created, then it cannot be the self that is designing the self. Since self-design is an act of conscious choosing it must be an act of the ego, of the "I." The freedom so favored by Nietzsche and the self-designers is the kind of freedom that is favored by the ego—a freedom of choice, of openness, of possibilities, of action. It does not want to find that there might be an actual self that was unchosen and which was largely determined by early childhood relationships and genetic givens. This kind of self—the kind that Kohut finds to be the truth of ourselves—is abhorrent to the ego and its supreme value of freely creating/designing itself. Kohut's self expresses a personal destiny; the designed self refuses to acknowledge any set of limitations as to what kind of life can be chosen.

The concept of the designed self involves a conspiracy between the ego, id, and persona. It carries a high responsiveness to desire and options for satisfying desire, especially within the realm of social status. Since the ego always has the underlying problem of legitimacy, it will seek to satisfy desires in a way in which both the id and ideals of social legitimacy are satisfied. The id produces a desire for food and, if I am wealthy, I can eat at one of the esteemed restaurants, seemingly satisfying both my needs for food and legitimation. Insofar as it is the psychological axis of ego/persona/id designing the self, it is not by accident that the cherished life must have both lots of success (ego legitimation) and loads of fun (id satisfactions). The male fantasy of the perfect life seems to involve becoming a sports or entertainment idol, having unbelievably voluptuous sexual adventures, owning multiple grand residences in the most desirable parts of the world, and having no desire go unsatisfied. Note how this fantasy expresses not only the ego/persona's need for legitimation and the id's demand for pleasure but also a pathological kind of narcissistic grandiosity which indicates an injury to or nonrecognition of the self. Note also how this fantasy has no recognition of selfobject needs.

Insofar as modern persons remain enthralled with the values of independence and self-design, they will have trouble locating and expressing the nuclear self. The self is not open to all possibilities, attuned to problems of legitimation, or interested in most desires. It has particular traits, ideals, and ambitions which need to be developed in commitments. As such, it can be felt as a limitation to possibilities. The self is not interested in optimizing opportunities for desire satisfaction but in finding ways to express and develop itself. It wants to be what it actually is and is not interested in designing a set of possibilities that can maximize the enjoyment of life. Often, the path of self-development involves anguish, dismay, failure, and difficult overcomings—just what the ego working under a pleasure principle and the idea of freedom as openness does not like.

In sum, we have seen how modernity opens up possibilities for self-expression but also undermines the self in its destabilization of home life, its negation of selfobject relations in the workplace, its conceptualization of individuality in terms of difference and radical independence, and its understanding of freedom as the ability to openly design one's life. It is now time to reconceive what life under modern conditions might look like if we make the nuclear self the central focus of lived experience.

LIVING WITH ONE'S SELF

The shift from defining oneself as a market individual to someone concerned with developing and sustaining a self involves, first, a shift in one's conception of what life is about from the maximization of pleasure and the optimization of professional opportunity to the values of self-discovery, self-expression, and the attainment of vital selfobject support. The market person seeks independence and success and is willing to give up selfobject connections in order to optimize opportunities; however, when we live with sensitivity to the self, we realize that our selves extend into our selfobject relationships. To live robustly as a self means to commit to sustaining these relationships, even if this means lowering our advantages in the socioeconomic world. In short, self-persons in distinction from market-persons attempt to locate what activities best express the self or support the self in distinction from what satisfies desire. In our more technical vocabulary, it means being able to distinguish between ego/id/persona motivations and self-motivations.

And this brings us to the major problem with a self psychologically focused ethics: the need for subjects to know who they really are, for this involves knowing the self and the self is largely unconscious. How are we to know which motivations are located in the self and which come from other parts of the psyche?

Let us, along with Plato and the later Freud, name the primary sign which indicates the presence of self-motivation, *eros*. To be erotic is to be in love, with all the sense of heightened life and vitality that comes when we find ourselves in love, whether it is with another person, an activity, a place, or a work of art. The state of eros differs from the pleasureful satisfaction of desires in a number of ways. First, desires seem to stem from a particular want or need or place in the body, but when eros is present, it seems to touch everything we experience. The birds seem to sing more brightly and flowers reach out to us with their shimmering colors. The pleasures from desires come and go, but eros can remain not only for a day or a year but a lifetime. Socrates fell in love with philosophy at an early age and every time a philosophical occasion arose he became an impassioned lover, to such an extent that at the age of seventy he would rather die than roam the streets of Athens without being allowed to do philosophy. Particular pleasures satisfy particular desires or needs in us, but erotic love satisfies us. We feel most ourselves and most vital when we are erotic.

Plato calls eros a *daimon*—a special spirit that is not a full-blown god (which for Plato had to be complete and eternal), travels between the earthly and the divine, and moves the soul to seek ever higher forms of beauty.[9] I think that Plato's *daimon* and what Kohut calls the self are one and the same. While animals have desires and the gods rest in their perfection, eros seems to be a motivation peculiar to humans and lures them into a form of existence very different from either gratification or perfection: development. All living creatures desire; but humans strive to realize themselves. For Plato eros seeks objects that will complete us, make us whole. In its best known form, eros is sexual desire seeking another person with whom to unite. However, as Plato and even Freud saw, sexual desire is just one manifestation of eros, one way in which we try to become whole by forming a union.

While Kohut does not speak of an urge to wholeness, he presupposes it when he says that the psyche seeks to achieve psychological coherence and can do this only if there is a coherent self at its fulcrum. Ever since

Plato's first great description of the psyche as containing multiple sources of motivation, the healthy psyche has been conceived of as one in which the multiple sides of psychic life are not at war with one another but achieve some kind of harmony. It might be a harmony with tremendous tensions, such as Hegel's dialectical soul, but when the conflicting parts are organized, it leads to a dynamic psyche, rather than one tortured by internecine battles. The psyche seems to have an urge—an eros—to overcome its diremptions and achieve a wholeness or working harmony.

The striving for wholeness was mistaken by the ancient philosophers as a striving for perfection or self-sufficiency. They believed that teleological striving which did not attain a final goal would be incomplete and irrational and, hence, held that the soul had to unite with the eternal—the Forms, Nature's higher laws (Stoics), or God. As much as I respect the wisdom in the history of philosophy, I think that the yearning for perfection is a regressive pull back to primary narcissism, a flight from mature living in the real world of change, multiplicity, finitude, and loss. Striving to realize the self is the ever expanding attempt to integrate the parts of one's psyche and to integrate oneself in the world. It is an adventure that is never complete, for the psyche can always explore connections beyond any state it achieves. If the self is not a thing but a dynamic process, then achieving wholeness cannot be conceived of as a static state of completion but as a temporal attunement of the parts whose future horizons seem to be real possibilities related to the present rather than abstract fantasies or dull repetitions.

In an age in which postmodernism has thoroughly critiqued the value of wholeness as being anti-diversity, anti-otherness, and anti-life, why should it be a value at all? Again, I think we need to specify the level of discourse in order to be clear. Fragmentation of the self typically results in the ego's erecting defensive apparatuses that limit the possibilities and spontaneity of a person. However, if the self is coherent and harmonious (its traits, ambitions, and ideals are aligned), then the person can be consciously spontaneous, adventurous, and open to otherness or diversity without fear of retraumatization. A person with a coherent self who experiences a significant degree of wholeness need not be inclined to impose values of sameness on others or herself.

As Plato recognizes in the *Phaedrus*, eros is a kind of divine madness. People in love appear to be mad in that they lose a rational orientation toward life, often foregoing food and sleep, happy to suffer countless miseries for just a glance at their beloveds. There is something divinely mad about the self and its erotic passions, for they are thoroughly singular and original. The spark of singular originality is always a bit mad, for it defies explanation according to codes or causal chains. No one can ex-

plain either to others or themselves why they have fallen madly in love
with a profession, another person, or a place. To be a self is to participate
in the mysterious. We are not to look to others, copy them, or dissipate self
energies in the mired codes of ordinary life. We are to discover our unique
selves and act with a spark of divine originality (Emerson), without worry
of what the They will think. Nietzsche has the overman laugh at himself
and life, for he acts beyond codes that define what makes sense. While
Kohut does not write about the self as a kind of divine madness, he does
think that having a mature self means that one must laugh, create, and
acknowledge death, and these acts are all tinged with madness.

When we erotically act from our original singularity rather than from
codes embedded in the social unconscious or plans devised by the rational
ego, we feel dynamically active. This feeling of being an active cause of
one's life is seen by a number of the West's foremost philosophers as the
central value of psychological life. For Plato, the essence of the soul is to be
"self-moving" and Aristotle's entelechy is a principle of growth from the
inside rather than growth in response to challenges from the world. For
Spinoza, we feel joy to the extent that we are the active cause of our actions,
pain to the extent we are passive. Most of the time we are in a mixed state—
our experiences are in part determined by what the world and our bodies
are doing to us and in part by our active response to these imposed conditions. This mixed state of dealing with our everyday desires, drives, wants,
and needs always has a sense of being caught in a web of necessity. It is only
when we find a different source of motivation in ourselves—one whose
motion comes out of itself rather than as a response to internal or external
pressures—that we become most alive and free.

Since eros is a force that is active and striving but also a state in which
one feels whole, there is obviously a tension between eros as completion
and eros as striving. I believe that this tension is part of what makes the self
so dynamic. The striving and sense of wholeness are not a contradiction
because the essence of the self is the realizing of its ideals and ambitions. In
striving to achieve its ambitions and ideals, the self is being itself. The feeling whole is in the striving. This is, of course, paradoxical, for to be striving
means to be not yet whole; but if the self's very nature is dynamic, then it
feels most whole, most one with itself, when it is actively striving to achieve
its ideals and ambitions. The self's being is its becoming.

Striving, insofar as it is in the service of the self's ambitions and ideals, is equivalent to self-development. Since development requires us to
strive beyond where we are now, it usually involves suffering and labor.
This is another way in which eros differs from pleasure-seeking. Freud
found that the pleasure principle is conservative—it seeks to remain in
a state of nontension—it does not like to struggle, for struggle is pain.
Indeed, even though erotic striving brings the most intense of pleasures

when self-fulfillment is achieved, what usually confuses us or stands in the way of self-development are the pleasures of relaxation, entertainment, and the familiar.

Self-development is a union of unconscious determination and conscious design. The self is not just anything, not a pure potentiality, but a set of definite and peculiar possibilities—its ownmost possibilities. The self has a fate, for it has just these ideals and ambitions and no others. While this fate resides in the unconscious nuclear self, a person must make conscious commitments to the fields of development where the self finds itself most alive in order for the self to come to full fruition. That is, the fullness of self-developmental activity is a joint production of the ego and the self.

In *Therapeutic Action* Jonathan Lear holds that commitments form the essence of who we are and that our commitments must be to activities or relationships in which development is possible. We can't be committed to hair brushing, for this is too simple, but we can become expert hair dressers. We can't be committed to digging holes in the ground, but we can commit to becoming fine gardeners. In short, in order for the self to develop, it must make commitments to develop within activities, fields of endeavor, or relationships.

I have had many student advisees express to me a horror at having to declare a major. They have taken great delight in exploring the rich and multifaceted liberal arts curriculum at Colorado College and do not want to limit their academic adventures. They are in love with the freedom of choice and do not want to be forced to take required courses in a single field. They are modern persons. Yet, without limitation and commitment their education will amount to little: thirty or so exciting courses, all soon forgotten as one course replaces another. If they do not commit themselves to a discipline, then little personal or mental growth occurs. Once they say, "I am a this"—a biology major or Renaissance scholar—then they grow. In short, development occurs within the commitments we make.

Desires do not demand commitment; eros does. I can desire a great Italian dinner tonight without being committed to fully exploring the realm of Italian food. Many people make commitments to a love relationship or a profession, but not to development in these commitments, as though they were stable things rather than dynamic activities. When commitment without development happens, the love or work can easily become stale and repetition takes over and the self fails to be fully nourished. I am alive in my marriage so long as my commitment makes me seek ever more complex levels of intimacy, although each move to a new level of love usually involves anxiously moving to more profound levels of vulnerability. As Nietzsche says, going beyond ourselves is the most difficult of tasks, but it is the only way to be fully alive and escape the possibility of life falling into an average everyday routine punctuated by frantic escapes into excitement. While our souls can be erotically stimulated whenever they encounter beauty, our erotic commitments must, by necessity, be few or else they will dissipate our energies.

When we add the notion of commitment to eros, our understanding of it transforms. Until now I have spoken of eros and the experience of self-realization in a highly romantic way—as exorbitant life, the feeling of radiance, profound embodiment, ecstatic presence, dynamic activity overcoming passivity, and so on. I believe that such extraordinary experiences are possible and that they have a powerful effect on the course of an individual's life, but, in the end, what counts is not having exceptional experiences but the ability to live in a heightened way in ongoing committed relationships and endeavors. Exceptional experience can reveal to us new and more profound ways in which the self can express its nuclear program, but the sustained life of a person requires that the self find a way to be present in the midst of the ongoingness of everyday life.

For Heidegger the everyday typically descends into busy routine governed by social pressures, but the dailyness of life need not be passive if one can develop a strong self/ego axis such that the self is present even when it is not engaged in one of its favored activities. Paying bills, cleaning toilets, washing dishes, shopping for food, taking the car in for an oil change, calling the insurance company and being put on hold, getting caught in traffic, scheduling dentist appointments around professional obligations and family commitments, and hundreds of other such daily experiences have the ability to pull us into a dull mechanical efficiency, put us in a mood of general irritability, or simply fragment us. When we have a strong ego/self axis, these distracting experiences have far less ability to drive us into a dull depressiveness with anger lingering on the edges, for they now occur within the context of a meaningful life.

In sum, we might say that the desiring-person finds gratification to be the essence of life. Desires provide the impetus to action, thought, and organizing the world. The desiring-person is always seeking stimulation and always fighting off a dread of emptiness or boredom. Her self-generating motion tends to be disorganized and conflicted, as many desires vie for satisfaction. She longs for excitement but has trouble with commitments and establishing values of sustained importance. Such a person has, in Plato's words, a democratic soul, for it pays heed to all of the claims that desires make on it. As such, this kind of person is the most colorful, energetic, chaotic, and adventuresome of all the kinds of persons, but she is also like a city in conflict and one constantly verging on a meaningless anarchy.

On the other hand, the self-realizing person with an erotic soul proclaims the development and expression of the self to be her primary aim in life. This kind of person distinguishes what she desires from what she loves and commits herself to the activities and relationships she most loves. She seeks to develop herself in her commitments and to achieve ever greater unifications of the psychic parts and between herself and the world. She understands that development always involves suffering, and she accepts—even cherishes—this as a condition of growth. In contrast to the desiring-person's seeking pleasure, the self-realizing person seeks the happiness that comes from growth toward an ideal. If the desiring-person seeks excitement, the self-realizing person follows her loves and grows through them. If the desiring-person colorfully explores everything, the self-realizing person focuses on her loves. In her self-given limitations she achieves strength, coherence, and meaning.

AGENCY AND FREEDOM

Modern persons, whose highest value is freedom, tend to associate being free with having open opportunities. When we shift to a focus on the self, however, we understand freedom in a different, more complex way, one which combines the modern notion of freedom as environmental opportunity with the classical conception of freedom as agency. To attain a full sense of agency, one's character, self, and ego must work together in a world that offers opportunities for self-realization.

While modern philosophers have tended to define freedom as an environmental condition—the condition of having open possibilities for choice in the world—the ancient Greek philosophers focused on the psychological conditions necessary for a person to be able to make a choice. Aristotle and Plato understood that even if the world provided opportunities not everyone was equally capable of having a self-directed life. They found the power of the passions to be so overwhelming that they could reduce life to a kind of blind pursuit of immediate satisfactions. Aristotle held that we needed the moral virtues to moderate the power of the passions to give reason a chance to think about what is best. It is the combination of the virtues moderating the passions and reason being able to deliberate about which choices were optimal that allowed a person to become a self-determining human being. An impulsive, rich teenager shopping in a mall might satisfy all the requirements for being free in the modern empirical sense but would not be an agent for Aristotle, as her desires are not really hers nor is she capable of organizing choices and desires into something that looks like "having a life."

Aristotle's account of agency, while being one of the most important ever developed in the West, has three crucial flaws. First, the virtues themselves are non-individuating, for any wise person who is virtuous and rational will tend to make the same choices. The virtuous person does not act from her singularity but acts the way a wise person ought to act.

Second, this kind of virtuous rational agency disallows freedom as spontaneous passionate expression. Spontaneity is the kind of freedom championed by the Romantics and naturalists and, while not the only kind of free act, is certainly an essential element of freedom. Third, neither the virtues nor reason can transform what Freud found to be the greatest hindrance to agency: unconscious pathology. A good, moderate person might rationally apprehend that a compulsive ritual makes no sense and is constricting his life, but this does not mean that he can choose not to perform the ritual. Aristotle goes a long way in describing the conditions that allow us to be agents, but we still need to know how individuated spontaneous agency is possible and be given a way to overcome the constrictions of unconscious motivation.[10]

Self psychology offers important responses to these problems with the Aristotelian account of freedom. First, it recognizes what is uniquely individual about persons—the self. It is the one part of the psyche that is individual, for the id is encumbered with common biological urges, the persona is bemired in social types, and the ego operates with a generalized rationality. Because the liberal empiricists and Kant did not recognize the self as a unique psychological structure, they tried to locate freedom in the realm of desires or a purified rationality, and both failed. When we turn to the self, we find that although it has biological roots and is inherently intertwined with others in its selfobject relationships, there is something radically original and singular about it. Even when the self is being built through selfobject identifications, it devours the selfobjects and turns them into its own protein. It actively resists inputs that are not aligned with its core, while it consumes and transforms what is. It asserts its particularity with vigor and seeks ideals that can express its unique talents and ambitious energy.

The self is the original individuality that Emerson exhorts us to realize, throwing off foreign models and socially coded shackles. Thoreau did not think that being natural and free was opening up to the id forces and spontaneously being sexual or animal-like. Being freely natural for him is finding the core self in distinction from the imposed model that society wants us to be. The expression of any other part of the psyche is tinged with passivity or the abstractness of rational decision making. Only the self has the divine spark of daimonic originality, and when it directs our lives, we experience a profound sense of being naturally who we are and free.

Genuine freedom is the ability to be who one is and to act in accordance with one's essential nature. When one says, "I cannot do anything else, given who I am," this is not a constriction of freedom but its highest statement. It is Socrates at his trial remaining true to his philosophic calling; it is Martin Luther proclaiming his faith before a papal tribunal, knowing that such a proclamation will lead to his excommunication; it is Fred Astaire dancing and Katharine Hepburn being Katharine Hepburn. It is, in Heidegger's terms, being true to one's ownmost possibilities. Since one is in part defined by a set of commitments, we are most free when we act within the limitations of our commitments.

When we locate the core of human freedom in a person's ability to realize her self and also understand that the self is largely unconscious, then we must take seriously the constrictions that can arise from defensive unconscious processes. Since it is an extremely rare person these days that does not harbor some unconscious injuries, the crucial question becomes how to overcome unconscious defensive constrictions. This is an extremely difficult question, for the very psyche that is trying to overcome its pathology is infected by it. I think that the psychoanalytic tradition in general and self psychology in particular are right in claiming that one probably needs a guide—a therapist—to help one out of these troubles. I would love it to be the case that humans could easily self-repair, but this hope embodies the old concept of the self-sufficient individual who does not need others. Minimally, the conception of freedom elaborated here makes us aware of unconscious limitations in a way that is not available in the empirical, ancient, or Kantian models of freedom. If we accept the need for social and political agencies to open up the realm of opportunity, we should be able to accept the need for therapeutic help in overcoming unconscious obstacles.

In sum, becoming a person capable of acting freely is a complex matter that involves the development of a coherent vital self, the development of the virtuous character traits, the maturation of deliberative rational capacities, and the continual opening up of opportunities for self-expression and selfobject relationships in the wider world. Without a self, freedom amounts to little more than opportunities for the satisfactions. It is the self's realizing itself that is the core to feeling like a free agent. However, the self without character will be overruled by the id passions; the self without a rich, open society will have few options for how to express itself; and the self without the powers of reason will not be able to make careful choices for how best to realize its nuclear program. And, we must remember, that much in life has nothing to do with self-realization. We make choices between items on a luscious menu that have more to do with our tongues and mood than with our deep core natures. Decisions about insurance policies, what kind of computer to purchase, which plumber to call, and so on have a lot to do with efficiency and getting the most for your money and very little to do with how to be self-determining. Hence, I do not propose that we replace modernity's conceptualization of freedom as choice between opportunities but add to it the freedom that comes from the self's asserting itself. It is especially crucial in an age where environmental influences are so pervasive and potent that we find some way to distinguish between motivation that is essentially mine from that which does not express anything essential about me.

CONCLUSION

I have tried to show in this chapter how modernity produces both material conditions and conceptualizations of individuality and freedom that undermine our abilities to develop, access, and assert the self. I have attempted to distinguish a life lived around the notion of self-development from that lived for the maximum experiencing of pleasure, and I have worked out what individuality and freedom mean from the viewpoint of self psychology. However, the possibility of having a world come into existence in which the focus of life is the self cannot rest merely in the hands of individuals changing their conceptualizations of what life is about. In order for a self-oriented modernity to come into existence, a number of social institutions and practices also must change. It is to these changes that we now turn.

NOTES

1. See especially Carol Gilligan's *In a Different Voice* (Cambridge, MA: Harvard University Press, 1981) and Ross Poole's *Morality and Modernity* (New York: Routledge, 1991).
2. Ross Poole makes these points in chapter 4 of *Morality and Modernity*.
3. Morris Berman, *Dark Ages America* (New York: Norton, 2005), 26.
4. See Levinas's essay, "Ethics as First Philosophy," in *The Levinas Reader*, ed. Seán Hand (Oxford: Basil Blackwell, Inc. 1989).
5. Martin Heidegger, "The Question Concerning Technology," in *Martin Heidegger: Basic Writings*, ed. David Krell (New York: Harper Collins, 1977).
6. Robert Putnam, *Bowling Alone* (New York: Simon & Schuster Paperbacks, 2000).
7. Kohut does not talk about objects having the capability of being selfobjects, but it is clear that some—especially music—can help restore self functioning in certain circumstances.
8. Carlo Strenger, *The Designed Self* (Hinsdale, NJ: Analytic Press, 2005), xiv.
9. See Plato's *Symposium*.
10. These same criticisms can be made of Kant's concept of freedom: it, too, is non-individuating, unable to accommodate spontaneity, and ineffective in dealing with unconscious constrictions.

EIGHT

SOCIAL TRANSFORMATIONS

When a major overthrow of a set of established conditions is proposed, it typically calls for some form of social revolution. Indeed, modernity and revolution seem to go hand in hand. The American, French, and British Revolutions destroyed monarchal and aristocratic privilege and instituted democracy as the regnant political structure of modern life. The Industrial Revolution fully transformed the nature of material life. The revolutions of 1848 had a significant impact on the further democratization of Europe. Marx called for a Communist Revolution that would overcome the evils of capitalism and establish a more equitable economic society. Such revolutions occurred in many countries, including two of the most important, Russia and China. In no previous age has revolution been so successful a tool of political transformation. Revolution has been such a powerful vehicle of change that some theorists have proclaimed that having a "revolutionary consciousness" is the most important way to be alive, for all established orders, no matter what they are, are deadly precisely in their being established and orderly.

I do not advocate a revolutionary overthrow of capitalist-based modernity for three reasons. First, violent revolutions, regardless of what they accomplish in terms of social change, always bring with them trauma, chaos, and the negation of the stable conditions that are necessary for the development of selves. Second, even with all the injustices, suffering, and disruption of traditions that a global market system causes, it still appears to be unrivaled as an economic system in its ability to produce an abundant material life. Third, I believe that modernity is the only form of human life (so far) that supplies the conditions necessary for selves to have the possibility for full actualization. It supplies these conditions by expanding the possibilities for working, recreating, and loving—for having a life—so far beyond what had been previously possible that it constitutes a new world. Being a self in the ancient world was more or less of an interior activity, as having a self-directed life in the world was something available only to an extremely small minority of privileged males. Modernity offers the possibility for "having a life" to immeasurably more people with immeasurably more choices for finding activities that resonate with the self.

What modernity needs is not a violent social revolution but a revolutionary conceptual shift from thinking about life fundamentally in economic terms to thinking about it psychologically. If this shift can be effected, then many of the problems we have seen that haunt modern persons will be alleviated without a concomitant loss of the genuine goods of modern life. What I propose is that we keep the material benefits and personal opportunities that modernity offers but reject its concept of human nature and its understanding of what it means to live a good life. This is not impossible, for the view of humans as satisfaction-optimizing organisms is not required by market economics, evolutionary theory, or liberal democracy. Modern people can readjust their final values toward being selves, establishing selfobject networks, and ethically recognizing the need for others to have these opportunities without having to relinquish a robust existence in the material world or giving up a naturalistic view of human nature. The modern world will, of course, be severely torqued, perhaps beyond easy recognition, as it makes profound adjustments to the loss of insatiable desires and the refusal of humans to be driven, compulsive workers who equate worth with monetary compensation.

Before elaborating the social conditions which I think must be transformed in order for the modern world to be genuinely responsive to the needs of the self, I should make one point clear. Just because modernity has lacked an adequate notion of self does not entail that modern persons have no selves. If we had no selves, we would be psychotic or borderline persons—that is, we would have no ground by which to organize experience and could not form a social order. Selves are not developed by "having an adequate concept of a self." They are formed through processes of nurturance, mirroring, idealization, and transmuting internalization. These processes tend to occur "naturally" in the bonding that occurs between parents or loving caretakers and children. If our psychological well-being depended on our holding correct theoretical ideas, we would not have survived as a species!

However, ideas about who we are and what constitutes a good life do affect how we live and what we most value. If our patterns of living based on these values result in systematically downplaying the needs of the self for mirroring, empathy, optimal frustration, commitment, and selfobject support, then our selves are more likely to feel under-supported, unrecognized, or, in more severe cases, traumatized. That modernity is producing a kind of person who is in a constant state of self-distress I take to be true from the prevalence of the symptoms I have mentioned—narcissistic vulnerability and entitlement, a dread of inner emptiness, an extreme tendency toward self-referencing, ungrounded restlessness, a parceliza-tion of life, and, of course, the tendency to cheat. These symptoms are not the result of an overvaluation of the self, as many of the communitarian thinkers seem to believe, but are the outcome of depleted persons at-tempting to compensate for the lack of a firm and self-affirming self.

When a person has attained a coherent self, found activities in which to realize her nuclear program, and developed relationships that can be counted on for trustworthy and consistent selfobject support, then experi-ence has a very different quality to it than what I have described as the typical modern experience. With a self at the psychological center, we do not have the same degree of personal vulnerability and insecurity that characterizes modern living. The self that is injured or under-developed always feels vulnerable, fragile, and capable of disintegration at any time. It feels it must ward off attacks and, hence, falls apart or gets overly de-fensive with criticism and is constantly fantasizing about sources of great-ness that might sustain it—fame, wealth, prestige, a mansion, a status automobile, and so on. An intact self is not as worried about attacks and seeks genuine self support from others rather than from images of great-ness. That is, a person with an integral self already feels her specialness and greatness and, hence, does not need surrogate images of it.

The crucial question that we must address is: "What transformations should modern society undergo to better foster persons' having selves?" Rather than proposing a massive social revolution in the name of self psychology, I wish to present six "little revolutions" in the way we struc-ture and respond to modern life. If all six little revolutions occurred, modern life would be transformed into a social world in which selves could much more easily flourish.

1. Restore the Family

The crucial years for the formation of the self are the first half decade of life. During this time children need consistent, empathic mirroring, sensi-tive care, the ability to merge with an idealized selfobject, safety, and the attention to the usual daily needs for such things as food and warmth. In general our society does fine in recognizing the material and safety needs of children but is negligent in recognizing the psychological needs of self-development. In order for these self needs to be met, parents or caregivers need to be profoundly and consistently involved with the lives of their children and to do this they must spend considerable time at home, some-thing very hard to do for the typical two–wage earner family.

In calling for the reinstatement of the primacy of family life, I seem to be echoing the program of conservative Christianity. While both self psychol-ogy and conservative religious groups champion the importance of family values, how they conceive of the optimal family is very different. The conservative patriarchal family is hierarchical and organizes itself through the imposition of superego values. It uses shame and guilt to achieve conformity to its vision of goodness. It does not affirm the narcissistic selves of children or delight in their idiosyncrasies and grandiose displays but attempts to make them conform to an ideal of what a good child ought to be in order that they might grow up to be what a good adult ought to be. What is most valued is a vision of "the right way to live" rather than the particular individuals who are in the family. This kind of atmosphere tends to produce considerable anxiety in children who must worry about whether they can ever be good enough or what punishments (especially the loss of mirroring affirmation) await them if they fail. This constrictive kind of family can be as damaging to the development of self-structure as the empty, under-nourished modern household.

In contrast, self psychology would have us affirm and attend to the particularity of the children before us, empathically responding to who they are rather than affirming them only if they fit an ideal of excellence. Of course, children need to be given guidance, values, and limits. Solving problems through physical violence is wrong; running out into the street is forbidden; stealing from other children is not tolerable, and so on. But setting limits and giving guidance are different from imposing on children an ideal for who they must be regardless of who they are.

Giving enough consistent and empathic care to young children for them to develop core selves seems to require more time, energy, and personal interaction than is typically available to young adults who are at the same time attempting to establish their careers. It is common that the parents of young children live away from their parents and so cannot count on grandparents to give consistent nurturance. Paid help is available in terms of nannies and childcare centers, but their quality of empathic concern is questionable. This problem of giving adequate care to children while establishing one's identity (and self!) in the professional world has torn sensitive young parents apart now for over half a century—ever since it became questionable for women to stay at home to mother. The women's movement was right in pointing out that the burden of parenting fell unfairly upon one gender and that women needed to have equal professional opportunities to those of men, but there was no one to lead the children's movement to demand what they most deserve—consistent and empathic love.

Here's the rub: modernity demands that young adults establish themselves in the socioeconomic world at the same time that it is optimal for them to begin a family. If we take seriously that the most important thing that can ever happen in life is for a person to develop a coherent self in early childhood and realize that this cannot happen without nurturing consistent care, then something must give way in the demands of professional life such that the selfobject needs of young children can be systematically met.

How can we solve this problem with the least disruption to present society? I feel uncomfortable as a philosopher whose job is to think carefully about important concepts to offer advice for how to construct institutions in the socioeconomic world, but I feel called upon to offer at least a few suggestions, all of which might work, especially in conjunction with one another, to help make family life stronger.

The least disruptive solution would be to allow dynamic young parents set on establishing their professional identities to be able to leave their children during work hours at selfpsychologically oriented daycare centers. These centers would be run by childcare professionals who know about the psychological needs of children, are especially empathic, and have strong selves to hold idealizations. Such people are, obviously, not easy to come by now, but I believe that when such persons are validated as worthy, they will appear and be able to enjoy this kind of important work. I would also recommend that the government subsidize the salaries of such trained childcare workers, since they will be some of the most talented, sensitive, and intelligent members of our society and young parents rarely have the financial wherewithal to pay them what they deserve.

This suggestion will, of course, hardly solve the problem, for the core of healthy childhood narcissism is the feeling that one is very special and it is difficult to have this feeling in a group situation. No one can have a gleam in their eye for a child like a mother or father can. The best solution to the child nurturance problem is simply the ability for parents to be home in an energized, available way as much as possible. The easiest way for this to happen is for as much work as possible to be done in the home or for businesses/professional institutions to offer highly flexible work hours such that one parent can be home in the morning, one in the afternoon, and so on. A less formal way of solving the problem is for young adults to live close to one of their sets of parents, so that grandparents can share more fully in the raising of the children.

A number of European governments have subsidies for stay-at-home parents and I think that such a social program is required if children are going to get the selfobject home milieu that they need. Rather than spending the massive amounts of money we are now putting into the penal system to punish persons whose psychological injuries have made them antisocial, violent, and immaturely narcissistic, why not use the funds to foster family conditions that would decrease the likelihood of criminality later in life?

2. Prioritize Selfobject Relationships

Even if strong selves are developed in early childhood, they need to be sustained through the rest of life with meaningful selfobject relationships. A selfobject relationship is not just one of support or care but an on-going relation in which we entrust a part of ourselves to another human being. Kohut's theory of the self involves a radical de-centering of the notion of self—our selves are not isolated identities in our psyches but are partly held in our relationships with others. Insofar as modernity values mobility, independence, and adventure over location, interdependence, and stability, it puts tremendous strain on sustaining selfobject relations. Further, the competitiveness of the workplace and the loss of relaxed friendship time put sustaining relations even further at risk. Without the safety of strong selfobject relationships, the self cannot risk being fully present in the world. It retreats and lets the ego take over experience. This retreat of the self and abandonment of experience to the ego perfectly coincides with the traits that economic society needs to run efficiently and productively. But the self goes wanting.

The general sentiment in modernity is that friends are replaceable. We pay "friendship" great lip service, proclaiming friends to be the most important thing in life, but in reality the mobility of modern economic society means that we have to be prepared to leave friends and they us at a moment's notice. The best friends of high school days are abandoned when we go off to college. College friends are abandoned when we leave to make our ways in the world. And adult friends are left when better opportunities become available. Such is modern life. Even spouses—the most crucial selfobjects—are replaced often enough in the contemporary world. This feeling that friends are variables who can be replaced is one reason why modern life does not feel quite real. If others really do hold parts of oneself, then to make them expendable is to make parts of oneself replaceable. We become so adaptable to the pressures of the market that we cease being actual beings and become, in Heidegger's words, "standing reserve."

The radical individualism and replaceability of all friends that characterize modern life means that our selves cannot risk exposing their vulnerability and leave experiencing to the ego. The ego, of course, not only can tolerate the making and losing of friends but rather delights in its adaptability. This is why the ego and the modern world are so in love with one another. But the self is left out, for it is not so adaptable. It has a definiteness which is partially defined by its particular selfobject relationships. When these are constantly severed or lost, the self then becomes less secure, and without security, the self cannot be fully at ease asserting itself in the world.

This little revolution of taking selfobject relationships seriously would mean that modernity's values of abstractness, adaptability, and mobility would have to be balanced by the self's need for stable ongoing selfobject relations. When we prioritize the importance of selfobject relations, it is not so easy to move away from one's parents, to change jobs, or to pull up stakes whenever one pleases. If organizations—especially businesses— prioritized the psychological health of their members, then they would be less inclined to disrupt their lives by demanding that they change location to advance in the company. Since this suggestion adds a balancing value to the key market values of productivity, efficiency, and profitability, it might sound utopist. However, there is strong evidence for the claim that persons who feel psychologically well-supported at work are also more efficient and productive.

Notice, I am not advocating a kind of stultifying stability in which all relationships must remain constant, for such a state is antithetical to the life of the soul. However, the modern world emphasizes change, disruption, and adventure so much that it negates the kind of social world that selves need to flourish.

3. Humanize the Workplace

The workplace has become increasingly professionalized, with only the values of functionality being permitted. We are supposed to do our functions as best we can, be judged by our productivity in those functions, and leave the rest at home. There are genuinely important reasons why the values of love, care, and emotional responsiveness have been forsaken in the workplace. Aside from their interference with the values of optimal productivity, they often lead to favoritism, sexual harassment, exploitation, and other forms of injustice. Women especially suffer when nonprofessional values are allowed to roam freely through the halls both in terms of the excessive empathy they are expected to give and the unwarranted sexual attention directed toward them. But getting rid of these evils has also typically involved lessening an ambience that is supportive of the self. The baby has been thrown out with the bathwater. Constructing an atmosphere in the workplace which recognizes and supports the needs of the self need not lead to sexualization or other forms of exploitation but precisely the opposite. It is people with injured selves who need to sexualize, diminish, control, and use others. The more the self is intact, the less it needs to desperately fill up an inner emptiness by displays of power or seeking sexual substitutions.

The workplace for many is not just a place for identity/persona formation but an important arena for self-expression. This is not just because professional life can offer particular fields in which the self can realize its nuclear ideals and ambitions but because it is one of the major areas in modern life in which we encounter situations of optimal frustration and achievement—the kinds of experience that are central to the developmental line of narcissistic grandiosity. Most of us feel a surge of greatness when we accomplish a difficult task that has social recognition attached to it, even if it does not involve the use of our favored talents or skills. These experiences of triumphant accomplishment help the self retain its buoyancy. Concomitantly, the workplace also seems to be a place where the self encounters defeats and blows to its esteem, for it is a place of competition and often others do better or get more recognition than we do. Whether for positive or negative, the workplace deeply affects our abilities to sustain our selves.

Given that the workplace is so central to the health and buoyancy of the self, it is crucial that it understand and know how selfobject needs operate and be able to offer appropriate selfobject supplies. This might mean little more than shifting from an attitude that at work humans are primarily functionaries to an attitude that sees workers as persons with vulnerable selves who have needs that functionaries do not. They are not needs for sex, special treatment, endless approval, or cheerful support but for respect, empathic concern, and care.

The above suggestion that the workplace be responsive to selfobject needs requires extensive qualification. If the selfobject needs exist at an immature level due to injuries to the self, then the workplace is not responsible for the transformation of these needs. It cannot take the place of a therapist. Also, insofar as selfobject needs get fused with sexual desire—not an uncommon occurrence—they threaten the stability of the workplace and open up the possibility for harassment and seduction. This is not tolerable. However, one can be empathic, caring, supportive, and interactive with other human beings without crossing over into other relational territories—friendships, sexual involvements, buddies, pals.

A widespread problem for selves attempting to survive and flourish in the workplace is the presence of a person who exudes a kind of poison to the selves of others. Someone is toxic to others when his general modus operandi involves undermining the self-esteem of others and lowering their sense of liveliness in order to gain power over them or assert their own pathological narcissism. For the most part the undermining, controlling, lessening activity is unconscious and not available for conscious adjustment. The toxicity is often hidden within legitimated forms of interaction, but one still feels one's confidence getting shaky, vitality draining, and rage emerging when in the presence of such people. In situations where toxic people have authority over one, life in the workplace seems almost unbearable.

Toxicity comes from injuries to the self that have as one of their outcomes a primitive envy at persons who have selves. This kind of person cannot tolerate the presence of what they do not have in others, and so they attempt to destroy the selves of others. I have found almost no way to confront this kind of toxic person with positive results. For the most part, I try to escape the poison by avoiding the person as much as I can. They certainly need help to repair their injured selves, but it is not at all clear how to get them to recognize their injuries and need for help. My guess is that for many, if not most, toxic persons, such help must be required by a superior or it will not be gotten.

4. Tolerate—Even Celebrate—Grandiosity

The fourth little revolution in modern life that I propose is to tolerate, even celebrate, the need of the grandiose self to display its specialness. We have inherited from our Puritan forefathers a dislike and distrust of any display of grandiosity, from making elaborate communion rails in church to celebrating one's achievements. Perhaps there would be far less pretentiousness in modern life if we knew how to foster and accept occasions of genuine self celebration. I admit to being nauseated by all the "We're number one" displays about everything from college football teams to first graders who win a spelling bee. The problem with "We're number one-ism" is both that it is a display of immature narcissism in that it typically involves primitive identifications with greatness and it occurs within a competitive context in which one's triumph implies another's defeat. While I think that the feeling of specialness is crucial to feeling a sustained vitality in life, I do not think that it must come at the loss of specialness on the part of others, although sometimes this is necessary. For Aristotle both boastfulness—an overestimation of one's specialness—and humility—an underestimation of one's greatness—are vices that miss the virtuous mean: a proper pride in one's accomplishments.

While Kohut validates our needs to feel special and grandiose, their expressions need to keep maturing to age appropriate levels. Gesticulating like a two-year-old when one is an adult is not a celebration of self but an exhibition of pathology. The mature narcissist both enjoys the feeling of specialness and understands that she is not special at all insofar as all people need to enjoy the same feeling. The mature narcissist can both celebrate the specialness of their accomplishments in the context of their own lives and know that others are just as special in the contexts of their lives. While achievements can and do produce feelings of specialness and need to be proclaimed, in the end what makes most people feel special is the experience that first made them feel special—the gleam in another's eye that announces "You are the most wonderful person in my world." We feel special when we are loved.

Finally, we can never forget that the self is always part of a self-selfobject complex. When I feel exuberantly alive, self-confident, and glow with the knowledge of self-worth, these heightened self states seep into the souls of others and help transform them. I typically feel myself stronger and more robust after I have been with someone exhibiting a vital self confidence and typically a bit less alive when I have been with someone who is depressed or suffering from impoverished self-structure. The radiance of a strong self shines on others and helps them grow into their own selves.

$$\mathcal{Q}\mathfrak{d}$$

5. Accept the Unconscious

Unlike the ego, the self is an unconscious dynamic structure that cannot be known directly through conscious introspection but which gives signs of itself in dreams, shifts in emotional response, altered moods, erotic attachments, anxieties, and so on. To be committed to discovering oneself and fostering the self as the *axis mundi* of life implies that one accepts the notion of unconscious mentality.

For Western culture to embrace the notion of the unconscious, so brilliantly excavated and rendered by Freud and the psychoanalytic tradition, is the most important and difficult of the little revolutions I am positing. While Freud remains ever present in our culture, his work is still the object of a persistent scorn and ridicule. His hypothesis of unconscious mentality has opened up possibilities of more profound self-knowledge and deeper forms of psychological well-being than ever before possible, yet it remains under strenuous attack on almost every front. Jonathan Lear points to three major reasons as to why the theory of the unconscious is not being accepted: Prozac and other psychotropic drugs, the policies of insurance companies, and the inflated claims psychoanalysis made for itself during the 50s and 60s.[1]

When modern persons encounter psychological troubles, they do not want to do the difficult, often lengthy and sometimes terrifying work of honestly remembering what has happened to them and owning the uncomfortable intentions and emotional presuppositions that they harbor. Rather, they wish to take a pill and feel better. Insurance companies support the pharmacological approach to psychological problems, for drugs are controllable and calculable; psychotherapy and analysis are not. How many sessions does one need to work through a failed idealized selfobject relationship in early childhood or an uncle's sexually abusing one as an adolescent? Factors such as the expertise and quality of empathy of the therapist, the fit between therapist and client, the strength and resilience of the defenses, and the coherence and complexity of the self at the time of the trauma will make major differences in how many sessions it might take to repair the injuries to the self. I have known some persons who with brief therapy experienced remarkable transformations, while others made little progress even after years of intensive psychotherapy or analysis. Drugs can make one feel better; the dose can be scientifically determined, and the cost is predictable—and this is what seems to count most to insurance companies. Hence, insurance companies typically cover psychotropic drugs and have ridiculously low limits on the number of sessions or total cost of psychotherapy.

Is feeling good what human life is about? Is the essential human task the one written over the gate at Delphi—to know one's self—or is it the utilitarian one of living in as much pleasure as one can? I can imagine a highly successful union of neuroscience and psychopharmacology that will produce drugs which have the power to make us feel good all of the time. This world was first imagined by Homer as the Land of the Lotus Eaters and re-envisioned by Huxley in *Brave New World*. We might be able to construct a life of pure pleasure and not have to worry about what human life means at all. Lear puts the problem this way:

> The real object of attack—for which Freud is only a stalking-horse—is the very idea that humans have unconscious motivation. A battle may be fought over Freud, but the war is over our culture's image of the human soul. Are we to see humans as having depth—as complex psychological organisms who generate layers of meaning which lie beneath the surface of their own understanding? Or are we to take ourselves as transparent to ourselves? . . . [We are] a culture which wishes to ignore the complexity, depth, and darkness of human life.[2]

Freud was right in announcing that the discovery of the unconscious was a narcissistic blow to humans, one on the order of Copernicus' eliminating their planet from the center of the universe and Darwin's negating their myth of divine origin. If humans harbor intentions, memories, emotions, dire sufferings, and wishes that are unknown to them and have a kind of mentality that produces symptoms and self-defeating behavior, then we can no longer think that we can be masters of our fates, rulers of our destinies. The discovery of the unconscious is the death knell of the Western imperative that we become full masters of our souls. It finds

Plato's hope to achieve a full rational command of psychic material to be unachievable.

Perhaps Sophocles was wiser than Plato. Oedipus declared that he would not accept his fate, for he thought that his rational ego had the power to escape what the gods had ordained and construct a new world based on his intelligence. Oedipus is the new kind of person being proposed by the philosophers, a human being who discovers the extraordinary powers of rational consciousness and proclaims that there is no higher power than the rational will. But Oedipus' denial that he had a fate did not mean that he did not have this fate. The contemporary denial of an unconscious mentality that largely dictates the contours of our lives does not mean that the unconscious does not exist. We, like Oedipus, deny it perhaps at the cost of our civilization.

This turning from the unconscious is partially motivated by a common human fear of the unknown. When ancient mapmakers drew uncharted waters they often wrote in them "There be dragons here." We wish to live in chartered waters without the dragons, but this is a wish to be something other than who we are. And, typically, where there are dragons, there is treasure. The self is the treasure of the unconscious, but it is often protected by dragon-like defenses and the revisiting of horrifying ordeals.

Accepting that there is an unconscious is difficult and a terrible blow to those who have identified with their egos or rational minds (a condition I find to be generally true for academics). Admitting that humans have unconscious mentality means that we carry "the other" within us, a foreigner who might subvert who we are, unconsciously derail our best plans, and cause us to seek repetitive situations of trauma and self destruction. It raises difficult questions, such as: Are we responsible for our unconscious intentions? If I do not know that I harbor narcissistic rage and covertly am attempting to destroy others, especially those who remind me of the perpetrators of my trauma, am I morally accountable for my deeds? How can I consider myself to be an agent if at any time unconscious intentions might be motivating my actions without my knowledge of them? These questions have answers,[3] but the answers will demand that we stop thinking about ourselves as being able to attain full mastery over ourselves and begin believing that life is highly circumscribed by fate.

Because the unconscious is so antithetical to the ego values of control and legitimation, it has either been derided in wonderfully clever arguments by masters of rationality or been treated as a plague. Indeed, most of the history of philosophy attempts to identify mentality with consciousness and then argues that if an item is not conscious it cannot belong to mentality. Even Freud seems to have fallen under the spell of this tradition when he declared that the aim of psychoanalysis is to make the unconscious conscious, to replace the id with the ego. If we interpret

Freud's dictum to mean that we need to achieve self-awareness (which is different from ego awareness) of our unconscious wishes, intentions, and organizing principles then his seminal idea is congruent with the self, not the ego, being the center for psychic activity.

This self knowledge is not easy to attain. To enter this wild world of symbol and dream, one needs both the understanding of scientist (in terms of grasping structures of unconscious dynamics) and the skills of a literary interpreter, the empathic compassion of a humanist and the rigorous search for truth of a researcher. It is not by chance that when Dante had to go into his Inferno, his guide was a poet of rigorous meter, Virgil. Nor is it by chance that Freud was as versed in the humanities as he was in the sciences. Kohut, too, was a scientist who was quite knowledgeable in the humanities.

I believe that the most alive life is not the life in which the ego takes rational control over all of experience. In this claim I have good company—Goethe, Dostoevsky, Nietzsche, Kierkegaard, Heidegger, Virginia Woolf, Ralph Waldo Emerson, and Thoreau—to name just some of the great thinkers of the past two centuries who declared the fullness of life had to be found outside the domain of rational consciousness—in the intuitive, creative, irrational, wild, painful, and/or the spontaneous. But this is the realm of the unconscious. We inherently have a part of our psyches that refuses to be dominated and controlled by rational bureaucratic forces. Interacting with it, delving into its depths, acknowledging its suffering, attuning to its creative urges, and listening to its erotic longings make us more alive. It does not make life more pleasant, for sure. But the aim of the soul is not pleasure; the aim of the soul is life.

To acknowledge the unconscious then is to make life more complex, less controllable, less knowable, and far more fascinating. It is to leave the disenchanted world of the rational ego and re-enchant the world with depth and strangeness, with dragons and adventures into the unknown, with the fascination of self-discovery and, often, with more profound suffering than the ego thinks it can tolerate. It is to catapult us out of the shallow pond of rational consciousness into the deeper, more turbulent sea of life.

6. Accept Therapeutic Help

The last little revolution responds to the basic problem that lies at the source of all the changes I have mentioned above: if modern people have injured selves and the self is an unconscious structure unavailable for consciously willed alteration, then how is it possible for modern persons to change into people who can organize life around the self?

One might be tempted to answer that this change can happen only in the next generation after this generation raises their children in optimal ways for the development of the self. This response is problematical because of a fundamental (and horrifying) truth that Kohut discovered about childrearing: children's psychological development depends more on the unconscious state of their parents' nuclear selves than on the philosophy of childrearing that the parents are following.[4] If the parents' selves harbor fragmentation, narcissistic rage, and disintegration anxiety, the children will feel anxious and unsupported, regardless of how well hidden these pathogenic states are. The parents might attempt to apply empathic mirroring as a valuable technique, but there is a difference between empathically mirroring someone from the depth of one's being and being empathic because one is employing a method. When methods are applied to people, they are objectified—are treated as objects. Even if the intent of the method is to humanize, the result of methodological relating to others is to reduce them to objects to be changed or altered through the use of the method. Only when a subject subjectively immerses herself in the subjectivity of another (empathy) does the subjectivity of the other gain vitality and strength.

To qualify the above: when speaking of human beings and their psychologies, one must not think in black and white, all-or-nothing terms. Parents with deeply injured selves can meet many, if not most, of their children's needs, if they are nurturing, thoughtful, and caring people. But some level of profound support, trust, and connection will seem to be missing—something that the children cannot avail themselves of—a merger with a vital, confident, coherent self.

The crucial question then becomes how is it possible for modern people with injured selves to restore them? If the self has not been traumatically injured but just lost in the rush of modern life, then a conscious reorientation that pays close attention to the difference between eros and desire, that fosters selfobject relations, and that is willing to make commitments to activities that foster the self can be transformative. But if the self is traumatically injured—as I think is true for a great many modern people—then help is required. Since both the defenses that are protecting the injured self and the self are unconscious configurations, they are not amenable to changes directed by the conscious will. When the psyche that is attempting to heal itself is traumatically injured, then it is a case of the blind leading the blind. Help is needed from those who know how to treat the self.

While Freud thought that narcissistically wounded persons could not be healed through psychological methods, Kohut discovered that narcissistically injured selves could be restored through a psychoanalytic process that understood the nature of the self, grasped its developmental genesis, and attended to selfobject transferences. Although the theory of the self is a great aid to understanding the landscape of the unconscious, it is the self psychologist's ability to nontraumatically confront the defenses and attune to the specific narcissistic transferences that allows a patient to reclaim her self. The heart of the process is not the application of a method but the ability to empathically immerse oneself in the unconscious subjectivity of another human being.

I am suggesting what seems to be outrageously utopist—that we need to have a self psychologist on every corner and that it should be a common practice for modern individuals to avail themselves of therapy that can restore and bolster the self. One might object that even if there were the need for such therapy, there are almost no self psychologists around and no way to train that many of them. Yet, one of the most amazing features of a market economy is how quickly it can respond to recognized needs. Thirty years ago there were only a handful of computer experts; now every institution of any size has a computer team and any sizeable town will have computer experts on every other block. Thirty years ago, very few people spent any income on computers and twenty years ago no one was purchasing Internet services. If Henry Ford had refused to mass produce automobiles until there were enough gas stations, we would still be getting around in horse-drawn carriages.

The key to an adequate supply of self psychologists is the recognition of the psychological need for them. And this is where the problem essentially lies. Modern people, by the very fact that they are modern, are prone to deny that there is anything wrong with them, and, if there is anything wrong, they can fix it themselves. This is the ego's assertion of its centrality, power, and control. Underneath this refusal to acknowledge the need for help lies Western individualism, its fierce sense of independence, and its understanding of all forms of help as dependence. Modern people like "self help" books, for with their advice, they can cure themselves. Meanwhile, the number of people being severely overweight goes up. Addictions to gambling, alcohol, sex, and illegal drugs continue to intensify and cheating is becoming a national problem. Entitlement behavior erupts everywhere from adult road rage to children demanding the latest fad toys. But everyone seems to think that it is not I who am entitled, addicted, a cheater, or out of control with my weight, but others. An essential part of every psychological defensive organization is the denial of reality.

Modern people, for the most part, do not like to spend money to fix their subjectivity. They like to spend it on objects or recreational services—travel, home, clothes, entertainment, automobiles, restaurants. It is an object-focused life; not an inward one. The key, in this frame of mind, to feeling fully alive is to be in the presence of extraordinary objects. We want to marry a stunningly beautiful mate, possess a great mansion, travel to the most exotic of places, discover a new restaurant, root for the dominant football team, go to a rock concert of the latest greatest band ever, and so on. If we can continuously put ourselves in the presence of such exciting, alluring, "grandiose" objects, then we can feel alive and whole. This modern frame of mind is strange, since one of the greatest discoveries of modernity is that it is nature of subjectivity that determines the quality of experience, not the object. The great continental philosophers from Kant to the present day have grasped this essential truth, but we live as though subjectivity were just there and the difference between alive experiences and dull ones is the difference of the objects of experience. Supposedly, a grand home produces more intense experiences than a small one; a beautiful partner produces a higher amount of desire than a more ordinary person. This is simply false. One can be as depressed in a large home as small; be as unable to participate in intimacy with a beautiful as a homely person.

What modern thinkers have discovered is that the key to the intensification and vivacity of experience lies in how subjectivity is produced by its unconscious organizing structures. If the self has been traumatically injured such that the unconscious organizing structures must participate in the psychological defenses, then, with almost any object, experience will feel distanced from reality, disconnected from others, somewhat depressed (because of the energy going into defensive work rather than out toward the world), and overly driven. The present will not be able to be fully experienced because it is always colored by repetitious expectations from the past. While there can be areas in which the self feels safe enough to express itself, for the most part, it must remain out of experience with the resulting loss of vitality and coherence that only a self can give.

In short, if the psyche contains unconscious trauma, our experiencing of objects, especially the most important ones—those whom we love—will be skewed. There might be anxiety about feeling strong emotions about anything, lest the traumatic experience be re-evoked. Or there might be a tendency to avoid situations like those that traumatized one, but these often are experiences of love and trust, the very experiences that give life its deepest intensity and meaning. Traumas make the self reluctant to be present in experience, and so whatever is experienced is not gathered into the self to give it nourishment.

This is all clear once the notion of unconscious mentality is accepted. And it is clear that to allow the self to be healed, the traumas overcome, and experience to be revitalized, the traumatized person needs help from someone who knows how the dynamics of an unconscious that revolves around the development of the self evolves. That is, the modern world needs self psychologists on every corner.

Of course, it is another one of those blinding partial truths to say that if one rids his subjectivity of psychopathology, then all will be well. The truth is that objects count, too. Experience is a joint production of subjects engaged with objects. It makes a difference whether one lives in ugly, noisy, crime-ridden, dirty conditions or bright, safe, quiet, uplifting conditions. It makes a difference whether one's partner is caring and empathic. Modernity is not wrong in stressing the idea that better objects make for better experience. Its error is in not emphasizing the even greater importance of subjectivity, especially unconscious subjectivity in the determination of the quality and vitality of experience.

I need to add a second caveat. In today's world of quality control and professional regulation, one usually knows what one is paying for when one purchases objects or services. It is different with psychotherapy and psychoanalysis, not because these fields do not have professional regulation but because they deal with the transformation of subjectivity rather than production of objects. The therapeutic encounter is between two subjects attempting to explore and heal one of the subject's malfunctioning psychological dynamics without reducing that subject to an object. Whenever subjectivity is engaged, the results are not fully predictable, for the variables are too vast, as life is engaging life with all its creative, spontaneous, sensitive, chaotic, elusive, and hidden forces. This is not the realm of science but of interpretation—not the realm of the standardized and predictable but the realm of mind. Some analysts who brilliantly help some people are ineffective with others. Care (and some luck) is needed in finding a therapist who can genuinely help one.

It becomes clear in elaborating this small revolution that it verges on the wildly utopist. It requires an acceptance that the core self and key psychological functions are unconscious and not available for consciously willed adjustments and that how we experience the world is more important than what is experienced. It requires the recognition of the truth of self psychology by the psychoanalytic and other psychological traditions (something that has not yet happened), the unprecedented development of self psychological training institutes, and the tremendous shift in capital away from paying for things and the opportunities to experience exotic objects (travel, entertainment) toward paying for the difficult, often long, work to heal one's psyche. In short, it requires changing from an economic society to a psychological one.

Yet, stranger things have happened in human history. I am sure that if a Roman of the third century were told that a totalizing otherworldliness would soon overtake the Empire and make prayer, worship, and preparation for an afterlife the central human activities, he would have scorned the possibility as an absurdity. Likewise, if a German monk of the thirteenth century had been told that the world would soon devote itself almost entirely to the acquisition of wealth, he would find such a possibility incomprehensible. Worlds are abandoned and others come into being—all of the time. The economic world can transform into the psychological world.

These six small revolutions—restoring the family, prioritizing selfobject relationships, humanizing the workplace, tolerating grandiosity, acknowledging the unconscious, and accepting therapeutic support for the self as a normal part of life—leave in place the modern political and economic structures that have brought so much opportunity and material well-being. However, they revolutionize how we think about ourselves, our relationships with others, and the highest goals of life. They constitute a conceptual revolution insofar as they prioritize the needs of the individual self as the fulcrum of a well-lived life. I believe that only with this conceptual revolution will we be able to genuinely address the profoundest needs of human beings and start to construct a social order that allows us to fully flourish as singular, vulnerable individuals.

NOTES

1. Jonathan Lear, *Open-Minded: Working out the Logic of the Soul* (Cambridge, MA: Harvard University Press, 1998), 17.

2. Lear, *Open-Minded*, 27.

3. See my book *Ethics and the Discovery of the Unconscious* (Albany, NY: SUNY Press, 1997).

4. See Kohut's *Restoration of the Self* (New York: International Universities Press, 1977).

BIBLIOGRAPHY

Arendt, Hannah. *Eichmann in Jerusalem: A Report on the Banality of Evil.* New York: Harper & Row, 1963.

Aristotle. *Nichomachean Ethics.* Trans. Martin Ostwald. Indianapolis, IN: Bobbs-Merrill, 1962.

Bauman, Zygmunt. *Liquid Modernity.* Cambridge, MA: Polity Press, 2000.

Berman, Morris. *Dark Ages America.* New York: Norton, 2005.

Callahan, David. *The Cheating Culture.* New York: Harcourt, Inc., 2004.

Confucius. *The Analects.* Trans. D. C. Lau. New York: Penguin Books, 1979.

Dobson, Marcia. "Freud, Kohut, Sophocles: Did Oedipus Do Wrong?" *International Journal of Psychoanalytic Self Psychology,* 2, no.1 (February 2007): 53–76.

Foucault, Michel. *Discipline and Punish.* Trans. A. Sheridan. New York: Vintage Books, 1979.

Freud, Sigmund. *The Standard Edition of the Complete Works of Sigmund Freud.* Trans. James Strachey. London: Hogarth Press, 1953–74.

Gewirth, Alan. *Reason and Morality.* Chicago: Chicago University Press, 1978.

Gilligan, Carol. *In a Different Voice.* Cambridge, MA: Harvard University Press, 1982.

Goffman, Irving. *The Presentation of Self in Everyday Life.* New York: Doubleday, 1959.

Goldberg, Arnold. *Being of Two Minds.* Hillsdale, NJ: Analytic Press, 1999.

———. *Misunderstanding Freud.* New York: Other Press, 2004.

Hare, R. M. *Freedom and Reason.* Oxford: Oxford University Press, 1963.

Hegel, G. W. F. *Phenomenology of Spirit.* Trans. A. V. Miller. Oxford: Oxford University Press, 1979.

Heidegger, Martin. *Being and Time.* Trans. Joan Stambaugh. Albany, NY: SUNY Press, 1996.

———. "The Question Concerning Technology," translated by William Lovitt. Pp. 287–317 in *Martin Heidegger: Basic Writings.* Edited by David Krell. New York: Harper Collins, 1977.

Jung, Carl. *The Essential Jung.* Edited by Anthony Storr. Princeton, NJ: Princeton University Press, 1983.

Kant, Immanuel. *Foundations of the Metaphysics of Morals.* Trans. Lewis White Beck. Indianapolis, IN: Bobbs-Merrill, 1964.

————. *Critique of Pure Reason.* Trans. Norman Kemp Smith. New York: MacMillan Press, 1929.

Kierkegaard, Soren. *Fear and Trembling.* Trans. H. Hong and E. Hong. Princeton, NJ: Princeton University Press, 1983.

————. *The Sickness unto Death.* Trans. H. Hong and E. Hong. Princeton, NJ: Princeton University Press, 1980.

Kohut, Heinz. "Forms and Transformations of Narcissism." Pp. 61–87 in *Essential Papers on Narcissism.* Edited by Andrew Morrison. New York: New York University Press, 1986.

————. *How Does Analysis Cure?* Chicago: University of Chicago Press, 1984.

————. *The Restoration of the Self.* New York: International Universities Press, 1977.

————. *Self Psychology and the Humanities.* Edited by Charles Strozier. New York: Norton, 1985.

Lear, Jonathan. *Freud.* New York: Routledge, 2005.

————. *Happiness, Death, and the Remainder of Life.* Cambridge, MA: Harvard University Press, 2003.

————. *Love and Its Place in Nature.* New York: Farrar, Straus, and Giroux, 1990.

————. *Open Minded: Working Out the Logic of the Soul.* Cambridge, MA: Harvard University Press, 1998.

————. *Therapeutic Action.* New York: Other Press, 2003.

Lichtenberg, Joseph. *Psychoanalysis and Motivation.* Hillsdale, NJ: Analytic Press, 1989.

Lifton, Robert Jay. *The Protean Self.* New York: Basic Books, 1993.

MacIntyre, Alastaire. *After Virtue.* South Bend, IN: University of Notre Dame Press, 1981.

Mill, John Stuart. *Utilitarianism.* New York: MacMillan Publishing Company, 1957.

Mitchell, Stephen. *Relational Concepts in Psychoanalysis: An Integration.* Cambridge, MA: Harvard University Press, 1988.

Moore, George Edward. *Principia Ethica.* Cambridge: Cambridge University Press, 1962.

Nietzsche, Friedrich. *Thus Spoke Zarathustra.* Trans. Walther Kaufmann. New York: Penguin Books, 1978.

————. *Genealogy of Morals* in *The Birth of Tragedy and The Genealogy of Morals.* Trans. F. Golffing. Garden City, NY: Doubleday, 1956.

Plato. *The Collected Dialogues of Plato.* Edited by E. Hamilton and H. Cairns. New York: Pantheon Books, 1961.

Poole, Ross. *Morality and Modernity.* New York: Routledge Press, 1991.

Putnam, Robert. *Bowling Alone.* New York: Simon & Schuster, 2000.

Rawls, John. *A Theory of Justice.* Cambridge, MA: Harvard University Press, 1971.

Riker, John. *Ethics and the Discovery of the Unconscious.* Albany, NY: SUNY Press, 1997.

————. *Human Excellence and an Ecological Concept of the Psyche.* Albany, NY: SUNY Press, 1991.

————. "The Philosophical Importance of Kohut's Bipolar Theory of the Self." In *Basic Ideas Reconsidered: Progress in Self Psychology,* vol. 12. Edited by Arnold Goldberg. Hillsdale, NJ: Analytic Press, 1996.

Santner, Eric. *On the Psychotheology of Everyday Life*. Chicago: University of Chicago Press, 2001.

Sherman, Nancy. *Making a Necessity of Virtue: Aristotle and Kant on Virtue*. Cambridge: Cambridge University Press, 1997.

Siegel, Allen. *Heinz Kohut and the Psychology of the Self*. New York: Routledge, 1996.

Stolorow, Robert, Bernard Brandschaft, and George Atwood. *Psychoanalytic Treatment: An Intersubjective Approach*. Hillsdale, NJ: Analytic Press, 1987.

Strozier, Charles. *Heinz Kohut: The Making of a Psychoanalyst*. New York: Farrar, Straus, and Giroux, 2001.

Strenger, Carlos. *The Designed Self*. Hillsdale, NJ: Analytic Press, 2005.

Teicholz, Judith. *Kohut, Loewald, and the Postmoderns*. Hillsdale, NJ: Analytic Press, 1999.

Terman, David. "Optimum Frustration: Structuralization and the Therapeutic Process." Pp. 113–25 in *Learning from Kohut: Progress in Self Psychology*, vol. 4. Edited by Arnold Goldberg. Hillsdale, NJ: Analytic Press, 1984.

Thoreau, Henry David. *Walking*. In *Ralph Waldo Emerson: "Nature" and Henry David Thoreau: "Walking."* Edited by John Elder. Boston: Beacon Press, 1991.

Weber, Max. *The Protestant Ethic and the Spirit of Capitalism*. London: George Allen & Unwin, 1984.

Wheelwright, Philip, ed. *The Presocratics*. New York: Odyssey Press, 1966.

Williams, Bernard. *Ethics and the Limits of Philosophy*. Cambridge: Cambridge University Press, 1982.

Winnicott, Donald. *Human Nature*. New York: Schocken Books, 1988.

Wolf, Ernest. *Treating the Self*. New York: Guilford Press, 1988.

INDEX

About the Author

John H. Riker has been a professor of philosophy at Colorado College for over forty years. He has won numerous teaching and service awards there, including having been elected Teacher of the Year three times. He has published three previous books, including *Human Excellence and an Ecological Conception of the Psyche* and *Ethics and the Discovery of the Unconscious*. He has also been the Kohut Professor at the University of Chicago. He and his spouse, classicist and psychotherapist Marcia Dobson, have initiated an undergraduate program in psychoanalysis at the Chicago Institute for Psychoanalysis. Marcia and John are also acclaimed ballroom dancers. They love hiking the mountains of Colorado, going to the opera, collecting art, snuggling up with their four Shetland Sheepdogs, and playing with their grandchildren.